The
Soul *of*
Michael
Jackson

Also by Rabbi Shmuley Boteach

The Soul *of* Michael Jackson

A Tragic Icon Reveals His Deepest Self in Intimate Conversation

Rabbi Shmuley Boteach

Skyhorse Publishing

To Prince and Paris,
who were my children's playmates, and
Blanket whom we never met.

May you be inspired by your father's virtue,
be cautioned by his excess,
and be the living fulfillment of his unrealized dream
of Healing the World by living lives of selflessness,
kindness, and compassion.

God watch over you and protect you always.

CONTENTS

AFTERWORD

I am going to say something I have never said before and this is the truth. I have no reason to lie to you and God knows I am telling the truth. I think all my success and fame and I have wanted it, I have wanted it because I wanted to be loved. That's all. That's the real truth. I wanted people to love me, truly love me, because I never really felt loved. I said I know I have an ability. Maybe if I sharpened my craft, maybe people will love me more. I just wanted to be loved because I think it is very important to be loved and to tell people that you love them and to look in their eyes and say it.

MICHAEL JACKSON IN CONVERSATION
WITH RABBI SHMULEY

I am like a lion. Nothing can hurt me. No one can harm me.
THE SAME MICHAEL JACKSON IN CONVERSATION
WITH RABBI SHMULEY

The
Soul *of*
Michael
Jackson

Michael Jackson as I Knew Him

The Morality Tale, Our Friendship, His Demons

The Morality Tale

How This Book Came to Be

This book is being published because it was Michael Jackson's desperate wish that it be so. It contains the most intimate, authentic, raw, painful, and insightful conversations for public disclosure that Michael ever produced. There is nothing like it, and since Michael has tragically passed well before his time, there will never be anything like it again.

In publishing this book not only have I not broken any confidences, I have fulfilled the desire of a man who wanted his heart to be known to a public whom he understood was deeply suspicious of him. The transcripts this book is based on come from tape recordings of approximately thirty hours of conversations that Michael Jackson and I conducted between August 2000 and April 2001 with the express purpose of having them published in book form and shared with the public.

The conversations focused on a wide range of topics all with the intent of revealing—and explaining—the man behind the mask.

So eager was Michael to have people understand who he was that for many of these conversations he held the Dictaphone we used directly to his mouth so not a single word would be lost. On other occasions he made me stop our conversation so he could turn down the air conditioning in his hotel room, because he was afraid the noise would drown out his voice on the recordings. If his children Prince and Paris, who were about three and two when we began and present for many of the recordings, got loud, Michael made sure to gently shush them so not a word would be missed.

Michael asked me to write the book because we were very close friends and because I was already an experienced author and values-based broadcaster and lecturer, and more importantly because the conversations would naturally parallel the steps he needed to take, with my direction and encouragement, to regain his health and equilibrium and redeem himself not only in the eyes of the public but also in his own eyes. In the months ahead it became a desperate spiritual journey to consecrate his celebrity to a higher end. He wanted to share a deeper side of himself that our friendship had begun to uncover.

I completed a working draft of the book in the year or two after our conversations ended. People who read it said they never knew Michael could be such a deep and inspiring personality. Many of my most well-read friends told me they cried through the manuscript. Like many others, they had earlier dismissed Michael as a mindless and shallow celebrity materialist who was hopelessly weird. The sensitive personality revealed in the conversations, however, was introspective, knowledgeable, forgiving, and deeply spiritual.

But events overtook the making of the book and I withheld it from publication. My relationship with Michael had deteriorated because I no longer felt I could influence him positively. He was closing off from his deeper soul and returning to the profligate ways of the self-destructive superstar the world had determined he already was. I felt he was losing the battle between dissipation and excellence, between going to waste and making a contribution, between being a caricature of himself and being an artist.

If an opening still existed to publish these interviews, it was slammed shut when, in November 2003, Michael, who had settled sexual abuse allegations out of court in 1993, was accused for a second time of child molestation. There was no way his views would be taken seriously on any subject.

It would be impossible for Michael to be heard talking about his views on the needs of children, innocence, and the childlike spirit he believed contributed to the greatness of so many people without his thoughts simply being dismissed as the rationalizations of an accused pedophile. Plus, anything that was published would simply become more fodder for the publicity frenzy surrounding the case, defeating the purpose of the interviews, which was to cut through the hype and hysteria to reveal the deeper man beneath the (albeit extreme) public image.

And then, eight years after the interviews, Michael suddenly and tragically died. My dormant feelings of sadness, anger, resentment, disappointment, and even love were awakened and intensified by the insanity surrounding his death and the distorted portrayal of his legacy. I was spurred to finally publish this book. Michael's wish should be fulfilled. The tapes needed to see the light of day. Whatever people think of Michael, there was good in him and it deserved to come out.

Michael was far from a saint and I for one have never whitewashed his sins. But there was a gentility and nobility of spirit that I found humbling and inspiring in a man so accomplished. I realized that the extraordinary things Michael shared with me in these conversations would serve to fill the three giant holes left open by the often tabloid and circuslike media coverage: The first, who was the real Michael Jackson? The second, what pain did he live with that he tried so hard to medicate away and which ultimately consumed him? And the third, what moral lesson could be extracted from his tragic death that could bring redemption to a life cut short?

The final question especially tugged at me. I watched only parts of his memorial service at the Staples Center. I dismissed it as an outrage, a moral affront. Here was a man who had almost certainly died of a drug overdose. Yet, rather than convey even a fragment of the degree of the tragedy, they made his funeral into a concert.

America had to read our conversations and learn about the real Michael Jackson. They had to understand he was never a freak. He was not born to be weird. Rather, fame—his drug of choice—and a rudderless life had destroyed him completely. His was a terrible loss of both innocence and talent. His senseless death cried out for redemption.

The principal tragedy of his life was to mistake attention for love, fame for family, material acquisition for true spiritual purpose. I will never forget how, when we first began our conversations that are the soul of this book, Michael said the haunting words that I used for the epigraph of this book:

I am going to say something I have never said before and this is the truth. I have no reason to lie to you and God knows I am telling the truth. I think all my success and fame, and I have wanted it, I have wanted it because I wanted to be loved. That's all. That's the real truth. I wanted people to love me, truly love me, because I never really felt loved. I said I know I have an ability. Maybe if I sharpened my craft, maybe people will love me more. I just wanted to be loved because I think it is very important to be loved and to tell people that you love them and to look in their eyes and say it.

I remember being stunned as a listened to him, his tear-ridden voice hauntingly describing the abject loneliness of his life. One cannot read his statement without feeling a tremendous sadness for a soul who was so surrounded with hero-worship but remained so utterly abandoned. Because Michael substituted attention for love he got fans who loved *what he did* but he never had true compatriots who loved him for *who he was*.

The ancient rabbis of the Talmud proclaimed that words which emanate from the heart penetrate the heart. Michael's admission to me of how all he ever wanted from his career was the love that had so eluded him as a child pierced my heart like a dagger and drew us closer as spiritual soul-friends. I was being summoned into his loneliness.

The Eulogy That Wasn't

I was filming a TV show with my family in Iceland when my office called and shared the terrible news of Michael's passing. My wife and children were with me in the van and we could scarcely believe what we had heard. The children all remembered Michael fondly. He had given them their dog Marshmallow, who is still a member of our family. My daughter teared up. My heart bled for his children, whom he adored and who adored him in turn. I thought of Prince and Paris who were my children's playmates, and their brother Prince II, known as "Blanket," who I never met, and how attached they were to a father who regularly told me that he knew that when they grew up they would be asked by biographers what kind of parent he had been. He wanted them to have only warm memories to share. Alas, the memories will remain largely incomplete.

Yet I was not shocked to get the news. I had dreaded this day and knew it would come sooner rather than later.

During the two years that I had attempted, ultimately unsuccessfully, to help Michael repair his life, what most frightened me was not that he would face another child molestation charge, although he did. It was that he would die. As I told CNN on April 22, 2004, in an internationally telecast interview, "My greatest fear. . . is that Michael's life would be cut short. When you have no ingredients of a healthy life, when you are totally detached from that which is normal, and when you are a super-celebrity, you, God forbid, end up like Janis Joplin, like Elvis . . . Michael is headed in that direction."

Michael's family publicly disputed any insinuation that he would die. As CNN reported in response to my interview "Jackson's family has denied suggestions that the pop star's life is unhealthy, insisting he is doing very well, particularly for someone who faces his unique pressures."

I was also rebuked in that same interview by Raymone Baine, Michael's spokesperson through the trial and for several years thereafter, who said I was being wreckless and irresponsible for saying that Michael was going to die. On May 6, 2009 Raymone Baine sued Michael for $44 million. Six weeks later it didn't matter much because Michael was dead.

I am no prophet, and it did not take a rocket scientist to see the impending doom. Michael was a man in tremendous pain and his tragedy was to medicate his pain away rather than addressing its root cause. He confused an affliction of the soul with an ailment of the body. But all the barbiturates in the world could never cure a troubled soul that had lost its way.

Yes, from the media's infatuation with every prurient detail of the aftermath of his death one would think that it was a cartoon character, a caricature of a real man, who had died rather than an actual person. Michael always had a mutually exploitive relationship with the American people. He used us to feed his constant need for attention and we used him to feed our constant need for entertainment.

Still, it would have been hard to believe that Michael's story could be more bizarre in death than in life. But from the mother of Michael's two older children "deciding" whether or not she wanted her kids; to his dermatologist leaving open the possibility that he is the father of Prince and Paris; to Joe Jackson talking up his new record label as his son's body lay unburied; to nurses coming forward to claim that Michael asked them to inject him with quantities of painkillers that would have felled a water buffalo; to doctors being pursued by the Feds for acting as medically sanctioned pushers, clearly the impossible has been achieved.

And just when you thought this theater of the absurd had reached its zenith, the news came that Michael's memorial service would take place at a basketball arena complete with twelve thousand fans and that the Ringling Brothers Circus would be occupying the same arena the very next day.

Were there no adults present to bring proper sobriety to the moment, to actually remind us that a human being had died, that a tormented soul had finally lost its battle with life, and that three innocent children had been orphaned? Was there no one to say that what actually destroyed Michael's life and what brought such untold misery to the Jackson family as a whole was an inability to cope with fame? Was there no one who saw that something important and lasting could be learned from Michael's passing by sending him off in a quiet, dignified, truly religious ceremony that focused on the silent acts of kindness he performed rather than the albums he sold?

To my mind his death is not just a personal tragedy but an American tragedy. Michael's story is the stuff of the American dream. A poor black boy who grew up in Gary, Indiana, ends up a billionaire entertainer. But we now know how the story ends. Money is not a currency with which we can purchase self-esteem. Being recognized on the streets will never replace being loved unconditionally by family and true friends.

When Robert Oppenheimer witnessed the explosion of the atomic bomb he had worked so hard to develop, he famously quoted from the *Bhagavad-Gita*: "I am become death, destroyer of worlds." Anyone who witnessed the tragic implosion of the life of Michael Jackson and its circus aftermath in the weeks following his death might amend the saying to read, "I am fame, destroyer of lives."

Michael was anything but a monster. He was a thoughtful, insightful, deeply scarred, and at times very profound soul who was so broken that he could find no healing. No amount of fame or screaming fans would ever rescue him from his inevitable descent into the abyss.

Michael deserved a different kind of attention, and the public deserved and needed to hear a different kind of message, a eulogy that could bring redemption to Michael's life. In my sadness and self-questioning, I wrote and published the following words on July 5th, two days before the funeral and memorial service:

The death of Michael Joseph Jackson is not just the personal tragedy of a man who died young. Nor does it solely represent a colossal waste of life and talent. Rather it is, above all else, an American tragedy. For whether we wish to acknowledge it or not, our obsession with Michael Jackson, our infatuation with every peculiar detail of his life, stems from the fact that he represents a microcosm of America.

It has long been fashionable to caricature Michael as an oddball, as a freak. But how different were his peculiarities to our own?

Michael's dream was to be famous so that he would be loved. Having been forced into performing as a young boy, he never knew a time when affection was a free gift. Rather, attention, the poor substitute for love with which he made do, was something that he had to earn from the age of five. Hence, his obsession with being famous and his lifelong fear of being forgotten by the crowds. And if that meant purposefully doing strange things in order to sustain the public's interest, he would pay that price too.

But how different is that from the rest of us, living as we do in an age of reality TV where washing our dirty laundry in public makes us into celebrities and competing on American Idol promises us that we can be the next Michael Jackson?

Of course, there was Michael's constant plastic surgery. How much could one man so hate himself, we asked, that he is prepared to disfigure his face utterly? But the same question could easily be asked of millions of Americans, especially women, who live with extremely poor body image, who starve their bodies and undergo extreme cosmetic procedures—including sticking a needle in their forehead—to rediscover lost beauty and youth.

Yes, there was Michael's troubled soul. Could a man so blessed with fame and fortune, we wondered, really be so miserable that he had to numb his pain with a syringe of Demerol? And yet, my friends, America is the richest country in the world with the highest standard of living. Still, we consume three-quarters of the earth's antidepressants and one out of three Americans is on an antianxiety medication.

As far as Michael's materialism and decadence, particularly when we watched him on TV spending millions of dollars on useless baubles, is it really all that different to the rest of us who have maxed our credit cards buying junk we don't need with money we don't have, to compensate for an insatiable inner emptiness?

There were also Michael's broken relationships. Two divorces, estrangement from brothers and sisters, and extremely questionable and perhaps even criminal sexual activities. Yes, few of us, fortunately, are guilty of such crimes. But the huge success of "barely legal" pornographic Web sites, Girls Gone Wild videos, and the sexualization of teens like Miley Cyrus should perhaps have us question the adolescent nature of our own sexual interests. As for broken relationships, Time magazine just reported that of every 100 marriages, 50 divorce, 25 stay together unhappily, and only 25 are happy.

In sum, my friends, we are fixated on Michael Jackson because he was always just a very extreme version of ourselves and compacted into his short life a supercharged version of all the strangeness and profligacy of a culture which puts attention before love, fans before family, body before spirit, medical sedation before true inner peace, and material indulgence before spiritual enlightenment. Perhaps the only reason the rest of us did not become as strange or as broken as Michael was that we simply lacked the talent and the resources to do so.

And therein lies a profound morality lesson. Where Michael goes, the rest of us go. Our obsession with Michael was always selfish. It was a focus on where we ourselves were headed, where our culture and our interests were leading us.

And now we have the power to take a senseless tragedy and give it meaning by learning from the heartbreaking demise of a once-great legend that life is not about fame and fortune but rather about God, family, community, and good deeds.

Rest in peace, Michael. May you find in death the serenity you never had in life and may they judge you more charitably in heaven than we did here on earth.

Our Friendship

How We Met

I first met Michael in the summer of 1999 through my friend Uri Geller. While much of the world knows Uri through his claims as a psychic, I knew Uri as a close friend who lived in a town not far from my family's home in Oxford, England. While I was born and raised in the United States, I spent eleven years at Oxford serving as rabbi to the students of Oxford University and as founder and director of the Oxford L'Chaim Society, a large organization of students that specialized in hosting world leaders lecturing on values-based issues. Uri and his family were frequent guests at our home for Friday night Shabbat dinners and we grew quite close.

In the summer of 1999, I was a scholar in residence for a program in the Hamptons with my entire family as we prepared to move back to the United States. Uri called me up and simply said, "Shmuley, you should go and meet Michael." I had known that Uri was acquainted with Michael Jackson and he explained that he'd told Michael about me and that Michael wanted to meet me. By that time I had authored more than a dozen books on marriage, relationships, parenting, and spiritual healing and I guessed that Uri felt Michael needed some guidance in his life and it would be good for him to connect with me.

So, arrangements were made. Although I was interested in meeting Michael, I did not feel awed at the experience. I had counseled many people who lived life in the spotlight and was already of the opinion that fame did more harm than good in their personal lives. On the day of my visit, I remember knocking on the door of the beautiful Fifth Avenue townhouse Michael was renting by Central Park. Frank Tyson (whose real name is Frank Cascio), who served as Michael's manager and who would later become a dear friend, opened the door, said hello, and let me know that Mr. Jackson had allocated thirty minutes for our meeting. Michael, who was languishing in his career and ostensibly working on a long-delayed album that finally emerged in 2001 as *Invincible*, was very different from what I expected—quieter, shyer, yet more open and more accessible than his public image would suggest. He introduced me to his children, Paris and Prince (then about one and two), showed me pictures that had arrived that day from a concert in Germany, and openly talked about a host of topics including raising kids, the challenges of living in a fishbowl, and my life and work as a rabbi.

The conversation was more pleasant and substantive than I had expected for a man I believed to be inordinately materialistic. Our meeting went well beyond thirty minutes and by the time I left I felt that, for reasons I could not explain, Michael, a famous recluse, was becoming close to me.

After that we spoke on the phone a few times and made plans for a second meeting. This time Michael himself answered the door, but only after checking that no paparazzi were standing outside. I had brought two small gifts with me. The first was a mezuzah, the roll of Biblical parchment that Jews affix to their door which brings the divine presence into one's home. Normally, only Jewish homes display them, but I said to Michael, "God is the source of all blessing. Let this mezuzah always remind you of that." He was moved by the gift and we jointly affixed it to his front doorpost. I also brought him a Chanukah menorah as a symbol of God's light that should illuminate his life and home.

Again our conversation was open, warm, and surprisingly trusting for a man I was told was so private. He showed me a full-page picture in *The New York Post* of him walking out of a meeting with the Dalai Lama the day before. He said that he found his conversations with me more enlightening than those he had had with the Dalai Lama. Flattered and a bit embarrassed, I responded that the Dalai Lama was a truly great man and that I was not in his league, not a guru of any kind, but simply a man who had chosen to be a rabbi as a direct consequence of his parents' divorce and that I was trying to figure out the labyrinth of life using the profound moral code found in God's law, the Torah. Along the way, I sought to share with others what I had discovered about mastering life and establishing an ethical and spiritual foundation into which we could all anchor our lives.

As I was leaving his townhouse, Michael suddenly said, "You know I'd really love to go to synagogue with you." Surprised at the statement, I asked him if he was serious. "Yes, Shmuley, could you please take me to synagogue?" I replied, "Sure Michael. It would be a pleasure. I will take you to a synagogue I love."

The next week was the major Jewish festival of Simkhat Torah, the happiest day on the Jewish calendar. I took Michael to the most musical of all the synagogues in New York City, the Carlebach Shule founded by legendary Jewish folk artist Shlomo Carlebach, whose beautiful and soulful melodies have become justly famous.

No one except the rabbi knew that Michael was arriving. Jews do not activate electronics on holy days, so we took no pictures, made no recordings, informed no press, and tried to make it a truly personal and spiritual experience. When he turned up, the congregants were excited to see him and welcomed him warmly. He, in turn, put away his shyness and seemed to feel at home, humming along with the music, swaying with the rhythms, shaking the hands of all who greeted him, and blushing all the while. In his speech, the rabbi said that he hoped "Brother Michael" enjoyed this somewhat different kind of music. Michael, looking blissful, seemed enraptured by the atmosphere. This was clearly a man with a spiritual bent who hungered to be reconnected. He later told me that that evening at the synagogue was one of the happiest of his life. And he told Frank, his mother, and others the same thing. That evening made a mark on him.

A week or so after his wonderful experience at the Carlebach synagogue, Michael invited me and my family to his home for dinner. I explained that we're kosher and he went out and got a kosher caterer. When we all had dinner with him, I really started to notice just how shy he was.

Sitting there altogether, I found it almost impossible to imagine him as a superstar. He seemed so utterly ordinary. He remained shy even in his own (albeit temporary) home and I noticed that he hated existing at the center of attention in an intimate setting. Having people look at him up close made him feel like he was being evaluated and he became reticent. I surmised that perhaps this was due to the fact that he believed people were looking at him as a freak. But then, as we were getting up from dinner, which he barely ate, he hummed a tune from one of his songs and in that instant the beautiful voice reminded me of his vast talent that was usually nowhere apparent.

On Thanksgiving, Michael invited my entire family to see Disney's *Toy Story* at a regular theater. Michael's family and mine came in once the movie started and everything was dark. The last few rows had been blocked off and the theater brought all of us popcorn and drinks. I sat one row in front of Michael as he laughed uncontrollably throughout the movie. At first it struck me as juvenile. After all, this was a kid's film and I was attending it only for the sake of my children. But to be honest, hearing Michael in fits of laughter in the seat behind me was liberating, like it was okay for adults to let their guard down and see the world through the innocent eyes of a child. Soon I was laughing as well. This episode made Michael more human and further endeared him to me. Just before it was over we left. We missed the very beginning and end, but no one ever knew Michael Jackson was in the theater.

Some other family "adventures" didn't feel as innocent and uncomplicated. There was a shopping trip to FAO Schwartz that Michael intended to be the toy spree of a lifetime for my kids. He said he often went there and they closed the whole store for him. "I love it there," he said "We'll go, just us, and the kids can get whatever they want." So my wife and I discussed it and decided we would join Michael but with an important caveat. We sat our kids down and explained that they could each spend 25 dollars maximum—two gifts, 12 bucks each.

The trip was an adventure. When we got to the store Michael came to life. He seemed to know it intimately and took us to every floor, trying toys, demonstrating how they worked, encouraging the kids to fill up their carts. Our children were showing the toys to us saying, "Ma is that too much?" Michael was watching and said to us it wasn't fair since they closed the whole store and we were barely going to spend 150 dollars. Some other kids came from another family and they didn't have the same constraints. But I was adamant. I said to Michael, "There's no negotiation on this. Everyone has sucked you dry. Believe me, there's a part of me that can be as materialistic as the next guy. But we're never going to have that type of relationship."

And this attitude was critical. I had already noticed that one of the biggest problems in Michael's life was the gravy train of hangers-on. If I were to ever become one of them, my very morality would be compromised, which would be terrible for me but even worse for Michael. He needed people with values in his life, not sycophants who could be bought. And I also detected Michael's inclination to buy friends, which was a sure sign of insecurity. He had to know that he was enough, just the way he was.

All in all, our families had become fairly close throughout the fall, having several Shabbat dinners at our house, and once a week Michael and I would get together to study and talk. Michael expressed his thanks for the inspirational dimension he said I brought to his life. In turn, I thought him the consummate gentleman, that rare Hollywood celebrity who actually cared as much for other people as he did for himself.

As a brief aside, I should mention that I never attempted to proselytize Michael to Judaism. Believing in the authenticity of any faith that leads people to God, Judaism is not a faith that seeks converts, and we are commanded, even if someone approaches us to become Jewish, to turn them away at least three times. I repeatedly encouraged Michael to return to his Christian roots, in particular to the Jehovah's Witnesses Church, where he had been raised. I brought him into our Jewish rituals, philosophy, and Friday night Sabbath table as a means to help him reconnect with the beauty of prayer and the moving sound of worshipful music, all in the wider context of inspiring him to bring spirituality back into his life. I certainly believed that Judaism, with its focus on family, community, and righteous action, could play a very positive role in Michael's life. But one does not need to be Jewish to be enriched by Judaism.

Before the Christmas and New Year's holidays, without having accomplished any real progress on his new album, Michael left New York and went back to California. We kept in contact by phone, talking about family and relationships.

Neverland

What transformed our relationship from one of a warm friendship to that of a truly intimate bond was Michael's invitation to me and my family to join him for a few days at Neverland in the summer of 2000. It was August and we were already in Los Angeles visiting my father and brother. Since we were just a few hours away and hadn't seen him for months, we drove up for a short visit, which ended up stretching to nearly a week.

I think Michael sensed that I had something he needed—perhaps it was a sense of purposefulness. I knew what I wanted to do with my life; I had been a rabbi at Oxford and had built an organization that had an effect on its students, Jewish and non-Jewish alike; and given my parents' divorce, I had dedicated a large part of my life to counseling couples and writing books seeking to increase the passion and intimacy of couples. I had a sense of mission, and Michael seemed to have lost his.

Michael rolled out the red carpet for us. When we arrived he was outside with his children, accompanied by animal trainers with deer and even an elephant, a horse and buggy, and chefs and footmen dressed in appropriate attire. Michael was out to make an impression and he succeeded. We were overwhelmed by this fantasyland we had just entered.

My impression as soon as we arrived at Neverland was that by building this magical paradise Michael was making a statement. He had created his own private universe, a world of children's laughter, fun and games, cartoons, and candy. A world with no pain.

Every human being and every culture has a different vision of paradise. A year later on September 11, 2001, the world would discover that for an Islamic suicide bomber it could be an afterlife filled with wide-eyed virgins. For a shallow materialist it might be a place where money grows on trees. For Jews it is a future where the predatory instinct has vanished and the wolf lies down peacefully with the lamb. For Michael Jackson it was a place where no one ever grows up.

Michael was a gracious host. He gave my family and me an extensive tour of the almost-three-thousand-acre ranch, showcasing his home, which was not all that large, the rides in the amusement park, the animals in the zoo, and the video and arcade room. I remember vividly how he took us to the reptile house and instructed the zookeeper to take out a poisonous rattlesnake, which Michael held with tongs. Contrary to all the press reports that Michael was a germophobe, afraid of his own shadow, clearly this was a man who was not easily shaken. He took us all around the property on his train, after which we toured much of the giant ranch on all-terrain four-wheel quads, with Michael in the lead wearing a large white helmet. We had dinner together that evening, and he told us how happy he was to have us at Neverland. But what interested me most was that even at Neverland, amid his graciousness, Michael, although more relaxed, still appeared shy, uncomfortable, and troubled.

A few days after we arrived, another family also came to stay on their first visit to Michael's ranch. I got the feeling that Michael invited the boy, Gavin, to Neverland solely to impress me with how devoted he was to children with cancer. Michael was hoping that I would vouch for him to the world. So I had to witness his commitment to the needy with my own eyes. Gavin was wearing a hat because chemotherapy had made him lose his hair. I watched Michael as he spoke to Gavin and encouraged him never to be ashamed of his baldness. I found it commendable that Michael would try so hard to give the boy a sense of his own beauty amid the ravishing effects of the treatment.

The whole atmosphere was relaxed with all the children enjoying each other's company. It seems incredible, in retrospect, that Michael's relationship with this family would lead to his arrest three years later when he would be accused of having molested that boy. Most of the time, Michael ignored both the boy and his family and I even found myself gently rebuking him for the neglect.

My children remember Gavin and his brother as being shy, and they remember how excited the boys were to have a sleepover in Michael's bedroom. My children were invited to join too, but being girls, and religious ones at that who are allowed limited contact with boys until marriageable age, they dismissed it outright and said no without further thought. I'm surprised parents would have allowed it, especially on their first visit, but nothing that happened during those few days seemed eventful. We were at Neverland the same night that the first abuse allegedly took place, in a room that was in the same guest suite as Gavin and his family. And it's equally hard to imagine that Michael was showing the boy pornographic materials while I was staying there with my family.

We soon discovered that our visit coincided with Michael's forty-first birthday, on August 29th. I was very surprised to see that nothing was being done to commemorate it. I wondered if being estranged from his family and with few close friends, he had invited us in order not to spend it alone.

I went to see him in his room. He told me, "In my family we didn't celebrate birthdays," explaining that it was a Jehovah's Witnesses belief not to make too much of oneself because it could lead to conceit and arrogance. I responded, "Well, in the Jewish religion celebrating birthdays is very important. It is the day you came into the world. It celebrates your existence. We have to grow on our birthdays, and growth, since it is always painful, should never be a solitary experience. It has to be shared." The kids of both families thereby went about arranging a small party that would take place that night for Michael's birthday.

My concern for Michael wasn't about his birthday, though. Something about the atmosphere of Neverland, combined with the long gap since I'd last seen him, raised my alarm. His lethargy was so pronounced it might have been described as lifeless. He wasn't so much sad as completely burned out, indolent, almost lazy, like a man who believed that life held no further mysteries or challenges. The only things that seemed to animate him were his children. He came across as a shell of a man, strangely incongruent with his electrifying stage presence and larger-than-life persona.

Michael's staff brought in the massive birthday cards and collages that his fans had either sent through the mail or left at the gates of Neverland. They were put up in the large kitchen for Michael to see, but he did not so much as look at them. He would wake up in the very late morning or early afternoon. Although he told me he was working feverishly to complete *Invincible*, I almost never saw work of any kind take place. A musician who had worked with Michael on several previous albums had come up from Los Angeles to work with him on new songs for the album, but he too spent very little time with Michael.

In the evenings he did become somewhat more animated. In his large, private theater, where we ate TV dinners, complete with small trays built for the occasion, he screened his old music videos for us. Often, my wife and my kids would make their way to bed, but Michael would continue to show me his past with relish.

I began to draw a number of cursory conclusions about his malaise.

First, whatever its merits, Neverland was not a good place for Michael. It was too isolating, too remote, making him into a hermit. It was an unhealthy escape that allowed him to run away from his responsibilities, even his professional ones. Indeed, it seemed that Michael was mostly wasting his life there. Neverland got stale for me and even my kids pretty quickly. It's one thing to visit Disneyland. It's another thing entirely to live in it. For the first few days the rides and attractions were fascinating. But after that they lost their novelty and Neverland came to feel like a giant cage.

Second, far more than the environment was affecting Michael Jackson. The great superstar was experiencing a malady of the soul, a sadness of the spirit. All the material blessings that surrounded him seemed to mean little, including Neverland. Only Prince and Paris were able to get him out of his room and give him some energy.

Third, Michael was at a critical point in his life. He seemed to be slipping quickly, dropping into a melancholic stupor of lethargy and inactivity. If he did not pull himself out he might never recover.

Fourth, while Michael might believe that a revival in his career would bring him happiness—as was evidenced by his nostalgia in persistently screening music videos from the height of his fame, back in the *Thriller* and *Bad* days—I was fairly convinced that this was not the case. I sensed that rather than more of the same, however glitzy and grand, what Michael needed was to take his life to the next level.

This would be a huge, perhaps insurmountable endeavor for Michael (should he have even a modicum of interest), given the crushing weight of negative judgment and lack of love he was experiencing. A surprising meeting gave even more weight to these thoughts.

On about the third day of our visit, an elderly gentleman arrived at the house for a meeting with Michael and Frank. It turned out he wasn't a record label executive as I had surmised. In fact, he was a low-level diplomat from an obscure European country whom Michael had surreptitiously met and whom he thought could help him get a UN Ambassadorship to fulfill his vision of being a kind of international spokesman on children's issues. Michael had asked me to join the meeting, I assumed, to vouch for his character. But in chatting with the man it quickly became clear that he was at such a junior station in the UN hierarchy that he had no means to really help. The whole situation was professionally sloppy and depressing.

Michael came across as desperate, thus conveying the impression even he acknowledged: given the 1993 allegations of child molestation (for which he never went to trial and was never found guilty), he was damaged goods and no one would be interested in him. But the meeting was extremely revealing in an important way.

I suddenly realized that this weight, this feeling of shame, was the major source of Michael's sadness. The 1993 allegations had compromised his integrity and squandered his credibility, especially in the area of children. Like all of us, Michael Jackson wanted to be thought a good person. Indeed, in my book *The Private Adam*, I point out that few things cause a man or woman more pain than to be thought of as wicked. We all attempt to tenaciously protect our reputations. Michael was crushed by the fact that people believed he was a pedophile. The pain was made all the greater because he wanted to consecrate his fame to a cause larger than himself. His celebrity, like Neverland, was a form of incarceration. He desperately wanted to use his fame to help the world's kids but was prevented from doing so because many thought him a monster.

Michael Jackson was no different than other men (and women) of accomplishment who suffered from the pain of a tarnished reputation. For example, Senator John McCain said that although he was a prisoner of war for five years in the Hanoi Hilton, suffering torture and the most inhuman deprivations, the pain was nothing compared to the accusation that he was one of the "Keating 5," a group of senators who had been accused of using their position to give favors to a savings and loan executive, although he was subsequently fully acquitted.

Thomas Jefferson, who led a life riddled with suffering, including the death of his young wife and all but one of his children, similarly said that the worst pain he ever faced was when he was accused of cowardice as Governor of Virginia during the American Revolution. Even the famous gangster Meyer Lansky, who wanted more than anything else to be known for his goodness in his service to society, once boasted that "Everyone who came into my casino knew that if he lost his money it wouldn't be because he was cheated." Lansky made sure to give large amounts of money to charity.

It was clear to me that Michael understood that he lived a profoundly contradictory existence. On the one hand, he was arguably the world's best-known entertainer and famous for loving children. On the other hand, average American parents would never trust him with their own kids and found his interest in children suspicious at best and criminal at worst. With the junior diplomat paying him a visit at Neverland, he was trying to restore his reputation.

On the day of Michael's birthday, I felt compelled to tell him that something seemed really wrong; some key ingredient of his life seemed missing. Going a step further, I said: "I was thinking what to get you for your birthday and I have discovered it's quite a conundrum. What do you give to the man who seemingly has everything? All I came up with is that you're not in need of any material gifts, but you are hurting deep down. If I could, I would offer you what I believe you need most—the gift of inspiration."

That comment was an icebreaker. Michael opened up to me more than ever before. The shyness and reticence disappeared. He began to tell me that I was correct about his deep pain and permanent sadness. "All I have ever wanted in life was to do something for the world's children. Fame, money, they mean nothing to me. I want to devote my life to helping kids."

While he did not say it outright, it was clear he realized that there was little involvement he could have with kids after the serious events of 1993, including the multimillion-dollar settlement with his accuser, which, while never officially made public, the whole world seemed to know about, down to the most intimate details. Those allegations, he said, were a lie. He repeated it over and over. They were designed to extort money. He could never harm a child. People were jealous of his success and tried to bring him down. His lawyers told him to settle because the media circus surrounding the allegations was destroying his life and ruining his career. And he repeated that he did not care about the money. He cared that people thought ill of him.

Up until that comment I was convinced that Michael could relate only to people who deferred to him or even fawned over him with a steady diet of compliments. While we had had many interesting conversations, and I'd given him some cursory spiritual direction and counsel that I hoped was helpful, I never expected our friendship to penetrate to a deeper level. It had been a year since we'd met, but until our trip to Neverland, I hadn't penetrated below the surface or broken any significant ground.

Soon I would return with my family to the East Coast, and Michael would go back to his life as well. Yet suddenly, Michael Jackson had opened up to me in a way that, I suspected, he had rarely done with anyone else before. I decided to rise to the challenge, beginning by sharing some of the distasteful truths about his life.

I looked at him and told him that, if he wanted to be a credible global spokesperson for children, he was going about things in entirely the wrong way. "You need a new approach to your project of helping children and to the entirety of your life," I ventured. "What you lack above all else is credibility. You are famous, sure. As an artist, they give you credit for your immense talent. But as a human being, the world thinks you are strange at best and a bit crazy at worst. They think there is something really fishy about you and kids and many even think you're guilty of the 1993 accusations. Only through a major lifestyle shift—a moral makeover—can you gain back the respectability you've lost."

At any moment, I expected to get the glazed look I had seen before when subjects came up that were either unpleasant or too much of a strain for Michael to handle. But I did not get that. On the contrary, he listened to every word I said and then eagerly asked, "Would you be able to help me do this?"

Whoa! Was he really listening?

"If you are serious, and you take it seriously," I said, "then, yes. I will be prepared to help you. I think you can do a lot of good with your life. God has given you a microphone to the world that few people in history have ever possessed. But you have got to get your life together if you are not to squander your potential. Today is your birthday and the clock is ticking." Right then and there I began to outline a program that Michael would follow for the next nine months.

I told him that the first thing he needed to do was get people to take him seriously. "Your life did not end in 1993," I said. "Even though the allegations against you were very serious, you were never arrested, charged, or convicted. If serious people take you seriously, and you undertake respectable actions and get away from your more frivolous pursuits, then the world will overlook your past and respect you again. If you're going to be a spokesperson for children, you need to surround yourself with respected thinkers, authors, statesmen, and, especially, childrearing experts. And you can never be alone with a child that is not yours, again. *Ever.*"

Michael immediately agreed with me. He verbalized his commitment to never being alone with kids.

I had a click of insight that the solution for Michael was to work with parents and caregivers rather than kids. After all, the problem for many kids was that they were being raised by proxy because parents were too busy, too stressed, or too uninterested to give children what they needed most—time and love, family dinners, bedtime stories. "Work on bringing your message to the world's parents," I said. "You will help the kids and the world will be grateful."

I then told him he had to get his energy back. "Neverland may be beautiful, but it is way too isolated. You have got to get out of here and be around people who inspire you. You are a person who thrives on that adrenaline rush that comes from crowds but here you are in this beautiful paradise. But you have to ask yourself, are you here because you love it or because you are hiding?"

Then I talked about the obstacles he faced. The world simply did not get what he was about. "Every day there are a thousand lies about you in the papers," I said. "I myself read that you have ten nannies for the kids, and that if one of their toys so much as touches the floor you immediately throw it in the garbage because you're a germophobe. From being here, of course, I have seen that all that is a lie." (Michael had one nanny, Grace, a sweet and highly intelligent woman from Rwanda who was responsible for sparking my considerable interest in the terrible Rwandan genocide of 1994, about which I would later write many columns.)

"And there are tons of other lies, as well. You have done a very poor job of explaining yourself to the world or responding to these incessant attacks. You have never explained why you have chosen to remain so childlike and people do not understand it. In light of the 1993 allegations, and in the absence of such explanations, people are bound to conclude that a forty-something adult who refuses to grow up is either spoiled or has a screw loose."

Finally, I told him that he had to make sure that he had the ingredients of a wholesome life. I could see that they were mostly absent. On his birthday, no family members came to visit. There was no regular Sunday church attendance. Indeed, aside from his personal faith, God seemed to be entirely absent from the life of Michael Jackson. He had no interaction with loving friends and seemed to take little satisfaction from his work. His children had no other kids to play with and their degree of isolation was anything but healthy.

Michael indicated that *this* would be a wonderful birthday present. "My whole life is about doing things for kids. If I can't help children, I don't want to live. I'm desperate and I think you're the only one who can help me. You're my friend. I love you, and I know you can help me."

To be sure, it was extremely seductive and flattering to have a man as influential as Michael telling me that I was the only one who could help him. It didn't so much feed my vanity, because my issue has always been insecurity much more than vanity (although the argument can be made that they are intimately intertwined). But it certainly made me feel special.

Was this a cosmic drama that was playing out? Could it be that a rabbi and a rock star could team up to help make the world a better place? Could the dream that I had harbored, ever since I watched my parents' divorce at the tender age of eight, of healing and strengthening families, come to fruition through the agency of Michael's fame and extend the effect of the writing and speeches I'd already been giving around the world? Or was my natural, internal brokenness, coupled with my desire to be recognized as an exponent of values, simply grabbing onto a rickety foundation to anchor itself? Only time would tell.

What was certain was that this was a unique challenge. An opportunity to help a man change and to help rehabilitate a person who was becoming a friend, who was a star, and who shared my love for children and the need to value them in our culture. I, after all, had seven (we now have nine, thank God). If Jay Leno owned seven antique cars, he was to be lauded for his impressive collection. But I went around apologizing for having overpopulated the world with seven kids. I was part of a religion that cherishes the innocence of children as the most spiritual of qualities. Why, even the Cherubim, the twin angels who sat atop the Holy Ark in the Holy of Holies, the most sacred part of the Temple in Jerusalem, had the faces of children. As a rabbi, I am the representative of a culture that values family and children above all else. And now I was being asked by one of the most recognizable names on earth to assist him in his work to improve the lives of children around the world.

I went back to my room and got my laptop, and, with Michael and Frank at my side, I started typing out a plan of action that could turn Michael's life around, leverage his fame to heal families, expose him to some of the world's most respected people, and bring sound healthy foundations back into his life.

Before I departed Neverland a few days later, Michael and I had further agreed that at some point soon he would come to New York for a few months and we would work hand-in-hand to help him regain his equilibrium and implement a plan of action to improve the lives of children and parents.

Most significantly, sitting in his bedroom and library before I left, we began the tape-recorded conversations that serve as the very soul of this book.

The Struggle to Do the Right Thing

Immediately after our family visit in August, and in order to continue the recorded conversations for this book, Michael and I arranged to meet in Los Angeles and again at Neverland, and by October or November he arrived in New York City, where he installed himself at the Four Seasons Hotel. Yes, he was coming to work on his album, but really he was coming so we could spend time together to implement our plan.

Throughout that late fall, we saw each other almost every day. Much of the time we were busy meeting with people who might help us or participate in a series of public events where Michael could show a much more serious side of himself. I brought Professor Stanley Greenspan, one of the top childrearing experts in America, to get to know him. I introduced him to my hero Elie Wiesel, the Holocaust survivor and Nobel laureate, and his wife. I took him to see a few friends of mine in finance to try and help him get his financial life under control. Nothing came of it, but they at least sat him down and told him his true situation, which basically was that he was bankrupt and on his way to financial oblivion. It was a complete effort on his behalf.

In addition, Michael stopped what I saw as his destructive secrecy. The trust between us was total—at least that's what I was led to believe. My access to him was unlimited. If I walked into his hotel room when he was taking a shower, he would pop out in a towel and yell, "I'll be out in a minute." Often I would arrive at his hotel suite and wake him up because I told him how important it was for him to break out of his pattern of staying up most of the night and sleeping most of the day (something for which Elvis was famous as well).

For those few months Michael probably came as close to living a normal life as he ever had or would. My objective was to stop getting him to see himself as an aloof deity who was beyond reproach. He was a man who happened to sing and dance better than almost anyone else alive. But he was a man nonetheless. He was not to be worshipped and he required the healthy ingredients of a normal life like anyone else. To achieve this end, we saw each other nearly every day, even on the Sabbath, when Michael would come to our home across the Hudson River in New Jersey with his two children for the Friday night Sabbath meal. Those Sabbath dinners were extremely important because Michael not only immersed himself in a nourishing, spiritual environment but also mixed comfortably with the other guests who regularly attended our Sabbath meals. This may sound like no big deal, but for Michael, who had rarely been treated as a mortal, sitting next to other people and simply conversing was a *very* big deal.

We would tell our Shabbos guests beforehand that a well-known personality would probably be joining us for dinner and would they mind simply treating him like everyone else. It was interesting watching Michael making small talk with people around the table. And after a few awkward starts—Michael was always very shy in public—he did a respectable job and charmed our guests. Friday nights I usually have a prayer service for members of our community at our home, and one Friday night when Michael came we were dancing and singing in a giant circle—about thirty of us—and Michael joined the circle and danced with everyone else. I remember how much he smiled that night, like it was liberating just joining, rather than always being aloof from, the crowd.

We'd also spend time talking about the basic requirements of a healthy life. I would say to him, "You have to get up at a normal hour, and you have to go to sleep at a normal hour. Life needs structure. Your kids have to play with other people's kids, and they have to go to parks and to school. Even if you are divorced, your children need access to both parents to grow up as secure and well-balanced as possible. You cannot isolate yourself. You need normal friends who can tether you to the earth and to whom you are accountable. You need family who will love you unconditionally, and you must reconcile with them if you have fallen out. Most of all, you need God, the architect of humanity and the source of all blessing, who gives us rules by which we all thrive. You have to stop making the rules up as you go along."

I talked to Michael about the importance of struggling to do the right thing, of replacing his desire for attention with a hunger for righteous action, and of understanding that the effort was as important for happiness as some perfect result.

I talked to him about one of the things that most distinguishes Judaism from Christianity. It is not the belief in Jesus as God or deity. Rather it's the belief in the *perfection* of Jesus. When Christians ask, "What would Jesus do?," they are using a model of perfection to guide their actions. And I think that makes a lot of people feel that they can never attain that high station of perfect action. I think in America we don't like ourselves. We harbor a high degree of self-loathing because we're not realistic about, and we dismiss, our humanity. What a shame that I have an ego; what a shame that I'm married and I'm attracted to people who are not my spouse.

In Judaism there are no perfect figures in the Bible. They are all flawed. The greatest of prophets, Moses, can't get into the Promised Land because of sin. We all struggle to do the right thing amid a predilection to do otherwise.

Christians define righteousness as perfection; Jews define righteousness as struggle. We wrestle with our nature; we try to do better always. We acknowledge from the very outset the tendencies within us that are altruistic, that are greedy, that are giving, that are self-absorbed, and that are selfless. There's a constant struggle and we do our best to make the right choice simply because it's right—even when we sometimes are falling very short of our own expectations. In that sense we are more forgiving of ourselves, although we are not forgiving of our unacceptable actions.

My point to Michael was that yes, he had demons, probably more than most. But that was okay as long as he wrestled to overcome them.

I quickly noticed that there were two Michael Jacksons: the shy, soft-spoken humble child from Gary, Indiana, whose only desire in life was to be loved and cherished and the raunchy, bizarre, aggressive, and aloof King of Pop whose principle desire was to retain the adoration of the masses at any cost. Michael need not feel defeated in having a bifurcated personality, and in Jewish thought much is made of the constant inner struggle between "the good inclination" and "the bad inclination." If Michael chose to struggle and ensure that what Abraham Lincoln called "the better angels of our nature" were mostly triumphant, he would not only be vindicated with a wholesome and blessed life but would also be righteous.

Strange as it may sound to the reader, I also believed strongly that Michael needed a wife, a soul mate who could share his journey and steer his broken existence back to a place of healing and redemption. My belief was that he could not rehabilitate his life outside of a meaningful relationship with a woman. I wished greatly for him to marry. Some would say that it was naïve to presuppose Michael's heterosexuality. But I never saw any indication of his being gay, and it is not for me to question a man's sincerity when he firmly avows to me that he is attracted to women and is fully capable of a loving relationship with a woman.

The Michael I knew and observed frequently remarked on the attractiveness of women and was open to thinking about the possibility for a better marriage in the future. Additionally, he never expressed interest in men or made any kinds of comments that would indicate he was homosexual or that there was some hidden truth about his sexuality. What I now believe is that Michael didn't trust women and thus did not feel safe with them. When I learned of Michael's use of pornography (which came out in his 2003 trial), and combined this knowledge with everything he told me about his childhood exposure to adult sexuality of a largely degrading, overwhelming kind, I could see how he may never have experienced a sense of innocence around sex or never matured beyond an adolescent sexual self.

I realize that one of Michael's most recent biographers claims to have evidence that Michael was gay. I never saw anything that would lead me to that conclusion. Michael never even hinted that there were any men around to whom he felt attracted and I never saw any man who could possibly have been Michael's lover. Michael knew that I have a gay orthodox Jewish brother whom I love and respect and he met my brother on several occasions, so he also knew that I would not have been shocked had he shared with me that he was gay. But he never did. I therefore pursued what I saw as my responsibility of encouraging Michael to rebuild his family with a wife. For the sake of his children as well, I was adamant that a maternal presence be introduced into his life. But he told me that while he was not averse to marriage—he had tried it twice and failed—he was very concerned that most women would marry him for his money.

There was one woman in particular who struck a positive note with Michael that fall, and his experience of meeting her gave me hope. I had known Katie Couric from the *Today Show*. She has interviewed me for two of my books and we stayed in touch. She asked if I would introduce her to Michael, so I arranged a lunch for the three of us that took place at Michael's suite at the Four Seasons.

The meeting was warm and pleasant and as soon as Katie departed, Michael turned to me and said, "Shmuley, you're always encouraging me to date. But the women I meet aren't right for me. Someone like Katie might be perfect. She was smart, natural, and wasn't intimidated being around me. She's obviously very special."

"Well Michael," I replied, "I guess they don't call her America's sweetheart for nothing. But are you seriously suggesting that you want to go out with her?"

"Yeah," Michael said, "maybe for coffee or something."

"Why don't you ask her?"

Michael giggled nervously. "Shmuley, you know how shy I am."

"Okay," I said, "do you want me to ask her for you?"

"Yes, would you?"

Wow, I thought, what do I do now? No doubt, Katie would find the invitation kind of strange, but what the heck. As a relationships counselor and author I had always done matchmaking. That night, I reached Katie at home. I said to her, "This is going to be one of the strangest calls you've ever received, Katie, but guess what, Michael wants to know if you want to go out with him for coffee?"

Now it was Katie who giggled nervously. "Shmuley, I guess you don't read the celebrity magazines. I'm dating someone." I knew, as everyone did, that Katie was tragically widowed and was raising her two daughters as a single mother. But indeed I had no idea that she was in a relationship. "I guess not," I said sheepishly, and I apologized for the call. "No, don't apologize," she said. "You had good intentions." And I would not have revealed this story if not for the fact that Katie told the story on the David Letterman show in August 2009. But clearly this and many other demonstrations of Michael's heterosexual leanings gave me a strong belief that Michael was attracted to women.

On my birthday, November 19, my wife made a party for me and invited close friends, including Michael and his children. It was fun and a perfect chance for Michael to participate in the everyday flow of family occasions and begin to establish a wider circle of friends. (It always struck me that November 19, 2003, my birthday three years later, was the day before he was arrested on charges of child molestation.)

Then we spent our second Thanksgiving together. He came over to our house just with his kids. Imagine, he had nowhere else to go, no family, no old friends. After dinner, I noticed something interesting. Michael had brought a goofy video for the kids to watch on TV. He sat down, and me, my wife, and my kids sat next to him. Michael practically sat on his hands, almost to show me that I had nothing to fear. And I felt bad for him. True, I never left him alone with my kids, but I didn't think he would ever have harmed them, God forbid. But to see that even in the full view of the parents he was trying to prove his uprightness was to see how damaged he'd been and how suspicious he thought the world was of him. It made me pity him.

In December Michael attended, at my invitation, his first big public event in many years where he was a participant—not the headliner. It was the Angel Ball fundraiser for research into cancer, with lots of A List guests in attendance. (Denise Rich's daughter, Gabrielle, a gifted and beautiful young woman whom I knew at Oxford when she was a student, died of leukemia at age 27, and the ball raises money to help fight the disease.)

We met President Clinton, and Elie and Marion Wiesel and Professor Stanley Greenspan came with us as our guests.

In the rush of celebrities who came over to meet Michael, at one point Michael was pushed so hard he claimed he injured his back and unfortunately was forced to leave the dinner early. When we got back to his hotel, I discovered for the very first time the drug problems that would later claim Michael's life. Coming back with us to the hotel were the Wiesels and members of my family. It was a great honor for Michael to have one of the most respected humans alive, and a recipient of the Nobel Peace Prize, befriend him and accompany him back to his hotel suite with his wife. We were all going to have coffee and chat. But Michael told me he had to lie down due to the terrible pain in his back.

Professor Wiesel offered to call his personal physician to attend to Michael, and about half an hour later one of New York's most prestigious doctors walked through the door. He went into Michael's room and spent about a quarter of an hour there. When he came out, he looked ashen-faced. He stood by the door of Michael's bedroom and said to us, "Michael has just asked me for a quantity of drugs that would kill a horse."

I was shocked. I ran into Michael's room. "Michael, the doctor just said that you asked him for enough drugs to kill a horse." Michael seemed very calm. "Shmuley, he's wrong. I have a very high tolerance. I'm used to this. I'll be fine." He was defending what he just asked for.

"Look Michael, what you think doesn't matter. Years ago you admitted to an addiction to prescription painkillers. Maybe your tolerance level is extremely high. But even the doctor doesn't want to administer the level of painkillers you're requesting. You're playing with your life here. This stuff is poison. You have to get off it. You're just going to have to get used to the pain. We live with our pain and we grow from our pain. You're not supposed to just medicate it away. You can't pay people to take it away. You can't dull it with doctors. And this doctor is a *real* doctor and he won't give it to you, and none of us will let you have it." The doctor departed and Michael did not get the medication he requested.

The next day Michael came to my home for Sabbath dinner with Prince and Paris and made a point of telling me that the reason he was standing, rather than sitting, at the table was that he did not take any painkillers for his back, as per our conversation the night before. He was trying to impress me with his capacity for growth. He wanted to show that he got it.

As the weeks progressed Michael and I continued to work on promoting our Heal the Kids initiative, which focused on inspiring parents to have regular family dinners together, read bedtime stories to their children, and provide them with a loving and protective environment. We met with many dignitaries who could be helpful to the organization and made plans for two major public events right after the New Year. The first was a seminar in parenting that would take place at Carnegie Hall and which would be introduced by Michael, and the second, a joint lecture Michael and I would deliver about a children's Bill of Rights at Oxford University in England.

Just before Christmas, Michael went home to Neverland for the holidays. That's when I got my first real view of how careless Michael was with money. He had a whole floor at the hotel, one of the most expensive in New York. He kept the floor for the three or four weeks he was away. When he came back, I asked him why he didn't give the rooms back. And he said, "What were we supposed to do with our stuff?" I said, "Michael, you pack it in suitcases and put it in hotel storage. Then it's ready for you as soon as you come back." It was yet another glimpse of the kind of recklessness that was undermining Michael's life and leading him down the road to bankruptcy.

And this financial picture is significant. One of the main factors that killed Michael was the crazy schedule of fifty concerts for 2009 in the O2 Center. Michael was not in the psychological, emotional, or physical position to get through one concert, let alone fifty. But he was forced to agree to it due to his horrendous finances, accumulated through years of reckless spending. And when Michael panicked under pressure, he turned to ever larger doses of prescription drug medication for salvation.

Making Changes, Making a Difference

I had always heard that Elvis met with spiritual personalities on a regular basis and his question to them was, "I was a truck driver from Memphis and then I became the most famous entertainer in the world. So why me? What am I supposed to do with this? To what purpose is the fame meant to be consecrated?" It was his inability to find a satisfactory and compelling response to this important question that made fame his incarceration.

When you can't devote your celebrity to a higher cause it becomes a terrible weight. You become a burden to yourself. You're the biggest star in the world, but you're imprisoned and can't even walk outside. To make matters worse, you become Elvis even in your own mind. You can no longer think of yourself in natural, organic terms. Rather, you see yourself from the perspective of your fans. You begin to lose your innate humility and regard anyone who doesn't treat you with due reverence as someone unworthy of your friendship and trust. Those who criticize you are quickly shunted aside. You gravitate toward sycophants. Now if you can liberate yourself by devoting that burden to something higher then you're free. But if you can't you get crushed under its weight. And that's what was slowly happening to Michael.

Michael returned to New York in January and we got into gear for the several major events we'd scheduled for February and March to launch Heal the Kids.

The first, on Valentine's Day at Carnegie Hall, was a large event where Michael and I invited leading childrearing experts, as well as personalities such as Johnnie Cochran, Judith Regan, and Dr. Drew Pinsky, to discuss how the romantic love between husband and wife should lead to the building of a stable family with children being nourished from the foundational devotion of loving parents. Then, less than a month later, on March 6th, we gave a major address together at the main debating chamber of the Oxford Union at Oxford University, where so many luminaries had spoken before him. The speech was largely on the theme of forgiveness and the importance of children refraining from judging their parents. I had written it for Michael based on our interviews for this book and his own thoughts about his desire to change and heal.

When people first heard that Michael was going to give a lecture at Oxford they laughed. But he received a standing ovation from over a thousand enthralled students and it was extremely well-received in the press. I worked harder writing that speech than almost anything I had ever written because I so badly wanted the world to see Michael in a positive light. Interestingly an excerpt from the speech was used in the opening to Ian Halperin's bestseller, *Unmasked.*

To my mind, his words can almost be seen as Michael's and my hope and wish for the new direction in his life. I had decided that the lecture should focus largely on the theme of children refraining from judging their parents so that Michael himself would seek to purge himself of all the unhealthy anger he harbored toward his father. If the broken parent-child bond was to be rebuilt, it could not be done against a backdrop of bitterness, disappointment, and recrimination. Children would have to learn how to put themselves in their parents' shoes, empathize with the challenges they faced as people and as parents, and try and understand why they made the bad mistakes they did as parents.

I told Michael that he would have to embody the lesson by not just preaching it but living it. He would have to reconcile with his father, with whom he had a famously tortured relationship. Michael had on many public occasions criticized his father and I had told him it was inappropriate. He owed his father gratitude rather than hostility, in accordance with the Fifth Commandment, in which God had commanded him to honor his father. Even if he didn't always feel love for him, he still had to honor him.

On the way down to Oxford, while we were just hours away from the lecture, I told Michael that the time had come. His lecture would be meaningless if he did not call his father before the event and tell him that he loved him and that he should never have judged him. That, because he hadn't lived his father's life, he couldn't possibly understand why his father did the things he did. He took a cell phone and called his father and reached him in Las Vegas.

Several of us in the car bore witness to Michael telling his father, perhaps for the first time, that he loved him and that his speech at Oxford that night would be all about him and how he now recognizes that he had no right to judge him. Michael always called his father Joseph, rather than Dad. When his father first answered the phone, Michael said, "I'm giving a speech at Oxford University tonight. And it's about you." His father immediately said, "Uh oh!" And Michael corrected his misconception. "No, it's nothing bad. It's to tell the world that I love you."

Michael's speech conveyed an important message of healing:

> *You probably weren't surprised to hear that I did not have an idyllic childhood. The strain and tension that exists in my relationship with my father is well documented. My father is a tough man, and he pushed my brothers and me hard, from the earliest age, to be the best performers we could be.*
>
> *He had great difficulty showing affection. He never really told me he loved me. And he never really complimented me either. If I did a great show, he would tell me it was a good show. And if I did an okay show, he told me it was a lousy show. He seemed intent above all else on making us a commercial success. And at that he was more than adept. My father was a managerial genius and my brothers and I owe our professional success in no small measure to the forceful way that he pushed us. He trained me as a showman and, under his guidance, I couldn't miss a step.*
>
> *But what I really wanted was a Dad. I wanted a father who showed me love. And my father never did that. He never said, "I love you," whilst looking me straight in the eye, he never played a game with me, he never gave me a piggyback ride, he never threw a pillow at me.*
>
> *But I remember once when I was about four years old there was a little carnival and he picked me up and put me on a pony. It was a tiny gesture, probably something he forgot five minutes later. But because of that one moment, I have this special place in my heart for him. Because that's how kids are. The little things mean so much to them, and for me, that one moment meant everything. I only experienced it that one time but it made me really feel a lot differently about him and the world.*

But now I am a father myself, and one day I was thinking about my own children, Prince and Paris, and how I wanted them to think of me when they grow up. To be sure, I would like them to remember how I always wanted them with me wherever I went, how I always tried to put them before everything, including my albums and my concerts.

But there are also challenges in their lives. Because my kids are stalked by paparazzi, they can't always go to a park or a movie with me. So, what if they grow older and resent me and how my choices affected their youth? Why weren't we given an average childhood, like all the other kids, they might ask?

And at that moment, I pray that my children will give me the benefit of the doubt. That they will say, "Our Daddy did the best he could given the unique circumstances that he faced. He may not have been perfect, but he was a warm and decent man who tried to give us all the love in the world."

I hope that they will always focus on the positive things, on the sacrifices I willingly made for them, and not criticize the sacrifices circumstances may have forced upon them or the errors I have made and will certainly continue to make in raising them. For we have all been someone's child and we know that despite the very best of plans and efforts mistakes will always occur. That is just being human.

And when I think about this, of how I hope that my children will not judge me unfavorably, and will forgive me my shortcomings, I am forced to think of my own father, and despite the part of me that denied it for years I have to admit that he must have loved me. He did love me, and I know that.

There were little things that showed it. When I was a kid I had a real sweet tooth—we all did. My favorite food was glazed donuts, and my father knew that. So, every few weeks I would come downstairs in the morning and there on the kitchen counter was a bag of glazed donuts—no note, no explanation—just the donuts. It was like Santa Claus. Sometimes I would think about staying up late at night so I could see him leave them there but, just like with Santa Claus, I didn't want to ruin the magic, for fear that he would never do it again. My father had to leave them stealthily at night so no one might catch him with his guard down. He was scared of human emotion, he didn't understand it or know how to deal with it. But he did know donuts.

And when I allow the floodgates to open up, there are other memories that come rushing back, memories of other tiny gestures, however incomplete, that showed that he did what he could.

So tonight, rather than focusing on what my father didn't do, I want to focus on all the things he did do, and on his own personal challenges. I want to stop judging him.

I have started reflecting on the fact that my father grew up in the South, in a very poor family. He came of age during the Depression, and his own father, who struggled to feed his children, showed little affection toward his family and raised my father and his siblings with an iron fist. Who could have imagined what it was like to grow up a poor black man in the South, robbed of dignity, bereft of hope, struggling to become a man in a world that saw my father as subordinate. I was the first black artist to be played on MTV *and I remember how big a deal it was even then. And that was in the 1980s!*

My father moved to Indiana and had a large family of his own, working long hours in the steel mills, work that kills the lungs and humbles the spirit, all to support his family. Is it any wonder that he found it difficult to expose his feelings? Is it any mystery that he hardened his heart, that he raised the emotional ramparts? What other choice does a man have when his life is a struggle just to get by? And most of all, is it any wonder why he pushed his sons so hard to succeed as performers so that they could be saved from what he knew to be a life of indignity and poverty? I have begun to see that even my father's harshness was a kind of love, an imperfect love, to be sure, but love nonetheless. He pushed me because he loved me. Because he wanted no man to ever look down at his offspring.

And now, with time, rather than bitterness I feel blessing. In the place of anger, I have found absolution. And in the place of revenge, I have found reconciliation. And my initial fury has slowly given way to forgiveness.

Almost a decade ago, I founded a charity called Heal the World. The title was something I felt inside me. Little did I know, as Shmuley later pointed out, that those two words form the cornerstone of Old-Testament prophecy. Do I really believe that we can heal this world that is riddled with war and hate and genocide even today? And do I really think that we can heal our children, the same children who can enter their schools with guns and hatred and shoot down their classmates like they did at Columbine; our children who can beat a defenseless toddler to death like the tragic story of Jamie Bulger [murdered in England by two ten-year-olds]? Of course I do, or I wouldn't be here tonight. But it all begins with forgiveness. Because to heal the world we first have to heal ourselves. And to heal the kids, we first have to heal the child within each and every one of us.

As an adult, and as a parent, I realize that I cannot be a whole human being, nor a parent capable of fully committed, unconditional love until I put to rest the ghosts of my own childhood.

And that's what I'm asking all of us to do tonight. Live up to the Fifth of the Ten Commandments. Honor your parents by not judging them. Give them the benefit of the doubt. Understand that they had their own struggles, their own pains, their own traumas, and still did the best that they could.

That is why I want to forgive my father, and to stop judging him. I want to forgive him because I want a father and this is the only one that I've got. I want the weight of my past lifted from my shoulders, and I want to be free to step into a new relationship with my father for the rest of my life, unhindered by the goblins of the past.

Shmuley and I, who are launching this initiative tonight, are members of the Black and Jewish communities, both of which have confronted horrors and atrocities throughout our histories. How do our communities forgive the horrors done to us without forgetting them altogether? By remembering. We pass along our stories. But we also rise above those stories. In a *world filled with hate, we still dare to hope. In a world filled with anger, we still dare to comfort. In a world filled with despair, we still dare to dream. And in a world filled with distrust, we still dare to believe.*

To all of you tonight who feel let down by your parents, I ask you to let down your disappointment. To all of you tonight who feel cheated by your fathers or mothers, I ask you not to cheat yourself further. And to all of you tonight who feel like telling their parents they can go to hell, I ask you tonight to extend your hand to them instead.

For in the exchange of pain the accounts are never balanced. Vengeance cannot bring restitution. By forgiving our parents, we are not denying that they may have wronged us. We are not whitewashing their sins or creating saints of sinners. But harboring resentment against your parents will never give you the love you so crave. Getting even will not make our lives better. Perpetual pain, perpetual suffering, the cycle never ends. There is a Bakongo proverb that says, "To take revenge is to sacrifice oneself." And friends, our generation has sacrificed and suffered enough.

Rather, I am asking you, I am asking myself, to give our parents the gift of unconditional love so that they too may learn how to love from us, their children. So that love will finally be restored to a desolate and lonely world. Shmuley once mentioned to me an ancient Biblical prophecy which says that the time would come when "the hearts of the parents would be restored through the hearts of their children." My friends, we are those children.

Mahatma Gandhi said, "The weak can never forgive. Forgiveness is the attribute of the strong." Tonight, be strong. Beyond being strong, rise to the greatest challenge of all: to restore that broken covenant by teaching our parents how to love. We must all overcome whatever crippling effects our childhoods may have had on our lives, and in the words of Jesse Jackson, forgive each other, redeem each other, and move on.

With the world press extolling his speech at Oxford and with his life making strides toward normalcy, things were looking up. Michael came with me to synagogue and regularly attended Shabbat dinner. He seemed directed and content. He listened to what was being planned and what the purpose was, and he'd agree.

There were also simple times when I witnessed Michael's extremely moving acts of humility and kindness. A neighborhood friend asked me if he could bring his thirty-something brother with Down syndrome to meet Michael. Michael was one of his idols and the brother could even do the moon walk. Michael was focused on finishing his album but told me he could do a short meeting. The man arrived and sang some of Michael's songs for us, did the moon walk, and in general imitated Michael on stage. Michael could not have been kinder to this special man with special needs.

After the man departed with his family I thanked Michael for his kindness. "You did a very beautiful thing today," I said. "I am truly grateful."

"No Shmuley," he replied. "You did me a favor by bringing him. I so enjoyed his company. I'm jealous of him."

"Why would you say that, Michael?"

"Because he will never grow up. He will remain forever young and innocent. I envy him."

There were many stories like these, special acts of kindness granted by a soft and gentle human being who had a soft and gentle heart.

The End of Our Relationship

As Michael become more motivated, energetic, and visible, those who had written him off suddenly started showing up again. You could see them saying to themselves: He's going places again. People who had been at their wits ends with his lack of productivity were ready to start making things happen. Managers and producers whom he had not heard from in quite a while were now visiting him in his hotel suite. The direct result was that my influence with Michael was now waning and he was slipping—missing meetings, not keeping regular hours, not showing his commitment, cringing and sinking into himself if I asked him about something to do with advancing our project to prioritize kids in the lives of parents. There was a growing tension between us. He started to disregard my advice to stay the course of the program we had devised on his birthday. And rather than being supported, I was being undermined by the people around him who accused me of diminishing Michael's star power.

I heard later that Michael had been introduced to concert promoter David Guest (best known for marrying Liza Minelli and the messy lawsuits that followed) on a trip to meet Shirley Temple Black. David started saying to Michael that they should do a concert together to mark his thirtieth year as a performer. Michael was afraid to tell me because he knew I would oppose the idea until he'd found a sense of spiritual renewal. I'd tell him: Don't go back half-baked. It killed you the first time; don't do it the second time.

Of course I knew some meetings were going on, but what I didn't know, and learned a few months later from Michael's parents at their home in Encino, was that some in Michael's professional team had started telling Michael that I was demystifying him and making him too available. The attitude was that the rabbi is well-intentioned, but he is cheapening your brand by getting you to do free lectures at places like universities when your real place is in front of hundreds of thousands of paying fans in stadiums.

During this time the British journalist Martin Bashir had his office call me as an intermediary about a possible documentary on Michael because one of the producers he worked with knew me from my years as rabbi at Oxford University. I told Michael it would be a disastrous mistake. "Don't even think of doing this documentary," I warned. "First, your life is not yet ready to be opened to scrutiny. Second, you don't need to be more famous and invite cameras into your life. You need to heal and to become more credible."

I didn't even bother calling Bashir's people back and thought the project was dead. Two years later, our mutual friend Uri Geller would persuade Michael to do the Bashir project, which would be aired in 2003 under the title *Living with Michael Jackson*. It would prove to be one of the single greatest catastrophes ever to befall him. Michael's comments about "sleeping with children" would be seen by millions worldwide and would lead directly to his arrest on charges of child molestation.

Uri and I remain good friends and I know he cared for Michael deeply. I never would have met Michael if it weren't for Uri. And it was for this reason that I made a point of showing constant gratitude by including Uri in everything that Michael and I did together, including and especially our trip to the UK for the Oxford lecture, where Uri joined Michael and me on the stage at the Oxford Union. I honored Uri's request to bring Michael to Uri's wedding as best man, and as Uri's rabbi I myself was honored to be asked to perform the wedding. Uri is one of the warmest and most loving people I know. But even with the best of intentions, his arranging for Michael to do the Bashir documentary was tragically misguided and catastrophic.

Michael's life was a complete mess. He was a celebrity spendthrift who had an as-yet unexplained relationship to children. Additionally, his many fears for their safety compelled him to hide his children behind veils. He had little communication with the normal, everyday, outside world, let alone his own family, and was desperately in need of healing in virtually every aspect of his life. Amid promising me that he would never again be alone with children, clearly this was a practice Michael was continuing, at least with Gavin, the boy we had met at Neverland. Michael desperately needed spiritual guidance and moral direction, not another camera crew. Never in my life have I seen a single TV program so completely polish off a man's future as did *Living with Michael Jackson*, which is not to fault Bashir and the people who made the documentary but rather Michael and his team for ever agreeing. It was most unfortunate that people who cared so deeply for Michael advised him so poorly.

As Michael moved back into his identity as a star, he became more secretive and secluded from me. For example, he had promised me that he would never again have plastic surgery. Yet I was told by people in his circle that he had had another procedure that he hid from me. It was partly out of embarrassment—he was ashamed to show me that he was not strong enough to keep to our goals and plan for him—and partly because, by now, he could not suffer my criticisms, which increased with time. Most significantly, whereas before he looked to me as a trusted guide and loving friend, he was now treating me as an irritant.

As I saw him falter—wake up late, miss meetings, spend money he didn't have—I began to offer ever-increasing rebukes. They were offered gently and lovingly, but they were rebukes nonetheless, and Michael had absolutely no idea how to handle them.

The day of our last planned event was March 25th. It was a community-based literacy and health initiative in Newark, New Jersey, and it was the straw that broke the camel's back. My dear friend Cory Booker was our partner in the event. At the time he was a councilman and today is the mayor of Newark and one of America's most admired, accomplished, and inspirational leaders. Although an African-American non-Jew, Cory was president of my student organization, the Oxford L'Chaim Society, when he was a Rhodes Scholar at the university. He is one of the most special, loving, and uplifting human beings I had ever met, and together at Oxford we hosted great world leaders, such as Mikhail Gorbachev, to lecture to our students on values-based themes.

Cory and I continue to be like brothers and Michael had met Cory several times at our home for the Friday night Sabbath dinner. Michael immediately saw in Cory what I had seen all those years before and many times commented to me how inspired he was by my soul-friendship with Cory. Michael agreed to distribute children's books to parents in Cory's ward of Newark. It was to be a beautiful opportunity to highlight the importance of reading children a bedtime story.

But by the time we actually went to Newark, Michael was already getting weary and wary of all the events he had to show up for—it had been a whirlwind six weeks of being in the public eye in an entirely unfamiliar role. I knew we were on our way out. He seemed to be slowly leaving the work we had launched together. He was going back to being a superstar.

The event at Newark with Councilman Booker was a huge success and hundreds of families were in attendance. We distributed thousands of books. But on the way back to his van, Michael barely spoke to me. I could tell he was angry. Always the gentleman, Michael never showed overt hostility and I never once witnessed him lose his temper. Rather, if he was annoyed he would simply withdraw. He would punish you by taking away the one thing that meant the most to him: attention.

We arrived back at Michael's hotel suite and I underwent one of the most painful experiences in my friendship with Michael. One of Michael's principal managers sat me down, with Michael looking on, and began explaining to me why Michael was upset. "Yes, Shmuley, Michael loves you but he is annoyed. You just don't get it." Carnegie

Hall and Oxford were one thing. But a bunch of families in Newark? Michael is the biggest star in the world. He doesn't do things like that. A councilman in a small New Jersey city? Michael is around presidents and prime ministers. I was debasing his fame, abusing his celebrity.

Then the manager said something to me that I shall never, for the rest of my days, forget: "You want to make Michael normal. What you don't understand is that he's famous because he's *not* normal."

Michael was silent as he listened. Clearly he had found someone to do his dirty work. This was a planned and sanctioned speech. So there it was. Two sides of Michael Jackson, forever in conflict, forever at war. The normal, cute, adorable child from Gary, Indiana, who just wanted to sing and make people happy versus the reclusive superstar who was prepared to walk with a giraffe, befriend a chimp, mask his face, and disfigure his countenance, all in an effort to be mysterious and aloof so the public would never stop focusing on him.

I pondered the words. *He is famous because he's not normal.* And in that statement I saw the full tragedy of Michael's life. Here was a man so bereft of love, so dependent on attention, that he would do almost anything to get it. If it meant becoming the world's biggest freak show, he would pay that price too. The public's opinion of him be damned. Just so long as they were still talking about him.

When I took him to Newark, New Jersey, to give out books to parents from low-income households to read to their children, I did so in the belief that he was more interested in doing good with his celebrity than pursuing fame. But the superstar had won out. The wholesome boy had been buried alive. And a superstar doesn't do mundane things like distribute books to a bunch of nobodies. And he doesn't do so for a mere councilman who is trying so hard to improve the lives of working families. (What a tragic irony to see all these years later that Michael is now sadly no longer alive and Cory Booker is hailed today as one of America's most accomplished mayors and is being spoken of in many circles as destined for national leadership).

So our relationship slowly unraveled and I finally decided that it was time to call it quits. I was there to help Michael improve his life and consecrate his celebrity to a cause larger than himself. If he could not sustain the effort, if I was to be told he only involves himself with causes that behooved his fame, if I was expected to become another silent hanger-on, I was going to *move* on. I left Michael's hotel knowing that in all likelihood we would never be close again. That the right thing to do when one could no longer assist someone in crisis was at the very least not to bless his decline by sitting and watching in complacent silence.

It was the last time I saw Michael.

Two weeks later Michael called from Miami. He said, "I'm sending a plane for you" and then he spent a half hour on the phone trying to get me to come, telling me he still wanted to do our work together. He blamed our rift on the people who surrounded him. I felt the tug. Plus, I was raised in Miami and still had family there I could visit at the same time. I said I would think about it, and I did. But ultimately, I decided not to go. If Michael was serious about rededicating himself to the work we had begun, it would manifest itself through tangible action rather than empty words.

I waited for him to return to New York, but time went on and the announcement was made for two thirtieth anniversary concerts at Madison Square Garden that were to take place in September.

I was disappointed in Michael. I felt he had misrepresented himself to me and misrepresented himself to the world. He made me believe that his first priority was to help the world's children and live a life of unequalled altruism. And while he may have believed that, in reality Michael could never fully overcome the gravitational pull of superstardom. More than anything else, Michael misrepresented himself to himself. He had two sides, the giver and the narcissist, but was blind to the latter.

My relationship with Michael wasn't quite finished, however. Summer came and my family was together on an RV trip. Frank called and said, "Michael asked me to call you. We can't do the concert without you. You're his closest friend, Shmuley. He wants you and the kids to be there. It just wouldn't be the same otherwise." I pulled off the highway to talk it over with my wife. I knew I had to decide right then and there. Thank God my wife was there. I wasn't sure I had the power to resist the magnetic attraction of a superstar. My wife, who is the most wholesome person I know and who has a complete immunity to all things involving fame and celebrity, helped me over the mountain and I decided that I would decline.

I was Michael's friend and rabbi, not his fan. My purpose was to redirect his life with a moral and spiritual foundation, not to clap when he moved his feet. I would not be a sycophant. I would never go back to our friendship unless I could influence him positively. I would not sit passively and watch his decline. I could never allow myself to be compromised in this way. I called my office and dictated the following message to be faxed to his personal assistant:

> Rabbi and Mrs. Shmuley Boteach thank Mr. Michael Jackson for his kind invitation to his thirtieth anniversary concert but regret that they will be unable to attend.

In the end it was a painful but necessary moment. I was acknowledging that something about Michael was beyond redemption and that if I returned to his orbit I would sink too. I later explained to Frank that I was never the friend of Michael Jackson the superstar. I loved and cared for Michael Jackson the man. Since he had buried that side of himself, I was moving on. I wanted to go back to what I had been before Michael Jackson: a rabbi who tried to spread the glory of God rather than bask in the glow of a superstar.

His Demons

There was a time when I felt Michael could redeem his life, and that I could be a strong, perfect, caring guide to help him. Many others thought they could play that role too—from his mother Katherine, to his first wife Lisa Marie Presley when he was coping with the 1993 allegations and his drug addiction, to Frank Cascio, whose devotion to Michael knew no end. But for all Michael's strengths—his fierce determination, his pure talent and charisma, his patience, his innate gentleness and love of children—there were forces in his life that he didn't want to overcome or didn't have the strength to—especially his own hubris, his use of drugs, and the stone around his neck with the 1993 and then 2003 molestation charges.

Messiah Complex

What most corrupted the life and career of Michael Jackson was his belief that he was different from ordinary folk—more elevated, more sensitive, more long-suffering—and thus not subject to rigid rules of right and wrong. His hubris knew no bounds. If you thought he was having too much plastic surgery, well, you could never understand the imaging needs of a superstar. And if you thought that sharing a bed with a child, however platonic, was morally deplorable, well, that too was because seeing it from your mortal vantage point could never enlighten you as to how the self-proclaimed "voice for the voiceless" saw it. While Michael could be forgiven for his naïve assumption that even hardened mass murderers have something good left in them, what is truly shocking is his belief that *he* could somehow have gotten through even to Adolph Hitler, as our conversations will later demonstrate.

To justify sharing a bed with children, he told boldface lies. For example, his telling Ed Bradley on *60 Minutes* that Gavin Arvizo arrived at Neverland in a wheelchair and had to be carried to places such as the game room was preposterous. The boy I saw that day in August 2001 was extremely active, running around from ride to ride, and might even have been construed as wild. It's not, I think, that Michael consciously wished to deceive. Rather, he was so insecure about himself that he had to always sound like more of a saint than he was. Michael's insecurity led him to being an extremist. It was not enough to be a humanitarian. He had to be the greatest humanitarian on the planet. It was not enough to give hope to a child with cancer. Always the martyr, he pictured himself carrying the child on his back through a parched desert with no promised land in sight.

With the passage of time, I watched Michael's unhealthy Messiah complex grow, no doubt egged on by ingratiating fans who never rebuked him for behavior, which was clearly self-destructive. He refused to accept responsibility for his actions and blamed others' jealousy for his incessant problems.

The Bible's word for an adulterous wife is *sotah*. It literally means "to stray, to turn aside, to depart the path of love and righteousness." It is a word that is relevant to the sins of Michael Jackson. For his sins—aside, of course, from the extremely serious allegations of child molestation—

were never crimes he committed against someone else. They were primarily crimes against himself, a departure from the way of light, a detour into an ever-thickening darkness.

He could never see that a man who spends tens of millions of dollars on himself per annum, sulks in the most lavish lifestyle, and even has his security people holding his umbrella for him while he is on trial (where you would think he might finally have learned to exhibit some humility) is hardly the Messiah. He's just another damaged and self-absorbed celebrity.

Drug Use

Michael confused his afflictions of soul with ailments of the body. But whereas once upon a time the light of celebrity was hot enough to make him feel better, he had reached a stage where even that no longer warmed him. Drugs became the only balm by which to dull pain. As time went on I understood why things like painkillers or plastic surgery were so attractive to Michael. *Michael knew nothing but pain.*

Michael's drug use was difficult to detect because of how spacey and out-of-it everyone expected him to be. Plus, it was easy to assume that Michael took strong painkillers only when he was in physical pain. In the time that I knew him, he always seemed intent on me having a positive view of him and nothing untoward was ever done in my presence.

In retrospect, there were more signs that he was on something than I or anyone around him recognized or acknowledged. Michael was very forgetful. He sometimes seemed woozy. His head once drooped completely at the home of a friend that I had taken him to meet. But I just thought that with the kind of crazy hours he kept—Michael was going to sleep at 3:00 or 4:00 in the morning—he was just always tired. Michael often called me and spoke as if he was either tremendously inspired or a bit off. "Shmuley, I'm just calling to tell you that I love you. *I looovvveee you. IIII llloooovvveee yooouuu. . .* " "I love you too, Michael," I would say. But by and large, those conversations were very short, and I thought to myself, yes, that's strange, but that's Michael. He's different. He's eccentric.

What perhaps should have made me most suspicious was Michael's constant physical ailments. He was always complaining that a part of his body was hurting or had been injured. This, of course, became a central staple of his trial. But the Angel Ball was my earliest exposure to it. Michael claimed that he had been slammed against a wall by fans and fellow celebrities trying to get his autograph. But even if that had happened, it seemed as though the smallest knocks could completely incapacitate him. And that was either true—Michael did have a very fragile disposition—or he was using these ailments, which in his mind were real, as an excuse to take more painkillers.

A few weeks before the major address Michael was to give at Oxford, when he was back in California and I was in New York, Michael called to tell me he had broken his foot while practicing dancing at Neverland. "Are you going to cancel Oxford?" I asked. "No," he said. "It's way too important." In due course, Michael arrived in Britain in a foot cast and on crutches. I heard him give a number of conflicting stories about how he had broken his foot, but again, I made nothing of it, thinking that Michael was forgetful.

A doctor traveled with him to England from the United States and stayed in Michael's hotel. Whenever he would complain of terrible pain from his foot, they would go together into his room and emerge, about a half-hour later, with Michael looking glassy-eyed. I asked the doctor about his background and his practice, and as I recall he seemed to give inadequate responses. He was a personal physician who practiced in New York. I wondered why he had accompanied Michael all the way from overseas just because of a broken foot. There were doctors in England if Michael needed one. But if he was being administered more painkillers for his broken foot, which is what I suspected, Michael was still nowhere near being so out of it that he couldn't function.

Michael did come three hours late to Oxford, which meant that he did not attend the dinner that was staged by the Oxford Union in his honor, and he did arrive three hours late at our mutual friend Uri Geller's wedding ceremony the next day where I officiated and Michael served as best man. But other than that, the trip to Britain went off without a hitch.

As I was about to embark on my return flight home, Michael, who was staying on in Europe, reached me on my mobile phone. "*Shmuulleeeey,*" he dragged out the word, partially slurring it, "yesterday at the wedding, I was just staring at you conducting the ceremony. I was staring at you because I love you, because you're my best friend. *I just loooovveeee you.*" I responded as I always did, "I love you too, Michael." "But no," he said, "you don't understand. *I loovvveeee yooouuuu,*" dragging out the words for effect. It was a flattering phone call, but it made me alarmed that Michael was on something very strong. I would continue having conversations with him about staying off the poison of prescription drugs. He never fought me and always agreed.

When Michael was inducted into the Rock and Roll Hall of Fame that March, he invited me and my wife, Debbie, as his guests to the dinner at The Waldorf-Astoria in New York City. Although he was still on crutches, he seemed completely lucid. I spent a few hours in his suite helping him write his acceptance speech and he seemed cheerful and in good spirits. The next time we did a public event together was a few weeks later when we went to Newark, New Jersey. Michael's foot had healed and he was out of the cast. On that day, Michael seemed fine. Confident, chewing gum, and irritated with me as I explained earlier, but nothing more. I was certain that whatever medication he was taking had been connected with his broken foot and was now in the past.

It was a few months later, after I had severed all contact with Michael, that reports started to filter back to me from one of Michael's closest confidantes that he was hooked on prescription medication and imbibing large quantities of them. It was getting much worse, this friend said, and it was destroying his life. Demerol and Xanax, among others, were mentioned. "Is there a quack doctor giving this stuff to him?" I asked. "No," I was told. "The doctors around him seem okay. He seems to be getting his own supply; no one knows from where. Michael is injecting himself with the drugs intravenously." "Well," I said, noting that Michael and I had no interaction and I could therefore offer little assistance, "you guys better do something and save him before he completely self-destructs."

Michael's parents, Katherine and Joseph Jackson, were also concerned and invited me to their home in Encino, where they asked me to reinvolve myself in Michael's life. Michael's parents related to me that Michael had deteriorated significantly since I had last seen him. His state was bad enough for them to have attempted a family intervention to break the drugs' hold on him. Michael's brothers, a few weeks earlier, had arrived at Neverland unannounced to try to get him into rehab, where he had gone almost ten years earlier after admitting to an addiction to prescription drugs. Michael, however, had heard that they were coming and fled.

His parents were concerned, and I felt for them. But this just reinforced my decision. Not only was I sure that Michael would not listen to me, I knew next to nothing about helping people in this situation except to get them into rehab. Perhaps I could inspire Michael to make that decision, and his parents thought I could at least help. But I knew they were wrong. Michael had long since ceased taking my counsel. He found my advice too demanding. I was an irritant and was treated as such. Katherine, who was the anchor of Michael's life and whom I knew from the long interview I had done with her for this book, and Joseph Jackson, who I was meeting for the first and only time, had much more sway with their son than I did, and it was imperative *for them* to save their son's life by becoming available parents in his greatest hour of need. And if his own parents could not persuade him to get help, how could I?

Joseph Jackson also raised the subject of Michael's management with me. He said he didn't approve of the people running Michael's career at present and that he wished to reinvolve himself in Michael's management. I told him sternly, if respectfully, "Mr. Jackson, your son doesn't need a manager right now. He needs a father. You should relate to him as the father he feels he never had."

I left that meeting shaken. How tragic for Michael, and how similar this was all beginning to sound to Elvis, a fallen star, in terrible emotional and mental anguish, turning to drugs for relief, until they eventually destroyed him. Would Michael end up dead at an early age as well?

According to someone very close to Michael, the year before his arrest, Michael got clean. This person told me that Michael had, by himself, "gotten off the stuff. . . he's completely clean." I was incredulous. "He didn't go for rehab?" I asked. "You're saying he got himself clean on his own?" "Yup," he said, "We're really proud of him. He's clean. I swear it's true." Well, that was good news.

I was therefore extremely troubled to hear, from the same person again, that shortly after the arrest Michael had gone back on "the same stuff. He's delusional. That's how he's coping with the case. He's out of it a lot of the time."

"Have you tried to get him to stop?" I asked. "Yeah, I had a meeting with him. I told him I was positive he was back on the stuff. He denied it, but I know what he's like when he takes that stuff. But he responded by sort of cutting me off from him. Now, I can't get access to him."

This, sadly, was a typical response to Michael hearing people criticize his behavior. He just shut them out. "Do the people around him know?" I asked. "I don't see how they can't," he responded. "He's drinking a lot of wine and mixing it with all this stuff." This last comment especially surprised me, because, to my knowledge, Michael never drank alcohol. Indeed, even when he came to our home for the Sabbath meals, he would reject the tiny quantity of sacramental wine I offered him, telling me that he never drank "the Jesus juice."

The fact that Michael Jackson had been taking large doses of prescription medication explained much of his erratic behavior. Why would the man who was so famously overprotective of his kids suddenly dangle his own new baby from a balcony in Berlin? Why would the man who was so famously reclusive agree to a British journalist virtually living with him for a tell-all television documentary? Michael always told me how much he hated the British press more than any other. He told me that "Whacko Jacko" had started in England. So why would he have allowed Martin Bashir to essentially live him for so many months? Indeed, Michael's decision to grant full access to Bashir will forever remain the professional decision that most unraveled his life.

When I watched the *60 Minutes* interview with Ed Bradley that preceded the trial, in which Michael accused the Santa Barbara police of locking him up for forty-five minutes in a feces-covered bathroom and roughing him up so badly that they dislocated his shoulder, it seemed so improbable that I suspected that Michael's reality had been impaired.

Sure enough, twice in the interview they showed Michael stopping the interview to complain about how much his back hurt. The old opportunities (excuses) to take more prescription medication were back. I called my friend. "Did the police do all those things?" "No," he said. "They were really nice to him. Michael is delusional." Now this report may have been inaccurate, but I doubt it.

In 2004 I wrote in a public article, "If the people around him don't save Michael from himself, Michael may be yet another superstar who dies young, God forbid, due to the quintessential celebrity-oriented diseases of drug and substance abuse. But a wall of silence around this problem, while it might protect Michael's image, will do nothing to protect him."

Attitudes Toward Women and Pornography

I expected that after the episode with his parents, my last major point of contact, Michael Jackson would be entirely absent from my life. But his deteriorating condition had strangely awakened within me much of my old affection for my former friend. Whether it was pity or nostalgia, I cannot quite say.

I have consistently said that I never saw Michael do anything that would lead me to believe that he molested children. But since his trial uncovered that Michael was apparently absorbing large quantities of pornography, I understood something that had previously puzzled me. Michael Jackson, in the time that I knew him, had no real relationships with women. And this hurt him terribly because it meant that he had few nurturing relationships in his life.

When I was around him, his inner circle consisted entirely of men. Indeed, with the exception of Elizabeth Taylor, whom I never met and never saw in Michael's company, Michael seemed highly suspicious of women. He would tell me that many women are interested in money and that some of his brother's wives, whom he believed were motivated by greed, had torn the once close-knit bonds of the Jackson family asunder. To be sure, Michael loved and respected his mother, Katherine, immensely, and for good reason. A woman of great religious piety and principle, she was arguably the only truly positive influence in Michael's life. But she, sadly, had little control over her son and Michael shunned her advice.

Men who constantly feed their minds with porn quickly lose respect for women. Pornography depicts women not only as sleazy and vulgar but as greedy and parasitical. The porn watcher never forgets that the women who are stripping for him are doing so for cash. He concludes, therefore, that there is nothing women aren't prepared to do for money. Unlike men who at least have some standards, women are motivated entirely by greed.

With Michael, unfortunately, such toxic imagery actually started early, as our conversations revealed. It was Michael's recollection that from a young age he had witnessed women stripping in nightclubs where the Jackson 5 performed. Michael came to equate adult sexuality in general, and women in particular, as prurient, manipulative, and even unclean. It may also explain why Michael may have, as some have alleged, gravitated toward adolescent sexuality, which was so much more innocent by comparison.

No doubt the pornographic images of women he was consuming helped to solidify that impression. Indeed, Michael's 2005 trial revolved around the question of whether the mother of his fifteen-year-old accuser was a gold digger who coached her children to lie about Michael to rip him off. The effects of pornography on the male psyche is something that I dealt with extensively in my book *Hating Women: America's Hostile Campaign Against the Fairer Sex*. But as it applies to Michael Jackson, these exploitative images could only have reinforced a preconceived notion that people in general, and women in particular, are out to use him and he'd better be wary.

King Solomon declared in Proverbs that "He who has found a woman has found goodness," and Michael's inability to have healthy attachments to women could only have contributed to his steady and sad decline.

Pedophilia Charges

Much of the world came to regard Michael as a pedophile. I never saw anything that would even remotely have me accept that conclusion. I never believed the allegations against him brought by the family of Gavin Arvizo. As I said, I was at Neverland with my family when the Arvizos arrived. Far from being too obsessed with Gavin, Michael disappointed me with his seeming lack of interest in the child, amid the occasional moving conversation trying to convince Gavin that he had no fear of looking bald from chemotherapy because he was a beautiful boy.

I will, however, confess to having been severely jolted by the testimony of Jordy Chandler's mom, the mother of the first alleged victim, in Michael's 2005 trial. It did seem from her testimony that Michael was erotically obsessed with her son. It is also possible, as I said earlier, that Michael was psychologically scarred by the damaging images of women performing striptease acts that he witnessed at such a young age at night-clubs, which may have led him to be turned off women in general and adult sexuality in particular. He may have come to associate adolescent sexuality with purity and innocence. But none of this is anything more than uncorroborated speculation. What is certainly unnerving is Michael's multimillion dollar settlement with Jordy Chandler, even amid Michael's constant protestations to me that he settled the case because his advisers forced him to for fear that a trial would destroy his career.

But while Michael may or may not be guilty of the accusations against him, he was certainly guilty of feeling that different rules applied to his re-lationship with kids, or worse, that there were no rules at all.

I thought often of those first days in Neverland after reading news ac-counts of Tom Sneddon's opening statement in Michael's trial in Santa Barbara. The chief prosecutor maintained that Michael Jackson invited his accuser and his family to his Neverland Valley Ranch in August 2000, and that the first night, at dinner, he asked the boy to ask his mom if he could spend the night in Michael's bedroom. Later, according to Sned-don, together with his employee Frank Cascio, Michael showed the ac-cuser and his brother pornographic photos off the Internet.

All this may be true, but when I first heard it, it sounded completely suspect. Michael was desperate to have someone of reputation vouch for him and serve as his mouthpiece. He wanted me to serve in that role and wanted to make a positive impression on me, and I even surmised that he had purposely invited the Arvizos to Neverland while we were there to show me how much he cared for children stricken with cancer. Would he really have begun showing the boy pornographic materials while I was staying there with my family? It is possible, but he would have to have been a complete fool to do so. But perhaps it was I who was the fool in overestimating what my opinion of Michael meant to him.

Frank Cascio, who remains one of my dear friends, was named as an unindicted coconspirator who allegedly participated in showing the kids pornography on that first night. (Frank told me after the trial was over, and subsequently stated in an ABC television interview, that pornographic images were pulled up on the computer, but they were pulled up by the boys, who were acting wildly.)

I know Frank well and he features prominently in this book because he served as Michael's closest confidante and personal aide. No one was more devoted to Michael than Frank. I liked Frank very much and tried at the time and ever since to play a role as a mentor to him, feeling as I did that he was a young man, with good intentions, adrift in the chaotic and frenzied life of Michael Jackson. Frank was in his early twenties when I first met him, yet he was basically in charge of nearly every aspect of Michael's life. I would regularly lecture him about the need to remain firmly connected to God, to go to church (he was from a Christian family), to put his own parents and siblings before his relationship with Michael, and to try and help protect Michael from himself.

One of my main points to Frank was to ensure that Michael was never alone with children, given the 1993 allegations, and Frank, caring deeply about Michael and being around him constantly, promised to always be present when Michael was with children. Perhaps that is why he was there that first night when Michael's accuser and his brother were in Michael's bedroom.

The idea, as later alleged in the trial, that Frank threatened the boy's family with harm should they testify against Michael, was always improbable to impossible. Frank was always extremely well-mannered and went to great lengths to be the counterbalance to Michael's narcissism. From my knowledge of Frank, he could not hurt a fly, and from the time I met him I endeavored to positively affect Frank, making sure that his life did not go down the tragic route that Michael's did, being destroyed by the vacuous and unprincipled world of empty celebrity circles.

Frank, who came to run Michael's career, was never malicious, and I never once saw him even lose his temper. He always behaved with maturity and impeccable manners. After the trial ended, Frank called me and offered something of an apology. He told me that he now appreciated how I tried to rehabilitate Michael when the three of us were close, regretted that he was too young to understand it at the time, and that later, after I departed, he gave Michael much the same advice that I had given him four years earlier.

Michael's Death

I did not expect to be as saddened by Michael's death as I turned out to be. Not that I am cold-hearted, but I lived in constant dread that his death was imminent. When I was close with Michael, there were just too many times that he walked out of a room with a doctor, after complaining that his foot or back or neck hurt him. There was no way that a body could survive so regular an assault. So after begging him to give up the poison and failing, I steeled myself against the inevitable by feeling angry and disillusioned.

Was Michael not the man who had squandered so many blessings? Was he not the friend who, after I had invested two years of my life into helping him rehabilitate his, treated me as if I were a nuisance because I dared to push him to fix his shattered existence? I would overcome my feelings of pity with a spirit of defiance. No, I would not cry. He hadn't earned it.

But then the news of his death came and I was devastated. Michael was accused of pedophilia. But my children and his children were playmates. Yes, I made sure to supervise. But the children did not see him as a monster. Michael brought cartoon videos for his kids and my kids to watch. We sat in my living room laughing and joking. And the children remembered him and missed him.

Once, when my son Mendy was eight years old, he accompanied Michael and me to a kosher restaurant in Manhattan. Mendy tried to order. The waiter focused on the adults. Mendy felt ignored. He kept on repeating his order. Michael heard him. He interrupted the waiter. "Excuse me, but this child is trying to order. Can you please listen to him?" It was not something you'd expect from a superstar. They were supposed to be utterly self-absorbed, right?

I did not think I would cry when Michael died. It was only when I went back and listened to the many hours of our taped conversations for this book that I peered once again into his soul. Hearing his voice, hearing him say, in his long drawn-out way, "Shmmuuulleeeey," that did it. The tears flowed. Yes, I was angry at him. Truly. He threw away his life. He had lived recklessly and orphaned his children. He had medicated his various psychosomatic illnesses until his body could no longer tolerate the abuse. He had played the victim, blamed all his problems on others, and squandered his limitless gifts and God-given potential. But he touched me nonetheless.

He made me softer and gentler. He was highly imperfect and was perhaps guilty of serious, terrible sins for which there might not be any redemption. But God, was he tortured! And that is no excuse because you dare not visit your pain on an innocent party. And he would have to be held accountable for his actions. However, did that cancel out the good he tried to inspire in others?

He used to watch me tell my children I loved them. He did not approve. "Shmuley, when you tell your children you *luuuvve* them, you have to look in their eyes. They have to know that you mean it. You have to focus only on them. You can't tell them and look somewhere else." And ever since then, I peer into their eyes.

God, I miss you Michael. I always believed that one day we would reconcile. That one day you would call me and tell me that you regretted not heeding the simple advice to get your life together. That we would have Shabbat dinner together again and our kids would play as friends and we would all laugh. Alas, all we have left is the image. The dark, tragic, sad image of the King of Pop. The master of an empty Kingdom.

A Note About the Interviews and This Book

The conversations that Michael and I taped for publication were volu-
minous, far-reaching, and covered many important topics. I have therefore divided them into two books. This volume, the first of the two,
deals with Michael the man. Who was he and what were the formative
influences of his life? What scarred him and why did he never find inner
peace? What was his worldview and how did he see God, human purpose, and his relationship with both? Michael discusses his childhood
and the all-important question of the relationship with this father. How
he lived at home well into his twenties and how he handled the growing influence of fame.

Michael illuminates some of the most important questions of his existence, such as his spiritual life, his relationship with family, fame, why
he hated his appearance, and the abject loneliness in which he lived. Why
only other childhood stars could understand him and why he learned to
be wary of women's motives. He addresses how he came to love strange
pets and what led him to become so dependent on attention from fans.
He talks about historical incidents, current events, and emotions such
as jealousy and hatred. Michael also discusses the differences that came
between him and his first wife, Lisa Marie Presley, and the chasm that
eventually developed between him and the Jehovah's Witnesses Church.
Most ominously, he speaks of his fear of growing old, his preference for
an early death, and his plans to one day disappear.

The second book is devoted in its entirety to Michael's view of children. In it Michael develops a complex and sophisticated philosophical
system of what adults can learn from kids and argues that the most successful adults are those who have never lost their inner child. Michael

delves deeply into the innocence of children and explains how he could never harm a child. He addresses why he always wished to be around kids and why did he not want to grow up himself. He gives surprisingly compelling answers but they only further enhance the question as to whether his interest in children was an unhealthy, even criminal, obsession or whether we were the ones guilty of ascribing impure motivation to someone who just wanted to help needy kids. His take on children and childlike qualities will leave you, depending on your perspective, either amazed at his profundity or disturbed at his capacity for intelligent rationalization.

The conversations presented here include the verbatim words Michael said with only the most minor, occasional edits for clarity. My questions and comments have been edited as needed, both for brevity and to enhance the experience and understanding of Michael. The conversations themselves are for the most part presented intact, but arranged thematically, and in a few instances, some conversations were divided thematically.

Together, the two volumes will present a Michael Jackson you never knew existed. They may also cause you, as they did me, to shed a tear not for the death of a superstar or cultural icon but for a tortured and broken soul who once had highly developed insight and sensitivity but who in the end represented a colossal waste of life and potential.

I trust that the conversations contained herein will lead you to see Michael's beauty, Michael's pain, Michael's insights, and Michael's ugliness all in equal measure, but that you will also learn to judge him far more charitably once you come to know the depth of his anguish. Because for all his money and all his fame, Michael Jackson lived with a level of unhappiness that most of us can scarcely comprehend. And now that he is dead, now that the demons of his life have finally consumed him, now that we know that he lived in such torment that he downed bottles of pills nightly and still had no rest, perhaps we can find it in our hearts to show him a morsel of compassion.

The Conversations

SETTING THE STAGE

The Writing Was on the Wall:
Talking About Dying Young

Michael always spoke to me about the power of mystery. He was not a recluse merely because he was shy but also because he believed in it. He had to keep his profile partially hidden to retain the interest of the public. In celebrity terms, overexposure was death. So I asked him. . .

Shmuley Boteach: So would you say the best thing that's ever happened to the Beatles is the fact that they broke up, and that's why they had this longevity, because suddenly, kaboom!, they weren't around anymore, so you could never get bored of them? They never fizzled?

Michael Jackson: Yeah, Marilyn Monroe died young. You didn't get to see her grow old and ugly. I mean that's the mystery of James Dean.

SB: And people say about the Beatles, "I wish they were together."

MJ: Yeah, yeah.

SB: And you [the fan] become part of the wish then. The public keeps them going because they so badly want them back together.

MJ: Absolutely, or else they'd be funky and old now and you wouldn't care.

SB: So is that an argument, Michael, for you to say one day, "That's it," and quit?

MJ: Yeah, I would like some kind of way to disappear where people don't see me anymore at some point, and just do my things for children but not be visual. To disappear is very important. We are people of change. We need change in our lives. That's why we have winter, spring, summer, fall.

Here, I started to get worried about what Michael meant by "disappear." It's one thing to leave show business. It's another to harbor a death wish. So I said. . .

SB: Okay, but you want a long life and a healthy life. You don't want to disappear like, God forbid, the way some of these stars have disappeared, the way Marilyn Monroe has. You don't want to die young?

MJ: Um, you're asking me an interesting question. You sure you want my answer?

SB: I do.

MJ: Okay, I'll give you my honest answer. Okay, um. My greatest dream that I have left—I have accomplished my dreams with music and all that and I love music and entertainment—is this children's initiative, is this thing that we are doing. But, um, 'cause I don't care about [anything else], I really don't, I don't care about [career], I honestly don't Shmuley. What keeps me going is children, or else I would, I would seriously. . . I've told you this before, I swear to God I mean every word. I would, I would just throw in the towel if it wasn't for children or babies. And that's my real, my honest [answer]. . . and I've said it before, if it weren't for children, I would choose death. I mean it with all my heart.

And his voice had the ring of truth. His comments were alarming in the extreme. Did Michael just tell me he would choose death? I couldn't believe it. So I asked him to clarify.

SB: Choose death the way Marilyn Monroe chose death?

MJ: Some kind of way. I would find a way to go away off the planet 'cause I wouldn't care about living anymore. I'm living for these babies and children.

SB: You see them as really a part, a spark of God here on earth?

MJ: I swear they are.

SB: So for you it's the most spiritual thing in the world?

MJ: There is nothing more pure and spiritual to me than children and I cannot live without them. If you told me right now, "Michael, you can never see another child," I would kill myself. I swear to you I would because I have nothing else to live for. That's it. Honestly.

I was startled and shaken. I had to bring him back to his senses, so I said. . .

SB: So do you want to have a long life?

MJ: Let me take back that word swear, 'cause I don't swear to God. I take that back. I don't want to use that word. Say this question again?

SB: You said you want to disappear. Do you think it's important to disappear?

MJ: I don't want a long [life]. . . I don't like, I don't, I don't. I think growing old is the ugliest, the most, the ugliest thing. When the body breaks down and you start to wrinkle, I think it's so bad. I don't, that's something I don't understand, Shmuley. And I never want to look in the mirror and see that. I don't understand it. I really don't. And people say that growing old is beautiful and it's this and that. I disagree. I totally do.

SB: So you would die before that happens?

MJ: Um. . . I don't want to grow old. I would like to get. . .

I know that I shouldn't have been cutting Michael off in the midst of such a seminal subject, but his hinting at suicide was extremely troubling, and I felt the immediate need to inspire him to choose life. So I said. . .

SB: What if you could stay young in spirit Michael?

MJ: Yeah, that's important to me.

SB: You may have wrinkles, but don't you want to see Prince and Paris grow up?

MJ: Yes, I do.

SB: Don't you want to see their children?

MJ: I just don't want to look old and start forgetting. I want to always be youthful and have the energy to run around and play hide and seek, which is one of my favorite games. I wanted to play it so badly at your house the last time we were there 'cause you have a nice big house for it. Um, I hate to see people grow old, Shmuley.

Yes, we could talk about hide and seek, but not when Michael was discussing the possibility of his suicide. So I brought him back again to the possibility of growing old yet remaining youthful and vibrant.

SB: Haven't you seen people who grew old but kept their youthfulness. They behaved like they were still young?

MJ: Yeah, when they have a youthful heart, I love that. When they start to forget and wrinkle, [and] their body parts break down, it hurts me. Or when they get. . .

SB: Who has that happened to among the people you've loved? Does your mother grow old on you? Your father? Any entertainers that you know in the industry who grow old?

MJ: Yeah, people I love very much that died and I don't understand why. I was in love with this man, in love with him. And he was my friend, Fred Astaire, and I don't understand. You see Fred, since I was a little, a kid, Fred Astaire lived very close to our house and he used to talk to me all the time when I was little and you know he would teach me things, he would tell me you know, I was gonna be a big star and all this stuff that I didn't even think about when I was little. And to see him dance in movies, I was like amazed. I didn't know anybody could move so beautifully, you know? And, um, when I see him get to the point. . . One day he said to me, "You know Michael, I, if I was to do one spin right now, I would fall flat on my face. My equilibrium is totally gone." And when he'd answer the door when I'd come to his house, this is how he [walked], just like this Shmuley. Little tiny steps and it broke my heart. That hurts me, and the day he died, it killed me, it killed me. It destroyed me. And that's. . .

SB: But what happened to [Princess] Diana, that was a great tragedy, Michael.

I was trying to remind him that no matter how painful it was to grow old, dying a young, tragic death was much worse.

MJ: That was a great tragedy. That killed me. That killed everybody, I think.

SB: It's not good to die young. It may make you into a myth, Michael. But life is too precious, no?

MJ: Life is very beautiful and precious.

SB: So you think one day you're going to become just a myth.

MJ: See, why can't we be like the trees? That come, you know, they lose their leaves in the winter, and come back as beautiful all over again in the spring, you know? It's a sense of immortality to them, and the Bible says man was meant for immortality. But through sin and all this, we get death.

I should have said at this point that the Bible, in Deuteronomy, indeed compares humans to the trees of the field, and developed the metaphor. A tree may eventually crumble and die, but it sows the seeds for the next generation of trees and plant life. It lives on through its offspring and through its oxygenation of the air, in other words, what it does for the environment, what it does for others. So too, we may die, but our good deeds live on. Humans may not be immortal, but they exist forever through the people they love and through the good deeds they do. But for some reason, even though I have written extensively on the subject, I didn't think of it.

SB: But maybe you go to a different place, to a higher place, and your soul, being suddenly unrestricted, can actually move closer to the people. Think about it. God is here right now, Michael. We both believe that, even though you can't touch him or feel him. Are the souls of our loved ones very different?

MJ: I would love to come back as, as, as a child that never grows old, like Peter Pan. I wish, I wish I could believe that that's true, that I keep coming back. I hope that's true, I would like to believe that, Shmuley.

SB: In reincarnation? You keep on being reincarnated as a baby?

MJ: Yeah, even though our, my religion [the Jehovah's Witnesses Church], talks against it, that there's no such thing as [reincarnation]. . . When you die, the soul dies and it's like this couch, the dead, you know? But there's the promise of the resurrection and all that.

SB: But for the Hindus, they believe you come back.

MJ: I'd like to believe that, and I like what the Egyptians and the Africans do, how they bury [their dead]. . . I'd like to see, we would all like to see, what the other side looks like. Don't we?

SB: We wish we knew what lies after life, what heaven is like.

MJ: Yes, because there are so many concepts.

SB: Do you think there are children playing in Heaven?

MJ: Oh, God, I pray that that is what it is like.

SB: Are there adults playing there, too?

MJ: I would think so and I would think that they are very childlike. Like Adam and Eve, it is just a happy garden, a perfect peaceful place. I pray that it is like that.

SB: Are you afraid of death?

MJ: Yes.

SB: We all are.

MJ: I always said I want to be buried right where there are children. I want them next to me. I would feel safer that way. I want them next to me. I need their spirit protecting me. I always see that in my mind and I see myself and I hate to see it. I see myself and I see children lying there to protect me.

In light of Michael's subsequent death just a few years after this conversation, these are obviously disturbing and haunting remarks. He said clearly that if he could no longer work with, or on behalf of, children, he would find some way to take himself off the planet. After Michael's arrest on the second allegations of child molestation on November 20, 2003, it was clear that he could never again work with children. So did Michael commit suicide? No. I firmly believe he did not. He loved his own kids too much to ever contemplate an *active* form of death that would orphan them. Rather, I believe that in the wake of the 2003 allegations, although he was later vindicated and found innocent, Michael lost the will to live. The vast increase in his drug intake shows that he lived much of his remaining years in a drug-induced stupor. There was no way he was unaware that consuming this huge amount of drugs could kill him. Michael often told me that he knew all about prescription drug medication, and he took enough to become an expert. So Michael did lose the will to live, and he slowly shriveled as a human being. He agreed to do his final concerts not because he had any intrinsic interest in his music or career but because he needed the money. The only question that still remains and which I cannot answer is why Michael's love of, and dedication to, his own kids was not enough to instill within him a continued passion for life. But alive or dead, it did not much matter to Michael, just as long as he could numb the pain with the poison that eventually killed him.

When Michael died I also faced a profound moral dilemma as to what to do with this conversation in which he says he wants to be buried near children. In the end, after consulting with people whom I respect, I decided that revealing it in the immediate aftermath of his death would not influence the family decision as to where he would be buried and would just subject Michael to public ridicule. I also do *not* believe that he should be buried next to children, whatever his wishes. Still, I was saddened to see plans being discussed to bury Michael at Neverland. The ranch was isolating and damaging to Michael enough while he was alive. Why condemn him to that eternal loneliness and oblivion just to increase Neverland's commercial appeal?

PART 1

CHILDHOOD FAME AND JOE JACKSON

Childhood, Loneliness, Cartoons, and Brothers

The most formative experience in Michael's life was being forced into entertainment from approximately the age of five. Michael felt he had been robbed of not just an essential part of life but the most magical part. He longed to recapture it and spent his remaining days doing just that. Some argued that Michael was a case of arrested development. I disagree. Michael Jackson *chose* not to grow up.

Shmuley Boteach: Was there an age at which you realized, "Oh my gosh, I missed my childhood?"

Michael Jackson: Yes, I remember distinctly. . . It's like being on a ride you can't get off and you think, "Oh my God. What did I do?" and you are committed and you can't get off. It hit me before I was a teenager. I wanted so badly to play in the park across the street because the kids were playing baseball and football but I had to record. I could see the park, right across the street. But I had to go in the other building and work until late at night making the albums. I sat there looking at the kids with tears running down my face and I would say, "I am trapped and I have to do this for the rest of my life. I am under contract." But I wanted to go over there so bad it was killing me, just to make a friend to say, "Hi." I used to walk the streets looking for someone to talk to. I told you that.

SB: How old were you?

MJ: It was during the *Thriller* album.

SB: So you were the biggest star in the whole world and. . .

MJ: I was looking for people to talk to. I was so lonely I would cry in my room upstairs. I would think, "That's it. I am getting out of

here," and I would walk down the street. I remember really saying to people, "Will you be my friend?"

SB: They were probably in shock.

MJ: They were like, "Michael Jackson!" I would go, "Oh God! Are
they going to be my friend because of Michael Jackson? Or because of me?" I just wanted someone to talk to.

Already in this comment you could see the development of the two
personalities that would forever collide in Michael's person. There was
Michael Jackson, the King of Pop, an aloof superstar who had everything and needed no one. And Michael Jackson, the shy kid under the
mask, who lacked even a single real friend.

SB: Did you find it?

MJ: Yeah, well, I went to the park and there were kids playing on
swings.

SB: So that's when you decided that children were the answer. They
are the only ones who treat you as a person?

MJ: Yeah. That's true.

SB: So that's the age that it hit you, "Oh my gosh. I did lose my childhood, because these are the only people I can identify with."

MJ: I suffered a lot in that way. I knew that something was wrong
with me at that time. But I needed someone. . . That's probably
why I had the mannequins. I would say because I felt I needed people, someone, I didn't have. . . I was too shy to be around real people. I didn't talk to them. It wasn't like old ladies talking to plants.
But I always thought I wanted something to make me feel like I had
company. I always thought, "Why do I have these?" They are like
real babies, kids, and people, and it makes me feel like I am in a
room with people.

Realize the import of these words. Michael Jackson was so lonely
that he turned to mannequins to feel like he had human company. That
is the degree of isolation he experienced (and it's an experience shared
by many who make it to the top and lose connection to family, friends,
and community).

SB: Why were you too shy to talk to real people? Was it because you had only ever learned to perform and you weren't given the opportunity to hang out?

MJ: That's it. There was no hang-out time.

SB: Do you still feel lonely?

MJ: Not nearly the way I used to. No.

SB: Clearly you have your kids, which makes a very big difference. But there is a part of us that isn't only a parent. There is part of us that needs other forms of interaction.

MJ: What kind of interaction?

SB: Someone you can unburden yourself to emotionally in a way that Prince couldn't understand or Paris couldn't understand.

I was alluding to an intimate soul mate.

MJ: Mmmm. Friends and certain people you can trust. Elizabeth [Taylor], or whoever. . . Mac [Macaulay Culkin], Shirley Temple [Black], people who have been there.

Amazing, the only people he thought could ever understand him were others who had been robbed of their childhood.

SB: So it is always people who have been there, all these childhood stars?

MJ: They [people who have not been childhood stars] say, "Yeah, I know what you mean," but they don't know what you mean. They are just trying to agree with you.

SB: Do you discuss with friends who were also child stars individual things that happened to them? Or do you not even need to say it: Do you sort of understand it?

MJ: You know, it's like telepathy. I wish you could have seen Shirley Temple and myself.

Just a few weeks before this conversation Michael had been to visit Shirley Temple Black in San Francisco.

SB: Are you still in touch with her?

MJ: I am going to call her. I've gotta call her again. I kept thanking her and she was saying, "Why?" and I said, "Because of all you have ever done for me."

SB: Do you think you will ever dedicate a song to her?

MJ: I would love to.

SB: So Macaulay Culkin doesn't need to say to you, "I was on the set and this happened with my father." You don't even have to have conversations like that?

MJ: Oh yeah. There is this precious sweet little soul who is a baby, Macaulay Culkin, who is wondering, "How did I get caught up in all of this? I never asked to be an actor." He always wanted out. You gotta watch that energy when he gets heavy on his father, man, it tears into him and that's what happens, you know. Oh, but I saw it myself with him. [Michael screams] "Mac get in here!" the screaming. . .

SB: So that reminded you of what you had to go through? He made a lot of the choices that you did. He tried to hold onto his childhood for as long as possible. But there are other childhood stars who didn't, like Brooke Shields, whom you were once close to. What about someone like Brooke Shields who to the world looks like she didn't make childhood choices, she didn't try to rediscover her childhood. Do you think it will exact a price? Do you think that Macaulay Culkin and you and others can be healthier because you understand what you are missing and you need to compensate?

MJ: You know, with certain people I understand and with certain ones I don't. With her she started out being a model, so it wasn't like being on the set all day, every day. She did modeling. She wasn't a movie star until she did, I think it was *Pretty Baby*, and she played a female prostitute at the age of. . . I think it started around twelve for her. There was a lot of photography, so it wasn't like all day like what we did, all day, from early to night. I think it affects people differently, but it is all the same. She is very sweet, smart. She is not an airhead. She is real smart. A lot of people think that when someone is beautiful they are like an airhead. She is very smart.

SB: What other childhood stars have you been close to?

MJ: Not a lot of them are left. That's what is scary. Most of them self-destruct.

SB: At age thirteen you became a character in a cartoon series. Was that hard to handle?

MJ: I woke up every Saturday morning. I couldn't wait.

SB: To watch *The Jacksons*?

MJ: To watch *The Jackson 5* cartoon. I felt so honored that I had been made into a cartoon. I was so happy, you have no idea. We didn't have to do anything. It was someone else's voice. They just animated us and used our songs off the albums that we recorded and it played for years and years. I remember I was in Brunei in a hospital doing a show for the Sultan. It was the most beautiful hospital I have ever seen in my life and I'm laying in bed and there's *The Jackson 5* cartoon playing on television and I'm like, I can't believe this. They show it all the time. The same company did *The Beatles*, *The Osmonds*, and *The Jackson 5*.

SB: So this is one of the things that you liked the most?

MJ: Oh, I loved it.

SB: Did that make you feel more connected with the children round the world? Because you know that children mostly are going to watch it right?

MJ: I loved it. It put me in another world. It was like, "God, I'm in another world." I felt special. I think I felt more special about that than the hit records and the concerts and everything. That impressed me more than any of the other stuff.

SB: Now, out of your five brothers you were getting more attention than any of them. You were becoming the star until you were spun off as a solo artist. Was that hard for your brothers to handle? Was it hard for you? Was there any analogy to the story in the Bible about Joseph getting more attention than his brothers, until they hurt him?

MJ: It didn't come into my mind and I didn't see it until later and then it showed up later. My mother saw it, but she wouldn't bring it to my attention. But I think the wives kind of instigated it. It is what broke us up as a group. Wives are what broke up the Beatles. It is what broke up Martin and Lewis. It's what broke up all of the great acts. The wives get involved and they start saying to one member, "You're the star. He needs you. You don't need him." Then he comes into work the next day puffed up with pride and they start to fight. And that's what happened with me and my brothers. They really did. I saw it happen.

This was the first instance where Michael would express his distrust of women and how he came to see many women as manipulative, conniving, and prepared to use their sexuality to gain power over men. Many today believe that Michael Jackson was gay. I personally never saw any evidence of it. On the contrary, Michael constantly remarked on the attractiveness of women in my presence. What I believe is that Michael was attracted to women, but did not trust them and thus could not share intimacy with them. His perception that women sought control over men and would abuse their sexuality to achieve it made him something of a misogynist, the exception being his mother Katherine, who Michael adored. But this perception that women could be sleazy and sexually manipulative developed when Michael performed in seedy nightclubs from a very early age where he recalled watching women stripping and sexually tempting men. If that happened, and I don't doubt Michael's description, he was clearly too young to witness such toxic spectacles and the damage that was done was lasting and in some ways irreversible.

SB: That's what turned you off marriage a bit?

MJ: It really did. I said, "I don't want no part of this." I said, "I am not getting married." I said it for years.

SB: Was there any way to have stopped it? Could you have said to your brothers, "Look! What is happening to us?" Could you have stopped it? They married young. They must have been lonely as well.

MJ: They married young to get away from my father, to get out of the house. We begged them not to get married and they did.

SB: Why did you stick around the house?

MJ: I was there at the height of *Thriller*. I thought I was still this little kid. It's not time for me to go yet. I'm still a boy. It's not time for me to leave home yet. I really felt that in my heart.

SB: But you were still afraid of your father? How does that come together?

MJ: He wasn't managing me at that time, but he was getting a royalty check. He was a little calmer and he was proud of me. But he wouldn't say it.

SB: Did you want to hear it from him?

MJ: I needed it.

SB: More than anyone in the world?

MJ: Yeah.

SB: He still never said it. And he doesn't say it now? Do you think that he knows that you are the biggest star in the world, or do you still think in his mind he doesn't get it?

MJ: He knows that but he finds it hard to give you a compliment and that's what made me into such a perfectionist trying to impress him. He'd be in the audience and he would make a face like this. He'd go [makes facial gesture] and it would scare the bejesus out of you and you'd think, "I can't mess up. He'll kill us." Everybody would clap and he would be like, "We're going to hit you hard. Don't you mess up." I'd be like, "God, I'm in trouble after the show."

SB: Given that there are two motivating forces in life, fear and love, could you have gotten even further if the motivation had been love? Like if your father had said, "Michael, I'll love you anyway, but you can do it." Sure, you can now decry the fear that your father instilled in you. But the problem with that is, you became the biggest star in the world. So maybe fear is a better motivating force than love. To be sure, I don't believe that. But does your example show that that's true?

MJ: I think there is a balance. Is it worth giving up fatherhood? Is it worth giving up the love I could have bestowed upon him, and having that camaraderie when we look in each other's eyes, walking through the park, holding hands? I don't think it is worth giving up all that. I am sorry. That's golden.

SB: If your career now suffers for being a hands-on father, you are prepared to accept that price?

MJ: No, I am not prepared for that. I can do both. I feel I have to.

SB: You feel that God gave you this potential, this gift, and you have
    got to do something with it?

MJ: I have to.

The Father-Manager

Shmuley Boteach: What if someone were to say, "Michael. Look. So
    you disagree with the way your father raised you. He was a strict
    disciplinarian. He could be tough and even mean. But his methods
    worked." And even you, now, you can say that professional suc-
    cess is not what primarily matters, and I would agree with you.
    But you were the one, in one of our first conversations, that said,
    "I owe my father a lot. He taught me how to move and how to
    dance." And being a big star, you've repeatedly said, is *very* impor-
    tant to you. So what if someone said, "You're wrong and he's right.
    He made you what you are today. So how dare you be so ungrate-
    ful?" Especially, Michael, since he grew up in such poverty and
    wanted to save you from his fate of working in the steel mills. He
    thought, "Better Michael practice and rehearse as a kid, rather
    than play on the monkey bars, because at least this will give him
    a good income later and he can live a life of dignity."

Michael Jackson: He did a brilliant job with training me for the stage as
    an artist, but [as a] father he was very, very strict. I hate to judge him,
    but I would have done things a lot different as a father. I never felt love
    from him. I remember being on the airplane and they used to have to
    carry me on the plane because I hated turbulence and I would be
    screaming and kicking because we would take off in storms. I remem-
    ber it very clearly. He would never hold me or touch me and the stew-
    ardesses would have to come and hold my hand and caress me.

SB: Was he an angry man?

MJ: I think he was bitter. I don't know why. Man, he is not like that
    anymore, but he was tough. The toughest person I have ever met.

SB: What if someone said to you, "Look Michael. You can't have it
    both ways. He was a great manager but not a warm and affection-

ate parent. He taught you how to move and he taught you discipline." Are you going to say that you would be prepared to give up being the biggest recording star in order to have had a loving childhood? Or do you feel the choice is not necessary, that you could have been who you are without?

MJ: He could have done all the other things with me and had time to be a father sometime—play a game or catch a ball. I remember I told you the one time he put me on a pony. I don't think he even realized how that is marked in my brain forever.

SB: That was one of the most moving stories about fatherhood that I have heard. That a single gesture on the part of a father to a son could make such an indelible mark is astonishing and very moving.

MJ: I think about it today and I wish he had done a little more, just a little more. To this day I would have felt totally different about it.

SB: And maybe you wouldn't have been as eager to prove yourself. If you were shown a lot of love as a child, maybe you wouldn't need the world to love you and you wouldn't be the superstar. Would you be prepared to give it up in order to be more loved as a child?

MJ: No. I would never give it up. That's my job. I was given this for a reason. I really believe it and feel it. . .

SB: . . . that God has chosen you, given you this special. . .

MJ: I really believe that. If you could see some of the faces around the world and people say, "Thank you, thank you for saving the life of me and my children. Can I touch you?" and then they start crying. It's like healing. We are given this for a reason. . . to help people.

SB: So what Shirley Temple did for you with those posters [that you could put up in your hotel rooms to feel safe], you are doing for people around the world and to a much bigger extent.

As you'll discover later, Michael instructed his advance staff to put up pictures of Shirley Temple on the walls of his hotel rooms before a performance.

MJ: Oh yeaaah. Oh yeaaah. That's it and I just wanted to say, "Thank you" [to Shirley Temple Black for inspiring Michael in his low moments] and I started to cry so badly that I just couldn't get the words out and she touched my hand and rubbed it like that.

SB: Michael, when you say to her that you didn't know if you could continue, and then you had a look at the posters of her movies when she was a kid, what was going to defeat you? What was it? The mean-spiritedness that people were showing? The fact that you always had to work to keep up to be the best? All those things?

MJ: Working hard, not having a chance to stop and play and have a lot of fun. We got a little bit in the hotels with pillow fights between me and my brothers and stuff like that and throwing stuff out of the window. But really we had hurt a lot. I remember we were on our way to South America and I was at home and it was time to go and I started crying so bad that I hid. I did not want to go and I said, "I just want to be like everyone else. I just want to be normal." And my father found me and made me get in the car and go, because we had to do a [concert] date. Then you meet people on the road, somebody on your floor, could be a family, and you know that you have to have as much fun as you can in a short time because you are not going to see them again and that hurts. You know that the friendship won't be a long one. That kind of stuff really hurts bad, especially when you are a little kid.

SB: Your whole life you have had to put your career before your nurturing relationships. So do you have something nurturing in your life today? A car can't run without gas, and you can't continue without love being given to you. You can't just give love and never get it back. And to say you get it from the fans is not enough, Michael, because they love you for what you do and not for who you are. They love you for the electricity and excitement you bring into their lives.

MJ: I get it back through the happiness and the joy that I see in the eyes of the children. They saved my life so I want to. . . give it back [Michael starts crying]. They saved me. I am not joking. Just being with them, just seeing them. It really has.

SB: When you grew up, did you feel promises were broken to you?

MJ: My father broke a big one that I'm angry with to this very day. He cajoled me into signing a contract with Columbia when I was eighteen with the promise that I'd get to have dinner with Fred Astaire.

Earlier of course, Michael implied that Fred Astaire lived in his neighborhood. I did not ask him about the discrepancy.

MJ: My father knew that I loved Fred with all my heart. He knew I would sign without reading the contract, and he walked away happy and he never did anything about it. He'd say he was sorry or whatever. It broke my heart that he did that. He tricked me.

SB: Did you ever tell him how upset you were?

MJ: No. He doesn't know to this day how much he hurt me. That's why I won't make promises I can't keep.

One of Michael's fatal flaws was his inability to see the corruption that was slowly overtaking his life. He swore he would never be like his father, and that meant never breaking a promise. But in his last years Michael was plagued by numerous lawsuits that claimed he regularly broke promises he made. A failure to honor commitments became something that marked much of his later life, which I too unfortunately witnessed. Michael meant well, but as in so many other areas of life, he could not summon the courage to live by his convictions.

Michael's Appearance: An Ugly Man in the Mirror

Shmuley Boteach: You have to live a long happy life. But do you really think that one day you will decide to become a recluse and disappear?

Michael Jackson: Yeah.

SB: Live at Neverland and lock up the gates. Will that be it?

MJ: Yeah. I know I am.

SB: But why? Because you don't want people to see you growing old?

MJ: I can't deal with it. I love beautiful things too much and the beautiful things in nature and I want my messages to get out to the world, but I don't want to be seen now. . . like when my picture came up on the computer, it made me sick when I saw it.

SB: Why?

MJ: Because I am like a lizard. It is horrible. I never like it. I wish I could never be photographed or seen and I push myself to go to the things that we go to. I really do.

He was referring to the public lectures I was having him do, like Oxford University in England and Carnegie Hall in New York. But it was very important that I push Michael to get out of his reclusive mode and to appear in public to serve a higher calling.

SB: Michael, some people have written that your father used to say that you were ugly. Is that true?

MJ: Uh-huh. He used to make fun of. . . I remember we were on a plane one time, ready to take off, and I was going through an awkward puberty when your features start to change. And he went, "Ugh, you have a big nose. You didn't get it from me." He didn't realize how much that hurt me. It hurt me so bad, I wanted to die.

SB: Was that a hostile remark aimed at your mother, "You didn't get it from me?"

MJ: I don't know what he was trying to say.

SB: Do you think it is important to tell children they are beautiful?

MJ: Yes, but not to overdo it. You are beautiful inside. Do it that way. Prince looks in the mirror as he's combing his hair and he says, "I look good." I say, "You look okay."

SB: Don't you think your father instilled in you a belief that you are not handsome? So you tried to change your appearance a bit, and you are still not happy. So really you have to begin to love your appearance and yourself and all of that.

MJ: I know. I wish I could.

SB: We all have problems with our appearance. Look, I have this scraggly beard. When I do TV appearances, the people I work with always tell me to cut it, to trim it. But my religion doesn't let me cut my beard, and it gets long.

MJ: Would you like to cut your beard?

SB: Yes, to be honest I would. Not completely. Just trim it. But God and my religion are more important to me than looks and appearances.

MJ: You are not allowed to?

SB: Essentially, no. I roll it up here. A lot of rabbis cut their beards and some don't. . . .

MJ: When they cut theirs, is that against the rules?

SB: The rules are interpreted differently by different rabbis. The Bible says you can't use a knife on your face. So some people take that to mean, literally, a knife. So these are the people who cut their beard with an electric shaver but not with a razor, a naked blade. To others the meaning of the verse is any kind of sharp object that cuts the beard. But my wife, Debbie, says, "I didn't marry a man who is going to try and conform to society. I married a man I wanted to respect and you are a rabbi. Be proud of who you are."

MJ: She doesn't mind the beard?

SB: Not only doesn't she mind, she would be very upset if I cut it at all. She said to me just this morning, "If you really love and respect me you would never say that because it bothers me that you want to trim your looks to fit in more." My wife wants me to live always by my principles.

MJ: That's amazing.

SB: The other night, Thursday night, you looked fantastic. [Michael had gotten all dressed up for Denise Rich's Angel Ball cancer fundraiser]. You were the best-looking guy there. So you don't like being photographed?

MJ: I wish I could never be photographed and I wish I could never be seen. Just for entertainment so I design the dance the way I want it to look, and the film the way I want it to look.

SB: Now you want to do movies?

MJ: I love movies, but I can control it, you see. I can't control how those pictures come out with the lighting and my expression at the time. *Arggh.*

SB: If a child said that to you, "I hate being photographed," what would you say to that child?

MJ: I would say, "You don't know how beautiful you are. It's your
   spirit that's. . . "
SB: So why are you prepared to say that to everybody except yourself?
MJ: I don't know.
[He said this in a voice of confusion and resignation.]
SB: You see from your fans that tons of women are throwing themselves at you. So that must mean that you are handsome and desir-
   able. You feel all the time that they want to fall in love with you?
MJ: When I think about it—I would never say this on TV—but if I
   went on stage thinking about what goes through women's heads,
   I would never go out on stage. If I was suddenly to start thinking
   about what they were thinking about. . . sex, or what I look like
   naked, then, oh God, that would be so embarrassing. I could never
   go out. That's so horrible.

Here again you see how Michael immediately associates women with
prurience. The sexual displays to which he was apparently subject as an innocent and vulnerable child in nightclubs may have done lasting damage.
As far as Michael was concerned, the screaming women at concerts
wanted to have sex with him. Sex, to Michael's mind, seemed to be what
was most on a *woman's* mind.

SB: A lot of people like being a sex symbol. You don't like it because
   you are shy about it. Do you know when some women speak to
   you that it's what's on their mind?
MJ: Umhum. They tell me.
SB: I want to have sex with you?
MJ: Aha.

Michael's Fear of His Father

Shmuley Boteach: You know, Michael, I used to judge my father a lot
   and one day I stopped judging him because he had his own challenges. He has had a very difficult life that began in abject poverty

in Iran. And it wasn't easy for Jews growing up in Iran. Who knows what his childhood was like? Do you still judge your father?

Michael Jackson: I used to. I used to get so angry at him. I would just go in my room and just scream out of anger because I didn't understand how a person could be so vicious and mean. Like sometimes I would be in bed sleeping, it would be 12 o'clock at night. I would have recorded all day, been singing all day, no fun, no play. He comes home late. "Open the door." The door is locked. He said, "I am going to give you five seconds before I kick it down." And he starts kicking it, breaking the door down. He said, "Why didn't you sign the contract?" I go, "I don't know." He goes, "Well, sign it. If you don't sign it you are in trouble." It's like, "Oh my God, why? Where is the love? Where is the fatherhood?" I go, "Is it really this way?" He would throw you and hit you as hard as he can. He was very physical.

SB: Did you begin to feel that you were a moneymaking machine for him?

MJ: Yes, absolutely.

SB: Just like Macaulay Culkin described? So you felt used?

MJ: Yes. And one day—I hate to repeat it—but one day he said, and God bless my father because he did some wonderful things and he was brilliant, he was a genius, but one day he said, "If you guys ever stop singing I will drop you like a hot potato." It hurt me. You would think he would think, "These kids have a heart and feelings." Wouldn't he think that would hurt us? If I said something like that to Prince and Paris that would hurt. You don't say something like that to children and I never forgot it. It affects my relationship with him today.

SB: So that if you didn't perform for him he would stop loving you?

MJ: He would drop us like a hot potato. That's what he said.

SB: Did your mother always run over and say, "Don't listen to him. He doesn't mean it."?

MJ: She was always the one in the background when he would lose his temper—hitting us and beating us. I hear it now. [Adopts female voice.] "Joe, no, you are going to kill them. No! No, Joe, it's too much," and he would be breaking furniture and it was terrible. I always said if I ever have kids I will never behave like this way. I won't touch a hair on their heads. Because people always say the abused abuse and it is not true. It is not true. I am totally the opposite. The worst I do is I make them stand in the corner for a little bit and that's it and that's my time out for them.

SB: I think you are right. I hate when I hear things like that the abused abuse. It means that you are condemned to be a bad person.

MJ: It's not true. I always promised in my heart that I would never be this way, never. If—and it can be in a movie or in a department store—I hear someone arguing with their child, I break down and cry. Because it reflects how I was treated when I was little. I break down at that moment and I shake and I cry. I can't take it. It is hard.

SB: When my parents divorced, we moved away and my father lived 3,500 miles away from us. And it was difficult to be close to him. But I love him, and I try never to judge him, and I have made a great effort to be much, much closer to him. We have to take seriously the Bible's commandment to always honor our parents. The Bible doesn't say, "Honor them if they've earned it." It simply commands us to honor them. Just by virtue of them having given us life they have earned it.

MJ: I am scared of my father to this day. My father walked in the room—and God knows I am telling the truth—I have fainted in his presence many times. I have fainted once to be honest. I have thrown up in his presence because when he comes in the room and this aura comes and my stomach starts hurting and I know I am in trouble. He is so different now. Time and age has changed him and he sees his grandchildren and he wants to be a better father. It is almost like the ship has sailed its course and it is so hard for me to accept this other guy that is not the guy I was raised with. I just wished he had learned that earlier.

SB: So why are you still scared?

MJ: Because the scar is still there, the wound.

SB: So you still see him as the first man. It is hard for you to see him as this new man?

MJ: I can't see him as the new man. I am like an angel in front of him, like scared. One day he said to me, "Why are you scared of me?" I couldn't answer him. I felt like saying, "Do you know what you have done?" [voice breaks] "Do you know what you have done to me?"

SB: It is so important for me to hear this. Because as your friend and as someone who is asked constantly about you, it is so important for me to understand these things. It is so important for the world to understand this. You see Michael, no one would have judged you as harshly if they had heard this. They would have made more of an effort to empathize with your own suffering rather than just condemning you. Do you call him Dad or Joseph?

MJ: We weren't allowed to call him Dad when we were growing up. He said, "Don't call me Dad. I am Joseph." That's what he told us. But now he wants to be called Dad. It is hard for me. I can't call him Dad. He would make it a point: "Don't call me Dad. I am Joseph." I love when Prince and Paris call me "Daddy," or when you hear little Italian kids call "Papa," or Jewish kids call "Poppy." Sweet, how could you not be proud of that? That's your offspring.

SB: From what age did he tell you not to call him Dad?

MJ: From a little kid all the way up to *Off the Wall, Thriller.*

SB: He felt he was more professional that way?

MJ: No. He felt that he was this young stud. He was too cool to be Dad. He was Joseph. I would hate him to hear me say this. . . .

SB: I read somewhere that your mother was thinking of getting divorced and she filed or something.

MJ: I don't know if she filed, maybe. No, no, she didn't file. She wanted to, many times, because of other women and because he was difficult. But in the name of religion she only can divorce on the grounds of fornication. And he has been in that area before and she knows it. But she is such a saint that she won't part with him. She knows he is out doing other things and fooling around and she is so good and he will come home and lay next to her in the bed. I don't know anyone like her. She is like a Mother Teresa. There are very few people like that.

SB: So she is a long-suffering, saintly kind of woman. Do you feel that she has suffered too long? That she shouldn't have put up with it?

MJ: We used to beg her to divorce him. We used to say, "Mother, divorce him." She used to say, "Leave me alone. No!" We used to say, "Get rid of him." We used to scream at her, "Divorce him" when we were little. But many years we'd hear the car coming down the drive. He always drove a big Mercedes and he drives real slow. "Joseph's home, Joseph's home, quick!" Everybody runs to their room, doors slam.

SB: You were that scared of him?

MJ: Yeah. I always said, "When I come home and walk through the door I want the kids to go "Daddy," and jump all over me and that's what mine do. I want just the opposite. I don't want them to run.

Protective of Janet

Shmuley Boteach: Let me just share one thought. You said your father would humiliate you when you were in concert and he would make you cry and push you out on stage in front of all the girls who loved you. . . to do what? To show his power over you?

Michael Jackson: Well, um, no. He wouldn't do it on the stage. Like, after a show, there'd be the room full of girls. He would love to bring the girls in the room, my father. And after the show we'd have something to eat, or whatever, and the room would be just lined with girls giggling, just loving us, like "oh my god!" and shaking. And if I was talking and something happened and he didn't like it, he'd get this look in his eye like. . . he'd get this look in his eye that would just scare you to death. He slapped me so hard in the face, as hard as he could, and then he'd thrust me out into the big room, where they are, tears running down my face, and what are you supposed to do, you know?

SB: And how old were you now?

[Prince in the background, "We're three!". . . laughing]

MJ: Uh, no more than like, twelve. . . eleven, something around there.

SB: So these were the first moments that you felt shame in your life? Really humiliated?

MJ: No, there were other ones. He did some rough, cruel. . . cruel. . . I don't know why. He was rough. The way he would beat you was hard, you know? He would make you strip nude first. He would oil you down. It would be a whole ritual. He would oil you down so when the tip of the ironing cord hit you [makes noise mimicking], you know . . . and it would just be like dying and you had whips all over your face, your back, everywhere. And I always heard my mother like, "No, Joe! You're gonna kill 'em. You're gonna kill 'em, no!" And I would just give up, like there was nothing I could do. And I hated him for it, hated him. We all did. We used to say to our mother, we used to say to each other, and I'll never forget this. Janet and myself, we used to say. . . I used to say, "Janet, shut your eyes." She'd go, "Okay, they're shut." And I'd say, "Picture Joseph in a coffin. He's dead. Did you feel sorry?" She'd go, "No." Just like that. That's what we used to do to each other as kids. We would like play games like that. And that's how hateful we were. I'd go, "He's in the coffin, he's dead. Would you feel sorry?" She'd go, "Nope," just like that. That's how angry we were with him. And I love him today, but he was hard, Shmuley. He was rough.

SB: But did you know that that was part of being corrupted as a child when you start feeling that way—hatred? Did you know, "I gotta get rid of this somehow. I gotta do something about this"?

MJ: Yeah, I wanted to become such a wonderful performer that I would get love back.

SB: So you could change him, you thought. If you. . . so you thought that if you became a great star, very successful, and were loved by the world, and were very successful, your father would love you too.

MJ: Aha.

SB: So you could change him that way.

MJ: Aha. I was hoping I could and I was hoping I could get love from other people, 'cause I needed it real bad, you know? You need love, you need love. That's the most important thing. That's why I feel so bad for those kids who sit in those orphanages and hospitals and they're all alone and they tie them to the beds—they tie them because they don't have enough staff. I go, "Are you crazy?" And I go to each bed just freeing them, releasing them. I say, "This isn't a way to do children. You don't tie them down." Or they have them chained to the walls in some places, like in Romania. And they have them sleep in their own feces and their tinkle.

SB: Do you identify more with people like that 'cause you're also that sensitive?

MJ: Yeah, I always hold Mushki [my eldest daughter who was about 12 at the time] the most 'cause I feel her pain. She's in so much pain. When Janet went through her fat stage she cried a lot, my sister Janet. She decided to just lose it all, "I'm gonna lose this," and she did it. She used to be very unhappy.

SB: Are you very protective of her as a younger sister?

MJ: Yeah, I was determined to make her lose weight. I was bad. I would tease her to make her lose it. I didn't like it on her. I didn't like it because I knew she would have a hard time.

SB: How did you get her to do something about it?

MJ: I said you have to lose weight 'cause you look like a fat cow. I would tell her and that was mean of me to say that. She would say, "Shut up," and I'd say "You shut up." But I was determined to make my sister look good because deep in my heart I love her and I want to make her shine and when she became a star on, you know. . . records, I was so happy and proud because, you know, she did it.

SB: Are you still protective of her as a younger sister?

MJ: Yes, yes. . . . I just wish that we were closer. We're close in spirit but not as family. Because we don't celebrate, we have no reason to come together now. I wish that was instilled in us. I love what I saw you guys do, that blessing thing that touches my heart a lot. I see why you're so close to them, it's sweet.

On Friday nights, as the Jewish Sabbath comes in, my wife and I bless our children, one by one, to grow to be like the great figures of the Bible, the patriarchs and matriarchs of the Jewish people. Michael witnessed this several times as a guest at the Sabbath table at our home. He would always watch intently as we blessed our children.

A Painful Blessing: All I Wanted Was to Be Loved

Shmuley Boteach: Has God always answered your prayers?

Michael Jackson: Usually. Absolutely. That's why I believe in it.

SB: Do you feel that he has been with you through some of the difficult things in life?

MJ: There hasn't been one thing that I have asked for that I didn't get. It is not materialistic. I am going to say something I have never said before and this is the truth. I have no reason to lie to you and God knows I am telling the truth. I think all my success and fame, and I have wanted it, I have wanted it because I wanted to be loved. That's all. That's the real truth. I wanted people to love me, truly love me, because I never really felt loved. I said I know I have an ability. Maybe if I sharpened my craft, maybe people will love me more. I just wanted to be loved because I think it is very important to be loved and to tell people that you love them and to look in their eyes and say it.

I remember getting shivers when Michael said this. I was sitting with the most famous celebrity on earth, an icon whom so many aspired to imitate. And here he was telling me that everything he had ever done—all the songs we had heard, the dance routines, the moonwalk—were all designed simply to feel a morsel of love. I thought to myself that Michael lived in a black hole of affection of such magnitude that few of us could scarcely comprehend.

SB: But the flip side of that, Michael, is that if you were given a huge amount of love as a child, then you might not have worked as hard to be successful.

MJ: That's true. That's why I wouldn't want to change anything because it has all worked out in its many different ways.

SB: So you were able to turn the neglect into a blessing?

MJ: Yeah.

SB: I remember a quote from Paul McCartney, who was asked about you when you became a big star. Someone said, "Michael Jackson, is he going to be like these other rock stars—God forbid, dead at thirty and drugs?" And McCartney said, "No. Michael, his whole character is different. He doesn't swear, he doesn't drink." He said this about fifteen years ago. Did you know that about yourself, that you had a character that, if it continued like that, wasn't going to be destroyed by fame and success?

Wow, reading this part of the conversation just eight years later really makes you sad. If only I had known at the time that this was exactly the fate that awaited him. But it was a different time, and Michael then was a very different person.

MJ: Yeah. I have always been kinda determined. I have always had a vision of things I have wanted to do and goals I have wanted to reach and nothing could stop me getting that. I am focused and I know what I want and what I want to achieve and I won't get sidetracked. And even though I get down sometimes, I keep running the race of endurance to achieve those goals. It keeps me on track. I am dedicated.

SB: If you are completely happy with who you are, what about. . . you said you wouldn't have done anything differently because you know that whatever experiences you had in your childhood led to who you are today, your success. So you wouldn't do anything differently?

MJ: No. I am so sensitive to other kids because of my past and I am so happy about that.

Rose Fine: Michael's Childhood Tutor

Michael and I were discussing Rose Fine, his childhood tutor who accompanied The Jackson 5 while they toured. Michael remained attached to her well after he had grown up and assisted in her financial support for the rest of her life. The conversation starts with me and Michael talking about air travel.

Michael Jackson: It left a terrible scar on me.

Shmuley Boteach: What?

MJ: Turbulence and being up there and thinking you are not going to live.

SB: Remember that story you told me about your Jewish tutor?

MJ: Rose Fine?

SB: You told me once on the phone that she used to say to you that if there was a nun on the plane that everyone was going to die.

MJ: She said, "We're okay, we're sitting on the plane and now we have so much faith. I have checked. . . there isn't a nun on the plane." I always believe that.

SB: Do you still look out for that nun?

MJ: I think about it! I never see a nun on the plane. She [Rose Fine] helped me a lot because she held my hand and cuddled me. After the show I would run to the room. We'd read and have warm milk and I needed that so badly. She would always say to me, "The door's open," and she would leave her door open.

SB: Is it possible if someone is not a biological parent to love a child as much as you love your own child? Do you love children as much as you love Prince and Paris?

MJ: Absolutely.

SB: I have always noticed one of the most impressive things about you is when I say something like, "Prince and Paris are beautiful," you always say, "No. All children are beautiful." You won't let me get away with just praising Prince and Paris.

MJ: They are to me. I see beauty in all children. . . they are all beautiful to me. It is so beautiful and I love them all—equally. I used to have arguments about it with people who didn't agree with me. They say you should love your own more.

SB: Rose Fine, although she wasn't your biological mother, was able to show you a lot of motherly affection?

MJ: And boy did I need it. I was never with my mother when I was little, very seldom, and I had a wonderful mother. I see her as an angel, and I was always gone, always on tour doing back-to-back concerts, all over America, overseas, clubs, just always gone. That helped me a lot. We took care of her [Rose Fine] until the day she died, Janet and myself. She just died recently.

SB: Do you think she should be mentioned in the context of our children's initiative?

MJ: Please do. She needs to be remembered.

SB: How old was she?

MJ: She would never tell me her age. I think she was in her nineties. She used to say, "When I retire from you I will tell you my age." But when she retired she still wouldn't tell me. She was with us all the way from the very first professional tour of The Jackson 5 until I was eighteen. The first tour was after we broke big—the first hit single. She would always have the power, like some of the concerts would start late and she would always have the power to stop the show because the Board of Education would say, "You kids cannot go past your time legally." She would always let it go on. She couldn't hurt the audience.

SB: And then she would teach you during the day?

MJ: Aha.

SB: Regular subjects? Mathematics? English? She taught all five of you together?

MJ: Yes together, three hours. She taught Janet, all of them.

SB: Tell me a bit more about her.

MJ: Yes, Rose died this year. Janet and myself, we paid for her nurse and her hospital care, and if her television broke down or the electricity, or there was anything wrong with the house, we would cover her bills. Now her husband is sick so I am taking care of him, and because we felt she is our mother and you take care of your mother.

SB: You really felt that?

MJ: Absolutely. She was more than a tutor and I was so angry at myself that when she died I was far, far away. I couldn't get there. I was in Switzerland and Evvy [Michael's secretary] called me on the phone and told me that she was dead. I went, "What? I am in Switzerland. I can't. . . ." It made me angry, but I did all I could.

It also hurt when I came to the door to see her and I went, "Mrs. Fine, it's Michael," and she would go, "You're not Michael." I would say, "It's Michael," and she would say, "Don't say you are Michael. You are not Michael." That kinda sets into the brain and they don't recognize you. That hurts so much. Growing old is not always pretty. It is sad.

SB: How would a child deal with something like that? You have tried to retain your youth, your playfulness, all the things that we talk about. Do you see it as a curse, growing old?

MJ: In a way, when the body starts to break down. But when old people return to childhood, I have seen them, they become very playful and childlike. I relate very well to old people because they have those qualities of a child. Whenever I go to a hospital I always find a way to sneak into another room to talk to the old people. I just did it two days ago because I was in the hospital and they were so sweet and they just welcome you like a child does. They say, "Come in," and we talk. They are simple and sweet.

SB: So life is almost like a circle. You start as a child and then you go through this adult phase, which isn't always healthy. There are a lot of negative things about it, and you come back, in elderly age, to that innocence, you become a lot more playful. You have a lot more time the way children have. I guess that's why grandparents get along so well with their grandchildren.

MJ: Old people and children are very much alike. They are carefree and play—free and simple and sweet. It is just a spiritual feeling. I don't visit the old people's homes as much as I have the orphanages. A lot of them get Alzheimer's and they don't recognize. But I have a great relationship with older people. I love talking to older people and they can tell you stories about when they were kids and how the world was in those days and I love that. There was an old Jewish man in New York a long time ago who said to me, "Always be thankful for your talent and always give to poor people. Help other people. When I was a little boy my father said to me, 'We are going to take these clothes and these pieces of bread and we are going to wrap them up and you run down the street and up the stairs and knock on the people's door and place it in front of the door and run!' I said, 'Why did you tell us to run?' He said, "Because when they open the door I don't want them to feel the shame. They have pride. That is real charity." I have never forgotten that [story of the old man]. That's sweet, isn't it? And he did that as a little boy all the time.

SB: So have you tried to do charitable acts that no one knows about?

MJ: Yes, without waving a flag. He [the man Michael is quoting above] is saying real charity is giving from the heart without taking credit, and when he ran they didn't know who had left it. It was like God had dropped it there, you know? It was so beautiful. I never forgot that story. I was around eleven when I was told that. He was old, really sweet, a Jewish man, I remember.

In the Jewish religion the highest form of charity is when the benefactor does not know the identity of the recipient, and the recipient does not know the identity of the benefactor. Hence, the Jewish custom of putting money every day into a charity box at home or into a publicly administered fund that is later distributed to the poor.

SB: Was she [Rose Fine] a committed Jew? Was she observant of her faith? Or was she more of a secular Jew?

MJ: What does that mean?

SB: Did she refrain from traveling on the Sabbath, did she eat only kosher food, things like that?

MJ: Not that I remember. She taught me a lot about the Jewish way. I don't know if she ate the kosher food, but I always felt so bad for her because her son suffered so badly. He was a doctor who died early and the day he died, I remember how deeply dark and sad she was. He was a wonderful doctor, went to Harvard, and he was tall and handsome. He had some kind of brain tumor. I can't imagine losing your own child like that, let alone losing any child.

SB: Did you find out anything about Judaism from Rose Fine?

MJ: She taught me about the Jewish culture and I will never forget when I was a little kid we landed in Germany, she got real quiet. I said, "What's wrong, Miss Fine?" You know how kids can tell when something is wrong with their mother? She said, "I don't like it." I said, "Why?" She said, "A lot of people suffered here." That's when I first learned about the concentration camps, through her, because I didn't know nothing about it. I'll never forget that feeling. She said she felt cold there, she could feel it. What a sweet person. She taught me the wonderful world of books and reading and I wouldn't be the same person if it wasn't for her. I owe a lot to her and that's why I am dedicating the new album to her.

SB: Do you think she saw you as her son?

MJ: She called me her son. Whenever you go on the plane you see these seven little black kids and a black father, all got big Afros, and this white Jewish older woman would be in the back. They would stop her and go, "Who are you?" She would say, "I'm the mother." She would say it every time and they would let her go. Sweet story. She was special. I needed her.

SB: Did she show you unconditional love?

MJ: Yes.

SB: So you think unconditional love can be shown even by two people who are not related by blood?

MJ: Oh my God, yes, of course. I think I learned it through her and I have seen it and I have experienced it. It doesn't matter with blood or race or creed or color. Love is love and it breaks all boundaries and you just see it right away. I see it in children's eyes. When I see children, I see helpless little puppies. They are so sweet. How could anybody hurt them? They are so wonderful.

SB: She died this year so that means you have to deal with grief. How does a child deal with grief? A child lives in a paradise, a perfect world that we are trying to describe. Adults are later largely corrupted through their wars and their jealousy and their cynicism, and suddenly along comes death and even a child has to deal with a death. So how do you deal with death? And how does a child deal with death?

MJ: Yes, I have had to deal with death and it is very difficult.

PART 2

JEHOVAH'S WITNESSES YEARS
AND RELIGION

Rejection by the Jehovah's Witnesses Church

Religion was a big part of Michael's life. He was raised by his mother Katherine to be a devout Jehovah's Witness. Michael took his religious commitments so seriously that even after the *Thriller* album he still continued to go missionizing every Sunday, knocking on people's doors, giving them copies of the *Watchtower,* and trying to convince them that God existed. But as time went by, Michael became alienated from his Church. It was a fateful estrangement. Michael, in my opinion, never recovered from the loss of his spiritual anchor and most of the bizarre elements that would come to characterize his life began with his exit from the Church.

Michael described his childhood experiences as a Jehovah's Witness in an article I wrote for him that appeared on Beliefnet.com, the well known spirituality website, on people's experiences with the Sabbath. His memories of that time were so vivid and meaningful to him that I thought it made sense to share a bit of them here:

When people see the television appearances I made when I was a little boy—eight or nine years old and just starting off my lifelong music career—they see a little boy with a big smile. They assume that this little boy is smiling because he is joyous, that he is singing his heart out because he is happy, and that he is dancing with an energy that never quits because he is carefree. But while singing and dancing were, and undoubtedly remain, some of my greatest joys, at that time what I wanted more than anything else were the two things that make childhood the most wondrous years of life, namely, playtime and a feeling of freedom. The public at large has yet to really understand the pressures of childhood celebrity, which, while exciting, always exact a very heavy price.

There was one day a week, however, that I was able to escape the stages of Hollywood and the crowds of the concert hall. That day was the Sabbath. In all religions, the Sabbath is a day that allows and requires the faithful to step away from the everyday and focus on the exceptional. I learned something about the Jewish Sabbath in particular early on from Rose, and my friend Shmuley further clarified for me how, on the Jewish Sabbath, the everyday life tasks of cooking dinner, grocery shopping, and mowing the lawn are forbidden so that humanity may make the ordinary extraordinary and the natural miraculous. Even things like shopping or turning on lights are forbidden. On this day, the Sabbath, everyone in the world gets to stop being ordinary.

But what *I* wanted more than anything was to *be* ordinary. So in my world, the Sabbath was the day I was able to step away from my unique life and glimpse the everyday.

Sundays were my day for "Pioneering," the term used for the missionary work that Jehovah's Witnesses do. We would spend the day in the suburbs of Southern California, going door to door or making the rounds of a shopping mall, distributing our *Watchtower* magazine. I continued my Pioneering work for years and years after my career had been launched. Up to 1991, the time of my *Dangerous* tour, I would don my disguise of fat suit, wig, beard, and glasses, and head off to live in the land of everyday America, visiting shopping plazas and track homes in the suburbs. I loved to set foot in all those houses and catch sight of the shag rugs and La-Z-Boy armchairs with kids playing Monopoly and grandmas baby-sitting and all those wonderfully ordinary and, to me, magical scenes of life. Many, I know, would argue that these things seem like no big deal. But to me they were positively fascinating.

The funny thing is, no adults ever suspected who this strange bearded man was. But the children, with their extra intuition, knew right away. Like the Pied Piper of Hamelin, I would find myself trailed by eight or nine children by my second round of the shopping mall. They would follow and whisper and giggle, but they wouldn't reveal my secret to their parents. They were my little aides. Hey, maybe you bought a magazine from me. Now you're wondering, right?

Sundays were sacred for two other reasons as I was growing up. They were both the day that I attended church and the day that I spent rehearsing my hardest. This may seem against the idea of "rest on the Sabbath," but it was the most sacred way I could spend my time: developing the talents that God gave me. The best way I can imagine to show my thanks is to make the very most of the gift that God gave me.

Church was a treat in its own right. It was again a chance for me to be "normal." The church elders treated me the same as they treated everyone else. And they never became annoyed on the days that the back of the church filled with reporters who had discovered my whereabouts. They tried to welcome them in. After all, even reporters are the children of God.

When I was young, my whole family attended church together in Indiana. As we grew older, this became difficult and my remarkable and truly saintly mother would sometimes end up there on her own. When circumstances made it increasingly complex for me to attend, I was comforted by the belief that God exists in my heart, and in music and in beauty, not only in a building. But I still miss the sense of community that I felt there—I miss the friends and the people who treated me like I was simply one of them. Simply human. Sharing a day with God.

Shmuley Boteach: Do you think a hatred of pride is still a relic of your religious upbringing?

Michael Jackson: It hurt me a lot and it helped me a lot.

SB: How did it hurt you?

MJ: Er [long silence]. When I did certain things in the past that I didn't realize were against the religion and I was reprimanded for it, it almost destroyed me. Certain things that I did as an artist in my music I didn't realize I was crossing a line with them and when they chastised me, it really hurt me. It almost destroyed it. My mother saw it.

SB: Their disapproval, their rejection?

MJ: When I did the Moonwalk for the first time, *Motown 25*, they told me I was doing burlesque dancing and it was dirty and I went for months and they said, "You can never dance like that again." I said 90.9 percent of dancing is moving the waist. They said, "We don't want you to do it." So I went around trying to dance for a long time without moving this part of my body. Then when I made "Thriller" with all the ghouls and ghosts, they said that it was demonic and part of the occult and that Brother Jackson can't do it. I called my lawyer and was crying and I said, "Destroy the video, have it destroyed." And because he went against my wishes people have "Thriller" today. They made me feel so bad about it that I ordered my people to destroy it.

Michael did incorporate, at the Church's behest, a disclaimer at the beginning of the "Thriller" video announcing that nothing contained therein constituted an endorsement of the occult.

SB: So you have seen two sides of religion, the loving side that teaches you not to like pride and humility, but you have also seen what you would describe as mean-spiritedness and judgmentalism.

MJ: Because they can discriminate sometimes in the wrong way. I don't think God meant it in that way. Like Halloween, I missed out on Halloween for years and now I do it. It's sweet to go door-to-door and people give you candy. We need more of that in the world. It brings the world together.

SB: Do you take Prince and Paris trick-or-treating?

MJ: Absolutely, we have a family that we go with in the area and we give them the candy. I want them to see that people can be kind. We get it in a bag and then [whispering] *I exchange their candy for candy eyeballs.*

SB: I was speaking to Andrew Sullivan late last night, the journalist who was the editor of *The New Republic*. We had a debate together on homosexuality at a university and afterward we were talking about you and he was surprised to hear nice things about you and he said, "So why don't I know any of this?" I said, "I don't know." Insights like that, Michael, "the essence of Halloween." You should do press releases about things like that. "The essence of Halloween is for children to witness the kindness of strangers." I like that. It's a nice thought. It elevates trick-or-treat-ing into something more meaningful than sponging candy.

MJ: I cry behind my mask. I really do when I go with them and peo-ple say, "Open your bag," and I think, look what I have been miss-ing. I didn't know that this.... I look at their face and they are giving you a gift. It's sweet. The kids come and they open their bags and then they go, "Oh look at this little one," and it is just sweet the way they respond. I think that's very kind. That part of America I am proud of.

Did Michael See Himself as God's Chosen? Did He Have Special Healing Powers?

Shmuley Boteach: Jesus said, "Suffer little children to come unto me." He had all these amazing quotes about children and most saintly figures are seen around children. Do you identify with peo-ple like that? Do you feel that God has given you more than just a talent for music?

Michael Jackson: Yes, absolutely.

SB: . . . Wait. I think you do have something special to do here on this earth. Every human being does. And we can't ignore the fact that you have a level of renown rarely seen before. And we have to channel that celebrity in the proper way. That's when you become a teacher, Michael, not just an entertainer, you have to identify what it is, what positive message, you wish to impart to mankind. That's when your celebrity becomes redemptive. In fact, I think the word *entertainer* for you is a bit insulting. You are not an entertainer and you should always strive to be much more than merely an enter-tainer. As you said to me many times, no one would do the things you do if you were just an entertainer. Eddie Murphy is an enter-tainer. He is great. He is funny. But no one camps outside his home. You know what I mean. So that's something very powerful and you have to determine what it is you want to achieve with that, to what healthy and Godly use can you put it? And it can't be about you. It has to be about something much larger than you—a goal that is lofty and goes way beyond entertainment. Do you see yourself in that guise? Do you feel that God gave you a certain healing power?

MJ: Yes.

SB: So when you speak to Gavin you are healing him, not just speaking to him?

MJ: I *know* I am healing him, and I have seen children just shower me with love. And they want to just touch me and hug me and hold on and cry and not let go. They don't even know me. You'll see sometime when you hang out, or we'll be in an open place, and mothers pick up their babies and put them into my arms. "Touch my baby, touch my baby, hold them." It is not hero worship, like religions try to say, like idol worship.

SB: It is *not* idol worship? Why, because they're not worshipping you? Because they're getting to feel better about themselves? By being closer to you they feel lighter than air, they feel like they can almost walk on water themselves. Why isn't it worship?

MJ: Yes, because my religion taught us that you are not supposed to do that. If I had gone to my church they would have *never* treated me the way your church treated me.

When I took Michael to a synagogue for the Sabbath, the people greeted him very enthusiastically. In the Jehovah's Witnesses Church, they made a point of never treating Michael any differently than the other worshippers. In the case of the synagogue, we purposely did not tell the congregants he was coming, as we wanted his visit to be low-key and I wanted Michael to experience the beauty and serenity of the Sabbath unencumbered by the noise of celebrity. But when people saw him, they rushed to welcome him and shake his hand.

MJ: They would have been kind after the ceremony. "Hi Brother Jackson. Are you okay?" But hugging and, "Oh, oh, we love you," they would never. They would feel that it was idol worship and you are not supposed to do that. It is wrong, that it is taking it too far. There is nothing wrong with saying, "Thank you, we love you so much. . . ."

This was a fascinating point. I had spent so much time trying to steer Michael away from his need for veneration and his growing Messiah complex. But here he was saying to me that he had been treated that way in a Jewish synagogue! What Michael neglected to mention was that he attended the same Jehovah's Witnesses church every Sunday, so people were accustomed to him. I assume that had he attended the Carlebach Synagogue on the Upper West Side of Manhattan with me every Sabbath, the people would have become largely immune to his celebrity. But Judaism definitely has the same rule against idolizing any human being. In fact, it invented the rule and it's the main reason that Jews reject the divinity of Jesus.

Feeling Godlike, Connecting to the Divine

Shmuley Boteach: Do you have fun when you perform and do your music?

Michael Jackson: Yes. I love it. If it wasn't fun I wouldn't do it. I do it because I truly love it. There is no greater bliss than dancing and performing. It is like a celebration and when you are caught up in that place, where certain performers go when they become one with the music, one with the audience, if you are on that level it is like being in a trance, it just takes over. You start to play off each other and start to know where you are going before you get there. They have got to know where you are taking it and respond. It's like playing ping-pong. It's like when the birds go [migrate] and they all know when they are going. Or like fish. They are telepathic, they are on the same line. That's what happens when you perform, you are at one with the musicians and the dance and the music and you are in this trance. And man, you have got 'em. They are in the palm of your hand. It's unbelievable. You feel you are transformed.

SB: What is that energy which takes you there? Is it divine?

MJ: It is divine, it is pure, it is revelation, without making it sound spiritual or religious, but it is a divine energy. Some people call it the spirit, like when a spirit comes into the room. Some people look down on it. Religions sometimes look down on it because they try to say it's demonic, it's the cult, it's the devil. It isn't; it is God-like. It is pure God-like energy. You feel God's light.

The Jehovah's Witnesses Church, Michael explained to me, became increasingly critical of his fame and the adulation shown him. They were aghast at his being treated like a god. Michael should have taken their critique to heart, and realize that aside from considerations of sacrilege, no man could endure such unnatural idolization and survive. Humans are flawed, require adjustment, are rebuked by friends and family, and correct course. But man-gods are perfect. They never correct their ways. They therefore crash and burn, their tragic end being almost inevitable.

MJ: When I perform certain performances, like *Motown 25*, or when I did *Billie Jean* and the Moonwalk for the first time on the stage, and the audience, I'd do a little step and they would scream and you'd flicker your hand and. . . "*Agggghhhhh*," whatever you do. I am like caught in a trance with it all. I am like feeling it but I don't hear it. I'm playing everything off feeling. At the end of the piece when I am done and you open your eyes and see the response, you are surprised because you were in another world. I was at one with the moment, working moment, right in the moment.

SB: So you weren't doing it to conform to anybody. Maybe that's your power as a performer. It was never about what people wanted, about conditioning, about accommodating what other people wanted.

MJ: No.

SB: Can you teach people how to get there? If there was any bitterness or hatred in your heart in moments like that, if they are, as you say, divine, do you find it just empties out?

MJ: It just empties out. You are above it all. That's why I love it because you are going to a place where [there is] nothing nobody can do. It's gone, the point of no return. It's so wonderful. You have taken off. You can feel it, and that doesn't mean. . . and everybody else who's up there with you play off of that, the audience play off of that. . . .

Michael's Relationship with Religion

It was reported in the press that I had tried to make Michael Jackson Jewish. Nothing could be further from the truth. While I did take Michael to synagogue and he became a regular at our Friday night Sabbath meals at our home, that has been the case with many of my non-Jewish friends, and indeed in the eleven years that I served as rabbi at Oxford University, my synagogue and Sabbath table had as many non-Jewish participants as Jewish. Judaism is not a proselytizing faith. Indeed, even when potential converts come to us to become Jewish we are obligated to turn them away at least three times. This is based on the Jewish belief that there is more than one path to God and we must honor our original incarnation. The way that God created us is the manner in which we can find the most meaning for our lives. I am a great admirer of the Christian faith and try and get all my Christian brothers and sisters to look first at their faith before trying to find spiritual meaning elsewhere.

I repeatedly encouraged Michael to return to the Jehovah's Witnesses Church, and through the ordeal of his arrest I publicly called on the leaders of the Jehovah's Witnesses Church to take him back and offer him the spiritual direction he so badly needed. When Michael was a Witness it grounded him and he flourished. Even after the *Thriller* album, when he had become the most successful recording artist in the world, he remained a devout Jehovah's Witness and it anchored his life in a spiritual community and spiritual values. Indeed, one can chart Michael's personal decline to the time when he left the church. Michael's opinion of Jesus and Christianity were therefore significant.

Shmuley Boteach: Michael, I saw in some article that you once compared the pressures on Jesus to those on a modern celebrity. Do you remember that?

Michael Jackson: No, I don't. When was it?

SB: I don't know. Could have been made up. Do you have a relationship with Jesus?

MJ: Jesus, yes. Absolutely. But you [addressing me] believe in Jesus, don't you?

SB: No, not in his Messiahship or divinity.

MJ: You don't believe that he existed?

SB: Oh, we believe that he existed. We believe he was a good man, a devout Jew, a great moral teacher. But we don't believe that he was the son of God or that he was the Messiah. I did a Larry King show just recently with one of Billy Graham's daughters about this.

Do you feel an affinity with Jesus as a personality? Do you feel that he was a *Kidult*, because he is portrayed as a very gentle creature who had a beautiful moral message, and was soft and vulnerable on the outside? Was he like the stereotype of someone with a child at his center?

MJ: Yes, absolutely.

SB: And that's why he loved being around children?

MJ: I think if I sat in a room with him I would follow him everywhere he went, feel his presence. I would behave just like a child, like Gandhi.

SB: Can you see him laughing?

MJ: Yes, and Gandhi when he is giggling like a kid. . . it is so sweet. This man came out of nowhere and he led the whole nation. He held no political rank, no government rank. I think that is real power. That's incredible. That was a phenomenon—Gandhi. It's amazing, that was a phenomenal movie, did you see the movie?

[I confirm that I did.]

SB: What biblical stories do you find inspiring?

MJ: I love the Sermon on the Mount. I love the story when the Apostles are arguing amongst themselves about who is the greatest and Jesus says, "Unless you humble yourself like this little child, be childlike. . . ." I thought that was the perfect thing to say. Return to innocence.

SB: Did anyone tell you that it appeared to them that you were trying to create a Garden of Eden here [the conversation was at Neverland], your own vision of a perfect paradise, a refuge from what you saw was the adult insanity of the world?

MJ: You were the first one.

SB: Does the story of Adam and Eve have any special meaning for you?

MJ: Of course. Of course.

SB: Did you see the childlike qualities in them straight away?

MJ: Yes, I wish I could have seen it. Was it symbolism? Is it real? Did it happen? I'm confused sometimes that there is a loophole. I had questions that sometimes even the elders [of the Jehovah's Witnesses Church] couldn't answer.

SB: Did you ask them lots of questions about the Bible?

MJ: Oh yeah. I'm the kind of guy who used to grab the microphone and say, "Well, what about this and what about that?" They would say, "Brother Jackson, we will talk to you later." They would come up with this other funny kinda answer that wouldn't drive the point home.

SB: Adam and Eve are two perfect beings who were like children. They are created as adults, but their situation is unique because they are also children. They have just been born, just been created. So their perfection lay in how they are adults and children at the same time. They represent the amalgamation of the virtues of both. So this is a central story to what we're trying to develop, of people being adults on the outside, but always retaining their childlike qualities on the inside. So was this always a story that meant something to you?

MJ: But [what doesn't make sense to me is that God] tested them [with the forbidden fruit]. And if you are God you should know the outcome. And if you are God, why test if you create a perfect being that should not be able to do any wrong? And why judge and thrust such anger on them and run them away and tempt them with a snake? Would a God do such a thing? Would I do that to your children? No I wouldn't. I am not here trying to judge God or criticize him in any way. But sometimes I think it is a symbolism to teach us certain lessons. I don't know if it really happened. I wouldn't take your little baby or any of them and have something see if they would do right or wrong. And then to have the two kids [Cain and Abel]. . . was it incest? And they were two boys, how did they have children? And all of those things that they couldn't answer for me.

SB: These are the questions you were asking the elders?

MJ: Uhuh.

Michael's questions are actually important enough to be asked and answered by some of the leading Jewish Biblical commentators of ancient times. For those interested in finding some answers to his questions, see my books *The Private Adam* and *Judaism for Everyone*, where I discuss Adam and Eve in the Garden of Eden. Also, Rabbi Joseph Soloveitchik's seminal work, *The Lonely Man of Faith*, brilliantly analyzes Adam and Eve in the Garden.

Religion and Finding God in Rituals

Shmuley Boteach: I always say that the main purpose of religion is to teach you in your twenties what you only find out in your seventies. Otherwise religion is not principally designed to offer cosmic secrets. It's straightforward and its profundity is found specifically in its simplicity: Be a good person, spend time with your kids, love God. You know all that at eighty, but you should know it in your teens and twenties, so you don't squander your life.

Michael Jackson: Right, I see it, I see it. That's what we're all talking about.

SB: You're one of the few people who seems to be religious without practicing, meaning, you have a very deep-seated sense of spirituality, but you don't undertake many religious rituals. You'll tell me things like, "Although I once believed God is in a church, I now believe that God is everywhere, he's in my heart. . . I now find God in those moments I spend with my children, I find God in the innocent."

This was quoted from the article about the Sabbath that I wrote for Michael based on our conversations.

MJ: Yeah it's true, it's true.

SB: See, you're very religious, but it's important to also connect with God through rituals. It's like [my wife] Debbie. Debbie's more spiritual than I am naturally. She just feels God more than I do. I need to do things to feel him often. I'm not the pure soul that she is. I am very different.

MJ: So you guys don't go to the. . . uh. . .

SB: We go to synagogue every week, yeah.

MJ: Every week?

SB: Absolutely.

MJ: What day?

SB: Friday nights and Saturday.

MJ: You do?

SB: Yeah, of course. Remember that service we had at my house?

Michael had come to a Friday night service at my home and danced in a large circle with all my friends.

MJ: And do all your children go?

SB: Yes, of course.

MJ: And how long do you stay?

SB: Friday nights, it's about an hour. Then about three hours on Saturday mornings. Then Saturday afternoon it's another hour.

MJ: And the children stay for three hours? And they do well?

SB: Yep.

MJ: That's why they're so well behaved.

SB: They're very good about that. They're very good. And once a month I don't go to synagogue and I stay home with them and practice their prayers so they know what to say in synagogue.

MJ: So you have these prayers?

SB: We do services at home once a month.

MJ: They must be some beautiful prayers.

SB: Oh they're beautiful, yeah.

MJ: I know they must be very beautiful.

SB: They're very simple. Jewish prayers are not about big things; they're about little things. The prayers condition us to find God in the minutiae of everyday life. He is all around us.

MJ: But they're beautiful aren't they?

SB: They're about thanking God for the rain, about thanking God for the cooling wind. They're about thanking God for all the miracles he gives the Jews in history.

MJ: Wow.

SB: The Jews have been around for a long time. He's looked after us. We're an ancient people.

MJ: Wow, and Mushki and everybody go? Baba? [Baba, our nickname for our daughter Rochel Leah, was three at the time.]

SB: Baba goes too. Baba doesn't go three times on the Sabbath, she goes once Saturday morning with Debbie. 'Cause Debbie's pregnant now, although she sometimes goes three times, now she just goes in the morning. You know, we walk, we don't use a car. We don't drive on the Sabbath at all.

MJ: How far do you walk?

SB: It's not that far. About a half a mile. It's not that far.

MJ: All the kids walk?

SB: All of them.

MJ: Really?

SB: In Oxford [where I served as rabbi for eleven years], it was very far. In Oxford we walked three miles each way.

MJ: You and the children?

SB: It was always raining. It was always raining.

MJ: Shmuley, you guys walked three miles?

SB: Three miles.

MJ: And they didn't complain?

SB: No. Sometimes they complained if we'd come back very late 'cause we used to eat with the students for the Friday night Sabbath meals, and often we'd walk home well after midnight.

MJ: I love your family.

Karma and Justice

Shmuley Boteach: I really like the fact that at Neverland the Security are called Safety… it's on their badges, uniforms, and hats.

Michael Jackson: I don't know.

SB: The fact that is says "Safety" rather than "Security," it's like, "We are not here to keep the world out, but simply to ensure the safety of everyone who is visiting here." It's less intimidating and more humane.

Children have a really strong sense of justice. The most common thing I hear from my kids is, "That's not fair." You just said that these people who did this thing at your performance got away with it. On the one hand children have this very strong sense of justice, and on the other hand we see how mean people get away with things and no one stops them.

MJ: It happens all the time. I think justice is important because there are many injustices in the world and I hate injustice. "I am tired of injustice" is the opening to one of my songs on my last album, called *Scream*. That's the first line I say. There's a line where Janet [Jackson] says, "Oh my God I can't believe what I saw on the TV this evening. I was disgusted by all the injustice," because I wanted people to know about that and people get away with it and I don't believe in karma. I think that is a bunch of crap, because so many mean-spirited, evil people are on top of the world and doing well and people love them, no matter how evil they are.

SB: I love it when you make strong statements like that.

MJ: Well, I'm sorry, it's crap. Karma is a theory like any other theory that some human made up.

SB: Well, "what goes around comes around" is ok, because there's great truth to that. But karma could actually be evil because karma says that handicapped children did something bad in a previous life.

MJ: That's a fine line and I'm sorry for talking like that. But I hate whoever says some thing like that. A child did something in a past life so God is going to handicap them? There were all these orphans in this one country coming to America to be adopted. The plane crashed. Every child on the plane died. Why? If you could save those kids, if you were in Heaven, you would say, "This one is not going down. Maybe another one, but not this one." I know I would.

SB: Did you ever have Eastern spiritual gurus who came to you and said, "Michael children get hit by trucks because they fornicated in a previous life?"

MJ: No, and if they did I would be furious and I would give them all the reasons why that is a bunch of crap. That's *doodoo*. That's a theory like any other man's theory about the universe. Some people believe in the Big Bang, which I don't, and some people believe in the Creation, that story with Adam and Eve, that this universe isn't an accident. To say this universe was created by a Big Bang or an accident is to say, "Okay, I want you to take a car engine and we are going to take each piece apart and we are going to put it in a bath tub, and I want you to shake it up." You can shake that tub 100 years and it will never become the perfect engine. All the pieces to come together and make an engine, that is like saying the Big Bang theory, and there was a big explosion and we got children, and trees, and plants, and the air we breath, and oxygen. Somebody had to create this, a designer had to create this. From our lashes to our mouths to our digestive system. Don't you agree?

SB: That's the most important of all religious beliefs, that God is the origin of life.

MJ: When I used to go door to door [Witnessing for the Jehovah's Witnesses Church] and people would say, "We are atheists," [I'd think] what? They don't believe in.... I heard it a lot and I had a brother who was an atheist for a while but I think he isn't now. Tito was an atheist even after being raised as a strict Jehovah's Witness. I know some of the famous directors, the guy who directed *Singing In The Rain* and who won academy awards, Stanley Donen....

SB: So what arguments did you have for people when you were Pioneering when they told you that they were atheists?

MJ: I tried to bring out the miracles of life, the children, look into their eyes, our bodies, how it all works just right, this can't happen on its own, come on, no way. Then there are the questions I have about why we are here and why we are allowed to destroy each other. Because we are the only species who destroys their own. Every species on this planet... I don't understand how all that injustice takes place. Why didn't something in heaven stop the Holocaust or some of the great genocides that happen in the world, from the lynchings and slavery, to all the great problems, to Stalin, to...? I hate to say this but Napoleon, too. He gets praised for all his genocide [I assume Michael means all the wars he caused], whereas Hitler gets called the Devil, which he was. But they both did the same thing. But one was doing it for his country and the other one was too! But a lot of people died with Napoleon. There are statues of Napoleon.

SB: Well, no one was ever as evil as Hitler. And Napolean, while being a man who started many wars, was still a benevolent dictator and in no way could he be compared to Hitler. Still, in his day, Napoleon was referred to by the English and by all the nations of Europe as "the beast." They called him the anti-Christ.

MJ: But he died a lonely man on an island all alone.

SB: Do you enjoy reading about history?

MJ: I do enjoy reading about history, but I don't know what to believe and what not to believe. Because I know how much that is written about me is twisted... about me... how much stuff in history is twisted. Because the way this country was taken away from the Indians and the way Australia was taken from the blacks and apartheid, how they killed so many blacks.

SB: You know that most of the death of the indigenous peoples here in the Americas, as well as most of the slaves who were brought from Africa, was through disease and germs. Almost ninety percent of Native Americans died because of European diseases. You see the Europeans had so much disease in their blood they developed immunity to it. But the Native Americans had no such immunity and European germs killed off about eighty seven percent of indigenous peoples in the Americas, and something like ninety five percent of the Aborigines died of disease. They lived in more wholesome environments without all the European illness.

MJ: I hate it. I'm sorry I hate it.

SB: You know, when I was in Australia recently they had this big debate about whether the government should finally apologize to the Aboriginal people.

MJ: I know all about this. I told Frank about it, remember? [Frank Cascio was in the room with us during this conversation.] They say that if they apologize then they have to pay them the way they are paying the Jews for the Holocaust. And they don't want to pay them so they can't say they are sorry. They made a mistake because they are worried that they will stick their hand out and ask for money.

SB: Do you think they should?

MJ: Absolutely, and I give the Jews credit for standing up for the past. Yes. The Germans paid the Jews $47 billion a year in taxes because of the Holocaust.

SB: It's actually nowhere *near* that much. But the Jews were never paid for their slave labor and certainly never accepted blood money for the six million killed. Rather, they were compensated for the tens of billions of dollars in confiscated property that was stolen and destroyed by the Nazis and their collaborators, and even then only got a fraction of what they lost.

MJ: But I hate when people to this day think that all Germans are bad, because they are not.

SB: In the Bible there is horizontal, rather than vertical accountability. So, if I saw you beating up Frank and I didn't stop you, I am also responsible because I was here witnessing it but chose to do so without stopping you. But Prince wouldn't be responsible just because he is your son. We do not visit the sins of the fathers upon the children. So, horizontal accountability, but not vertical. He can't be accountable for what his father does. So we of course don't hold this generation of Germans responsible for what their parents did. But we do hold the generation who perpetrated it, and those who watched in silence, we hold them accountable.

Racism, Religion, and Anti-Semitism

Michael was heavily criticized for using *kike*, a term of derision for Jews, in his song "They Don't Care About Us." Indeed, many Jewish people, when hearing that we had become friends, wrote to me and told me that Michael was an anti-Semite. But with all the flaws I admit existed in Michael's life, being an anti-Semite was simply not one of them. If anything, I believe Michael had an intuitive affinity with Jewish people. He greatly respected the fact that I was a rabbi and did much to learn from the wisdom I had as a scholar of Jewish texts. And yes, I am well aware that in 2006 Michael left a voice message on a recording machine disparaging Jews. But while I'm not here to defend such a repulsive action it has to be remembered that by that time Michael was often stoned out of his mind on prescription medication and who knows who was feeding him these lines. Michael always demonstrated the highest respect for Jews and Judaism in my presence.

Shmuley Boteach: So you have been the voice for a lot of the people who have been left out. Like in the song "They Don't Care About Us," the main message being they don't care about who? The poor? The third world?

Michael Jackson: Well I'd say, they don't care about us, those who are treated unjustly, those who have been bastardized, being called "nigger," being called the word that they misunderstood me for when I said those who say "kike" to people. When I was a little kid, Jews, we had Jewish lawyers and Jewish accountants and they slept in my bed next to me and they would call each other "kike." I said, "What is that?" and they said, "That's the bad word for Jews. For blacks they say 'nigger.'" I said, "Ohhh." So I always knew when people had been bastardized, they've been called "nigger," they've been called "kike." That's what I'm saying and they used it. They took it all wrong. I would never. . . you know?

SB: You were trying to stand up for those with no voice?

MJ: Yeah, who don't have a voice. I would never teach hatred, ever. That's not what I'm about.

SB: Are you proud to be an American? When you did all these concerts abroad in foreign countries, did you feel like you were some sort of American representative?

MJ: I hope you don't take this wrong, what I am about to say, but I feel I belong to the world and I hate to take sides. Even though I am an American and I was born in this country and there are a lot of things about America I am proud of, and there are a lot of things I am not proud of. . . ignorance . . . like that [Norman] Rockwell painting of the little girl trying to get to school to learn and they were throwing stuff at her.

Rockwell had painted a black girl going to a recently desegregated school in the deep South, surrounded by Federal marshals who were there to protect her from attack. Michael and I had gone to see it at a private gallery.

MJ: I don't understand racism. My mother—and she is an angel and a saint—she was pulling out of the market and it was a block from my house in Encino and she was in her Mercedes. And my mother loves everybody, and this white man in a car screams out, "Go back to Africa, you nigger." It hurt me so much that that happened to my mother. . . this was no more than five years ago, because he was jealous.

I know stories of my brothers in their Rolls-Royces get out of the car and lock the door and when they come back they find that some guy had taken a key and scratched the car because there is a black man driving it. I just hate anything like that because the color of a person's skin has nothing to do with the content of their character.

I love the Jewish babies and the German babies and the Asian and the Russians. We are all the same and I have the perfect hypothesis to prove it. I play to all those countries and they cry in all the same places in my show. They laugh in the same places. They become hysterical in the same places. They faint in the same places and that's the perfect hypothesis. There is a commonality that we are all the same. Because I have heard that the Russians are hard-nosed and the Germans have no feelings and emotions. They were just as emotional [at my concerts]. . . even more so. Some of my most loving fans are in Germany and Russia. They will stand out in the cold and in the rain to get a glimpse. They scream, "We want to *Heal the World*. We love you." And these are young people, you know, who had nothing to do with the war and all that crazy conditioning. They are different, you know. The new breed is different. They are wonderful. I feel like a person of the world. I can't take sides. That's why I hate saying, "I am an American." For that reason.

SB: Do you think the fact that you were one of the first incredibly successful and famous black men affected your career to an extent? Some of the unfair things that people did, was that partially racism in the way that your mother experienced it?

MJ: Yes, because before me you had [Harry] Belafonte, you had Sammy [Davis, Jr.], you had Nat King Cole. You had them as entertainers and people loved their music. But they didn't get adulation, and they didn't get [people] to cry and they didn't get, "I am in love with you, and I want to marry you." They didn't get people tearing their clothes off and all the hysteria and all the screams. They didn't play stadiums. I was the first one to break the mold, where white girls, Scottish girls, Irish girls screamed, "I am in love with you, I want to. . . " And a lot of the white press didn't like that. That's what has made it hard for me, because I was the pioneer and that's why they started the stories. "He's weird." "He's gay." "He sleeps in a hyperbaric chamber." "He wants to buy the bones of the Elephant Man"—anything that turns people against me. They tried their hardest. And anybody else would be dead as a junkie right now, who'd been through what I've been through.

SB: What gave you the strength to persevere?

MJ: Believing in children. Believing in young people. Believing that God gave me this for a reason to help my babies.

SB: So even though the older people were mean you still believed the younger generation had a kindness in their hearts?

MJ: Absolutely. I am still to this day trying to figure it out. I am having problems in my heart with the Jewish thing. I am having a big problem with it.

SB: What Jewish thing?

MJ: When I found out the count of how many children in the Holocaust alone died. . . . [starts to break down]. What man can do something like that? I don't understand. It doesn't matter what race it is. I don't get it. I don't understand that at all. I really don't.

What kind of conditioning. . . I don't understand that kind of thing. Does someone condition you to hate that much? Is it possible that they could do that to your heart? They can't do that to mine. Could they do that to yours? I'm sorry.

SB: They could only do it to us if we made ourselves susceptible or if we severed our connection with a God who demands righteousness.

MJ: Hitler was a genius orator. He was [able] to make that many people turn and change and hate. He had to be a showman and he was. Before he would speak, he would pause, drink a bit of water, and then he would clear his throat, and look around. It was what an entertainer would do trying to work out how to play his audience. He would go into this fury of the first words he would say and he would hit them hard. But where did he come from? I know he failed school and he wanted to be an architect. He failed a lot of things. But I think it all happened in prison, the whole *Mein Kampf* thing, didn't it? I really believe that.

Michael's analysis of Hitler as showman was brilliant. I subsequently watched many of Hitler's speeches and Michael was absolutely right. Hitler would get up to speak, pause, make the crowd eager with breathless anticipation, and only then would he slowly begin.

SB: Where he first wrote the book and began to formulate his ideas?

MJ: Yeah, yeah. He built that anger, so strong, while [Nelson] Mandela did the opposite. He became a lamb in prison. He had no bitterness, to this day saying even though he is eighty and his youth is gone—because he was in prison so long—he doesn't regret any of it.

SB: But is his youth gone?

MJ: [No], he is sweet, very childlike.

SB: Does he like to giggle?

MJ: He loves children because when I went to see him I had some kids with me and people were saying the kids have to stay, but Michael Jackson can come. I said, "I'm sure Mr. Mandela wouldn't mind seeing children. I won't go in unless the children go too." I remember his representatives looked at me like this [makes stern and suspicious facial expression] and they went back and then they said, "Everybody come." The first thing Mandela did is run to the children and pick them up and hug them. I knew he was that kind of man and he loved them. He was talking to them and *then* he shook my hand. I knew I was right.

SB: Are you the opposite of Hitler? God gave you this phenomenal charisma and while he [Hitler] brought out the beast in man, you want to bring out some of that innocence and goodness in man. The darkest most malignant forces were unleashed within the Germans at Hitler's direction. Now God gave you phenomenal charisma as well. Are you using it to bring out the innocence and goodness in man?

MJ: I believe that. You can change them because going to my show is like a religious experience because you [go in] one person and come out a different person. You really do.

SB: Is that one of your objectives, to try and pull that out of people, not just give entertainment?

MJ: Absolutely, and we do it. I wish you could have seen some of the things we have done in concerts. Like we have had a huge tank on stage like an army tank and a soldier gets out and points it at everybody. And then he aims it at me and then the whole audience starts booing. This happens in every country. . . and I take the gun and I put it down and they start screaming. And then a little girl—I always have a little peasant girl—with a flower comes up and brings it to the soldier, right in his face, and he breaks down on his knees and he starts to cry. And the crowd goes crazy every time. Then I start giving this speech, and another little boy comes forward and he starts doing this speech in sign language and you look in the audience and everybody is crying. It happens in every country. That is part of *Earth Song.* I have been an ambassador of goodwill all over the world spreading this message. Then we do *Heal the World,* children of all nations circling this huge globe, and we have a big screen showing all the world leaders in the back and it is just amazing stuff. When other singers are singing about sex and *I want to get in a hot tub with you baby and rub you all over* and [yet I'm the one who] gets battered in the press as a weirdo. Does that make any sense to you?

SB: No, of course, not right.

MJ: It is not right, is it?

SB: It is changing in front of your eyes.

At that time, through our efforts to have Michael speak at places like Oxford, and surround himself with credible and respected statesmen and childrearing experts, he was beginning to get positive publicity. He was regaining lost respect.

SB: What if they wouldn't understand? What if they were like the Nazis, just evil people?

MJ: I can't imagine that I couldn't reach their hearts in some kind of way.

SB: So you believe that if you were face-to-face with Hitler you could . . .

MJ: *Absolutely*. Absolutely! He had to have had a lot of *yes* people around him who were afraid of him.

SB: You believe that if you had an hour with Hitler you could somehow touch something inside of him?

MJ: Absolutely. I know I could.

SB: *With Hitler?* Come on. Michael! Hitler?! So you don't believe there is anyone who is completely evil and there is no way to touch them. So you don't believe in punishing the wicked because then. . .

MJ: No, I believe you have to help them, give them therapy. You have to teach them, that somewhere something in their life went wrong. They don't see what they do. They don't understand that it is wrong a lot of times.

SB: But Michael, there are clearly people who are irredeemable. Like Hitler. He was evil incarnate. There was no humanity there for you to address. You'd be speaking to the abyss, to a darkness like you never before witnessed. What about someone who has killed a lot of people? Don't you believe that there should be no therapy for them? They are murderers and they need to face extreme punishment.

MJ: I feel horrible about it. I wish somebody could have reached their hearts.

SB: What if they have done it already? They've already killed their victims.

MJ: If they have done it already, it is wrong.

This was crazy stuff. A man who believed he could change Hitler in an hour. Hitler, the most evil man that ever lived. A man who systematically gassed and murdered six million Jews, including a million children, as well as six million other civilians. Michael can be forgiven for being naïve. But a man who's convinced that he can transform darkness into light and evil into goodness might take the next step to believing that normal rules of right and wrong need not apply to him. He might also believe that he had a very special healing power with children which others might see as wrong but which he understood to be comforting. Truth be told, I should have challenged Michael much more forcefully on his Hitler comment. I should have said to him outright, "Michael, you're not the Messiah. You could not have prevented World War II. So let it go." I blame my own cowardice for not having done so. Still, I decided to approach the issue with determination but using soft gloves.

SB: I am going to clarify this. The interesting thing about how you look at the world is that you view it through a child's eyes. Okay, the other side of that is that just as children would find it difficult to grasp that someone can be truly evil—which is why kids are so trusting—you have the same issue. Even when evil stares you in the face you want to say it has some good. So I wouldn't ask someone like you to construct a whole judicial system of punishment because that's not what your contribution to the world is, and frankly, you'd do a bad job. A punishment comes into the world once you have adultlike gestures that are cruel, and then you need punishment. But then in a child's world those things don't really exist so you don't need the same punishment. But come on Michael, do you really think you could have gotten through to Hitler?

MJ: Uhuh. Yes.

SB: By finding the good in him somehow?

MJ: Yes, I think I could have. I really do, I think. Nobody really talked to him. I think he was surrounded by, I hate to say this, brownnosers. But that's what they were. That's what he wanted. That's what they did.

SB: He was never challenged?

MJ: There were Germans against him. They even tried to kill him, remember?

SB: Yeah, Claus von Stauffenberg. But he and his plotters numbered, at most, a few hundred out of a population of tens of millions. On this one there is simply too much distance between us, Michael. Hitler was intrinsically evil. You could never have gotten through to him. The only thing to do with people like that is purge them from the world.

So you have forgiven everyone in your heart except for certain members of the press who are mean and people who hurt children?

MJ: Yes.

Following the Golden Rule—With All People

Shmuley Boteach: Let's get back to justice. When you see so many injustices with no recourse to justice, when people are killed and their murderer is never found, when garbage is written about you and people get away with it, in fact they are promoted, how do you continue to believe in justice?

Michael Jackson: I don't believe in justice. I believe in it but I don't believe that. . . .

SB: You don't believe that the righteous are going to be rewarded and the wrongdoers will be punished? That good people should prosper and wicked people should founder and sink?

MJ: All these are man-made things. I think evil is in people's hearts. This is where you and I might disagree. I don't think there is some devil out there manipulating our thoughts. That is what I was taught.

SB: Judaism doesn't believe in the devil. So we don't disagree nearly as much as you might think. Where we do disagree is in the belief that people who do very evil things eventually internalize those evil things to such a degree that it becomes an inextricable part of who they are. They may only start out *doing* evil, but after a while they *become* evil. A famous Jewish philosopher named Maimonedes said "Habit becomes second nature" and they become one with what they have done. They become evil. There is no hope for people like Hitler. And no one, not even you, can get through to them. They are evil to their very core.

MJ: I thought the devil is very evil. He is in this room and he is behind all the evil in this world. The devil is awfully busy. Look how everyone is turning gay and look at how women are doing this. I think the devil is man himself.

On the gay comment, I think Michael was paraphrasing what people who blame everything on the devil might say, rather than expressing his own view. Certainly, Michael never made anything like a homophobic comment to me, and it would be highly out of his character to have done so. He was not judgmental in that way, although he would sometimes play a guessing game as to whether some men he met were gay, based on their growing too attached to him.

SB: How can we get people to sustain a belief in justice in such a cruel world?

MJ: Follow the Golden Rule. Be kind to your neighbors, love them as much as you would love yourself, do unto others. . . .

SB: How do you feel when you see people get away with cruelty? Are you angry? Do you say, there is no justice, these are mean people?

MJ: I get angry, yeah. But I know that is the way of the world. That's the theme of my world show: Be kind, heal the world. Let's walk out of here a different human being. Let's love. It's like going to church, but I do it without preaching. I do it through music and dancing. Marilyn Manson says onstage, "Kill God. . . take your Bibles and tear them. . . ." Yet the press doesn't attack *him!* And he has got breasts on just like a woman. . . .

SB: So when you see people who are mean, who are very prosperous, do you ever look at God and say, "I can't figure it out?"

MJ: No, because I know how I feel.

SB: So what do you do at moments like that?

MJ: I believe there are some good people in the world and I do believe there is a God. I don't believe that God judges. I don't think that He is upstairs going, "You are alright. But I am going to tear you up." I wouldn't do that.

SB: There is no hell in Judaism either. There is punishment for the sake of cleansing, but no punishment for the sake of damnation.

MJ: Really? I think that is all beautiful because we were all taught to believe in the devil and Lucifer and the burial ground, where you never get resurrection and judgment. There is a decision being made right now as we talk. Jesus is putting certain people on the left and certain people on the right, and when the end of the world comes all those people on the left will be swallowed up and they will be dead forever.

That's not fair is it? There are a lot of beautiful, good people in the world no matter what religion, no matter what race. If there was really such a thing as real true heavenly justice, I don't think Hitler would have got away with what he did as long as he did. Then you get those people who say, "It happened for a reason, to teach the world never to let it happen again." My foot! You don't need a million of those little kids to die to teach the world. I am not going for it. They let him get away with it.

SB: One day when this is over we will get Elie Wiesel to take you to Auschwitz, where so many of those children died. That would be poignant. You have to read his book, *Night*. His book is one of the most influential books of the twentieth century. He was sixteen years old when he was at Auschwitz. He is the most famous Holocaust survivor in the world.

Professor Elie Wiesel is a prince of the Jewish people and one of my greatest heroes. As I mentioned earlier, I introduced Michael to Professor Wiesel, the Nobel Peace laureate, and they had several meetings. Wiesel was my guest over two visits while I was rabbi at Oxford, and we have become close friends. It was my fervent hope that Professor Wiesel would take Michael under his wing, and it was Michael's great honor to have one of the world's foremost humanitarians believe in him for a few months. Later, when Michael got arrested on charges of molestation, I called Professor Wiesel and apologized for vouching for Michael and what I thought to be his sincere intentions to help children. Professor Wiesel once told me that he saw compassion in Michael's eyes, but also cautioned me about celebrities in general. He has always been a wise counselor in my life and I continue to be blessed with his inspiration and guidance.

MJ: He is not bitter. He is like Mandela in that way.

SB: So you don't believe in justice? You have seen it subverted too many times to believe in it?

MJ: I believe there should be justice but I don't believe in the justice system. That's what I should say. You have seen the things that go on in the world and how people get away with them.

SB: The majority of the good people that you have met, have they prospered?

MJ: Absolutely.

PART 3

FAME IN ADULTHOOD

Thinking About Ambition, Success, and Honesty

Shmuley Boteach: So ambition can be a good thing so long as it is not ruthless, so long as it doesn't involve jealousy and envy?

Michael Jackson: Yeah, so long as it is not hurting anybody. Ambition is a wonderful thing. To know how the mind works and the power of thought and how we create our own circumstances in life. And to know all those goodies about the brain because we don't come with instructions when we are born. You have to find the truth to life and once you know those things, it's amazing you know your possibilities.

SB: So you want to foster that ambition in children, not stifle it?

MJ: They have it. You have to just will them on.

SB: Another thing. Let's talk about honesty. One of the most child-like qualities is brutal honesty. Sometimes telling our children the truth hurts. But they always say it like it is. Especially before they're old enough to learn how to lie. If you are fat they will say you are fat. If you are ugly they will say you are ugly. If you smell they say you smell. Is that always a good thing, or do we have to be more diplomatic?

MJ: I think we have to teach them to be kind and teach them how you can hurt other people's feelings. We went there [to the recording studio] yesterday, Prince and I. One of the musicians who works with me is fat, very fat, and Prince said, "He has a stomach which looks like a balloon." I said, "Prince, you are right. But if you see him don't say it in front of him because you could make him cry." He said, "Okay, I promise." Just teach him that you can't hurt people.

SB: Okay, but what about encouraging our children to tell the truth? So you are not saying to Prince that that is not true because that

is not a childlike quality to make him lie. You are just saying sometimes you hold the truth inside. You didn't say to Prince, "He's actually fine the way he is. He's not fat."

MJ: I did not.

SB: So it's important to be truthful. Let's say you have a musician
who isn't up to speed and he is holding back the whole album.
What do you do?

MJ: I just went through it in there with the string players. One lady
was playing completely off rhythm and I told the guy, "Let her
continue. But the next day we just can't have her come," and she
wasn't told that she could come the next day. But we did it quietly.

SB: So you do sometimes have to deal with these difficult situations
and you deal with it with honesty but without trying to hurt them.

MJ: You have to do it without hurting them.

SB: So there is a way of being truthful without being painful?

MJ: Absolutely. I don't go on the casting calls for my short films
[Michael always called his music videos "short films"] especially
when there are children being cast. I don't want to stand there and
say, "Okay let's see what you can do," and they do it and they
don't get a call back. Then they'll say, "Michael Jackson turned
me down." I have somebody else tape everybody and I look at it
at home and I decide. I cannot face the pain of them not being accepted. I always have to do it that way.

It eluded Michael that what he was really saying was that he hated
confrontation and he let his underlings do his dirty work. This contributed to the multitude of Michael's inauthentic relationships. He attracted sycophants who toadied up to him rather than giving him honest
criticism because they saw from the outset that the only way Michael
handled confrontation was to withdraw behind his curtain of handlers.
If you criticized him, even as a friend who really cared, you'd never hear
from him again. But being surrounded by brownnosers has never contributed to anyone's mental health and stability.

SB: So, honesty is very important in the way you raise Prince and
Paris.

MJ: [Turning to Prince] Doo-Doo has been on that Prince. That's full of doo-doo. Don't put it on your hair. That's the dog doo-doo shovel. Don't put it in your hair.

I left this in because of all the lies in the media about Michael being a germophobe and how his kids were not allowed to even touch a toy that had been on the floor. Here, Michael's son was playing with one of the dog's excrement shovels and Michael simply told him, in the middle of our conversation, to put it down because it was dirty. They didn't disinfect the boy.

SB: By the way did you hear what I said earlier that Paul McCartney has supposedly one of the biggest cartoon collections? You were saying about these great artists being childlike?
MJ: Yes, yes. He loves cartoons and takes them very seriously. He collects them. Mine is bigger than his now, if you go into the video library we have got rows and rows because I love cartoons. It is a great escape for me, the world of cartoons.
SB: [In thinking about your success] did you say something to yourself? "I was fortunate, it was from God, it is not just me. This is a divine gift. I have no right to be arrogant?"
MJ: Yeah. People always ask me how I didn't let it all go to my head. Um, because obviously it's not me. So how dare you think this is your doing, it's not me. It's not Michelangelo. He was touched with divine inspiration. That was a gift. I think you can cultivate something to a certain extent. But to be given real genius, that's like a gift.

Michael's response is at once humble and troubling. Yes, he believes that God has given him a gift, his talent, and that since it has been bequeathed to him he must eschew arrogance. But in the same sentence, he compares himself to Michelangelo. Perhaps Michael really is an artistic genius. But his delusions of grandeur, his need to constantly elevate himself into the world's foremost pantheon of artistic geniuses of all time, was one of the main factors in his rapid decline. Simply put, humility is protective and arrogance is corrosive. But maybe I was just being judgmental, so I said. . .

SB: Judgmental people are always small-minded people. They are nitpickers. How did we go from being big to small, Michael? As we mature, our bodies get bigger but often our minds seem to get smaller. Do you feel that children have bigger hearts than adults? What causes them to shrink?

Why didn't yours shrink? The more famous people become, the less love they have in their hearts because they become more self-absorbed. What makes people go from being big-minded to being small-minded, to being petty? Because they feel intimidated. They feel that their dreams were not realized and they become defensive. So your defense mechanism is to judge, to dismiss. What makes us get smaller and why didn't you get smaller? Why didn't you become more self-absorbed as you became more famous? Why do you care about the rest of the world? You have helicopters and private jets. Why would ordinary children suddenly figure in your life?

MJ: You know why, Shmuley? When you have seen the things I have seen and traveled all over the world, you would not be honest to yourself and the world to be that way. I just couldn't see myself not being touched by the things I have seen, like that village in China, and the things I have seen in Africa and Russia and Germany and Israel.

My wife Debbie and I married in 1988 in Australia. On the way back to the United States, we stopped in Hong Kong for a lecture I was to give and we took a day trip into China. A tour guide took us to a mud hut in a small village and showed us a picture of the woman who owned the hut posing with Michael Jackson. It was the strangest thing. What was Michael Jackson doing in this woman's hut? Well, apparently a few years earlier he had taken a private tour of the region. The elderly woman who owned the hut had an emaciated cat. Michael took out a $100 bill and told the woman to feed the cat. She kept her promise, but when it was fattened up, she ate it. When I met Michael I told him the story. He remembered the village, but was disheartened to hear the cat had been served up as dinner.

MJ: I remember this newborn baby fighting to live, newborn with all the things in the nose, in a hospital in Israel. How could your heart not go out to something like that? I said to everybody, the kids, everybody, "Come here kids. You have to see this," because I think they understand the sensitivity of how children are important, helping others, reaching out to the world, to the underprivileged. Being materialistic and showing this sense of me-ism all the time [is something I deplore].

SB: Why didn't your success go to your head? You pride yourself on not being arrogant. How did you retain your sensitivity? Why didn't it go to your head? Why did you visit orphanages? Why didn't it happen to you? How did you remain large, how did you remain grand and nonjudgmental when you should have become more self-absorbed? It's happened to everybody else. You've seen it happen to your friends, I'm sure, who've had success.

I recognize that this question goes against my previous point that Michael's self-absorption as a superstar made it impossible for him to take criticism. Both are true. When I conducted this interview, I had a lofty view of Michael. I was amazed at how humble and approachable he was. And it wasn't an act. There were always two sides to Michael, the soft gentle boy who hailed from Gary, Indiana, and the superstar who believed he deserved nonstop adulation. As time went on I would see less of Michael and more of the superstar.

MJ: That's hard to answer. I am just more sensitive to people's pain and love. I think it's just inside me.

The Pain of Performing, the Pressure of Staying on Top

Shmuley Boteach: Do you always feel that you are always proving yourself, that you are always having to perform, that there is never rest, that you were never given that period where you could play without having to worry and to impress?

Michael Jackson: I love art. I love it too much. My mother knows that about me. I love painting and sculpting and all that stuff. I always got an A in Art and English. They were the two classes I always got an A-plus. I had very little school schooling other than my tutor. But the years I did have it, the teacher always used me as an example to the class of good English and good storytelling because we all had to write the same stories. But she used to make me go out front—which I hated—and read my story to the class and I would get huge applause. Not because of who I was but because they truly enjoyed the stories I wrote. I had a portfolio of all of that stuff because I am an artist, too, and I like to draw and paint. And somebody stole it and it broke my heart because I always wanted to save it. One day it will pop up somewhere because I am a realist and I am not abstract. There are people that I am in love with, totally in love with them. I would die for them. I love Michelangelo. I love Charlie Chaplin with all my heart. I love Walt Disney. These are the people I am nuts over. These are my people. I love the great ones.

SB: There is this phenomenal pressure. Do you always have to be Michael Jackson, 100 million album sales?

MJ: And the press, they wait with knives.

SB: For you to fail?

MJ: Absolutely. They try and shred me apart so it has to be beyond expectation, beyond brilliant. I give everything I have.

SB: But it wears you out?

MJ: Yeah. Because when you are the top-selling artist of all time, the records that are broken, they wait. . . you are the target.

SB: What gives you rest, what gives you strength? Is it Prince and Paris?

MJ: Prince and Paris and children all over the world. Not just Prince and Paris—all children.

SB: Do you feel that if the next album is not amazing that you are not going to be special?

MJ: It would be a terrible blow to me [if I did not perform as well as I wish] because I put real pressure on myself and I demand the best out of myself. I really do. The best of the form or the medium that I work in, and I put a lot of pressure on myself. So to have that happen, if that was to happen, it would be psychologically destroying for me.

SB: But do you feel that people would still love you if you were not as successful? Would you still feel loved? A child has to feel loved even if he or she doesn't do well at school.

MJ: Yes, I would, because of the past work. But I wouldn't be comfortable with it. I try not to look at the past.

SB: Do you think that because of some of the things that you described to me, a very difficult childhood—without the birthdays, without the Christmases—that is why success in your career has become so important?

MJ: Probably. I think so.

SB: Do you think you punish yourself a bit too much, that's why there is so much pain? You punish yourself immensely if things aren't perfect?

MJ: I really do. I know that's true. I'd rather be the one responsible for it because I have the final say and the final cut on everything. In the past it has been very successful. Oh God, but if that [diminishment of success] was to happen, I don't know what I would do.

SB: But don't you see, Michael, that's what you have to get over.

MJ: I know, but I can't get over it. It's me. I'm not made that way.

The Master of Mystery

What was undeniable about Michael was that he rose to the very top of his profession worldwide. One of the most important ingredients in his remaining at the top was his intuitive understanding of the power of mystery. It was a subject I wanted to get into deeply with him.

Shmuley Boteach: Alright, I want to speak about something with you which is crucial to this book. Of all the things I've seen about you, I have to tell you, I have never seen anyone who understands the power of mystery the way you do. In other words, in the Jewish religion the use of mystery is very important. The prophet Isaiah says that angels, the Seraphim, have six wings. Why six? Well, "With two he covered his face, and with two he covered his feet, and with two he flew" (Isaiah 6:02). Isn't that amazing? The angels are so modest, so mysterious, that they use their wings to cover up.

Michael Jackson: That's beautiful.

SB: I've written about this extensively in my books, Michael. Mystery is one of the principal ingredients that I prescribe for relationships. The holy is always mysterious. It's always covered. And the Torah scroll, the Bible scroll that we read from in the synagogue is kept covered and hidden away by multiple layers, in the ark, concealed by curtains, veils, and doors. It's like three things you need to take away in order to see it. And similarly when Rebecca and Isaac meet in the Bible, before they get married and fall in love, the first thing that Rebecca does upon encountering Isaac is to cover her face. The same thing is true when Moses sees the burning bush. What's the first thing he does? He turns away and hides his face from seeing God.

MJ: I love those stories.

SB: So in the Bible mystery is very important. I've never seen anyone who understands the power of mystery like you. I'll give you some examples and I want you to comment on them. Number one, my kids are walking around Neverland. There's candy everywhere. My kids love it because they've never seen this, there's popcorn machines and there's snow cone machines, and as long as stuff is kosher, they're eating this and eating that. And although Prince and Paris are surrounded by all this stuff, you say to them, "No, only on your birthday you can have this." Grace told us they aren't allowed to use the swings and all that so that they don't get bored of it. And whenever we go to FAO Schwartz, Prince can buy toys but he has to wait to open them. And especially when it comes to your career, you've understood the power of being hidden. Like now, I look at all these new acts, even 'N Sync and even Britney Spears [whom Michael and I had just met in his hotel room], and I was watching them on *Entertainment Tonight* and they did an interview and I said, "My gosh are they short-sighted. You should do what Michael does. Never be ubiquitous." But they can't because they so badly need the attention, they can't hold back.

I had learned this from Michael. We were once in his hotel room and Britney popped up on TV doing an interview. Michael commented to me that she was everywhere and it was going to hurt her career. "I would never do what she's doing. In a few years no one will want to hear her anymore. She knows nothing about mystery.'" And this was years before her crotch-displaying antics.

SB: So there are two things I want to ask you. Talk to me about mystery and what it means to you and how did you get the discipline to hold back when you know that every TV show wants you? I mean, gosh, we're being pounded by every single show in America right now to get an interview with you. How do you, where does that discipline come from? Especially Michael, this is important to comment on, because people, your detractors will criticize you and say, "Michael's a child, he behaves like a child" when really the only definition of maturity that everyone agrees on, is that maturity involves a capacity for delayed gratification. When other people act impetuously, and you can be patient and wait for things in their proper time, that's considered the essence of maturity and self-control.

MJ: Thank you.

SB: And your career is built on that and I'm not just saying that to flatter you. It's true, I'm amazed at it. So talk to me about mystery. How do you know this, where did it come to you, the power of that which is concealed?

MJ: Wow, you're so observant. It's amazing how you notice details. Um, I studied. . . I love psychology, I love magic, I love. . . I love real beauty. I love real talent. I love when something's miraculous, when something's so beautiful you shouldn't get it. What I love about Halley's Comet, and I always say this to my lawyer, Halley's Comet is no more of a miracle than the moon or the sun. But we make a big deal about it because you see it once in a lifetime and everybody's out there to see it. You know astronomers and fans and people and it's this thing that circles around the solar system but you see it once in a lifetime. If it happened every night nobody would care, but to me the moon is just as miraculous. I always talk about deer and dogs and cats. A lot of people go, "There's a deer! There's a. . . " 'cause they're shy, they're always hidden. It's a big deal to see a deer, I mean, and I appreciate that, how people should appreciate real ability and I always say I don't care if you're the most talented person in the world, if you come on the television everyday people will regurgitate you. You have to know how to play your audience. You have to know that and it's true, Shmuley. And it's not just a game. But it's real for me, it's real for me. It really is.

SB: How do you know that? For example, I had to be taught this. I write about this a lot in my books but I began to develop a lot of my ideas on it from insights from other writers, thinkers, philosophers, etcetera.

MJ: [If you remain mysterious, people will be] more interested, yeah.

SB: Look if a woman is always taking off her top, no one's going to want to see her breasts.

MJ: That's right.

SB: But if she does it once in a while, that's what makes it so exciting. That's what makes it erotic.

MJ: That's right.

SB: But when it's, everyday. . .

MJ: That's right.

SB: Like you go to the African tribes and women walk topless, it's nothing.

MJ: Nothing, nothing. Leave something to the imagination. I believe in that and people are all. . .

SB: Did someone teach you that?

MJ: No. No, it just, looking at. . . learning from nature and learning you know, just watching and studying, being a serious observer. And umm, you can say to somebody, you can go, "There's six doors, you can open any of those doors. But the fifth door, don't open it. Don't open the fifth door, no matter what." Of course everyone is going, "What's behind door number five?" because it's the great mystery. And that's, everyone wants to expose door number five because you know. . . And I love that and it's not like a game but I want people to appreciate talent and ability. I only do an album every five years. Other artists do an album every year and my albums outlast and outsell all the other artists. And people wait for it. There's like, you know, a whole pulse going on about this album. [Michael was working on completing *Invincible* at the time.] Its like a fever, they're waiting, they're waiting. It's important to wait.

SB: So what is it about the hidden which makes it outlast the revealed? What is it about holding something back that people want it suddenly?

MJ: I just, I love, I do love the power of mystery, I really do. I think it's very powerful.

SB: Is it spiritual? What is it?

MJ: It's spiritual, it's, it's people conjure up all these ideas, people create it themselves. They conjure up all these ideas in their head about what's going on. I mean they used to say, you know, Howard Hughes is up there and he owns the hotel but he stays on that floor, he doesn't come down. He's in the dark, he's in the corner in the bed with long nails and hair down to here and he's hooked to an IV. So the brain would just go crazy conjuring up all kinds of crazy stories, and I love that. I love Howard Hughes 'cause he played this big thing. I mean, to me he's like one of my masters. But, I don't know, this is the first time I've ever said this Shmuley, I love Howard, he's a genius.

SB: Because what? Because he knew the power of mystery?

MJ: How to play people, yeah. He knew how to make the public interested. P. T. Barnum was pretty good at it himself.

SB: Is it a matter of just withdrawing? Is it that simple? For example, this book came along called *The Rules,* and I debated the people who wrote it twice. And they said the way you get a guy to marry you is by playing hard to get. He calls you up and you say, "Sorry, I'd love to go out to dinner but I'm too busy." He leaves messages on your answering machine and you never return his phone calls. You hear of the book? It's a very controversial book. Is it that simple?

I am actually a critic of *The Rules,* believing that manipulation is the worst approach to relationships and that there is a far better alternative, namely, for a woman to indulge her natural feminine mystique.

MJ: I don't, I don't totally agree. It depends on the individual.

SB: But with you, when you say it's become about playing the public, is it as simple as withdrawal and they want more? And more ways how to reveal yourself?

MJ: It's rhythm and timing. You have to know what you're doing. Like you never see me on award shows saying, "The nominees are . . ." And I get asked to do every show. Now they don't even ask. They know I don't do it. Or to host the show or to come out and say like, "Coming up next, Michael Jackson to present the record of the year." You never see me coming out and doing the nominees. I don't do it. They know not to even ask me. It's not what I do.

SB: You will never do something which makes you be the means to another end. You're either the end or you're not. It's either about you or you're not going to be the road.

MJ: Yeah, and I'm not trying to say that I'm holy or God or. . .

SB: But you're not going to belittle yourself either.

MJ: I'm not going to, I want. . . you know? People should respect, you know? Ability and talent, and it's all for the sake of goodness, really 'cause my message is for goodness.

SB: I agree with you.

MJ: But really. I'm just trying to conserve and preserve. . .

SB: This, by the way, is a whole book unto itself, how you have learned the power of the hidden, of the mysterious. Look out there in New York. Right now as we speak there are hundreds of thousands of woman who want to get married and guys won't commit to them. And do you know one of the main reasons is because they'll have sex with them anyway.

Years later I authored a book called *The Kosher Sutra,* which outlined all the erotic principles of attraction, with mystery, forbiddenness, and sinfulness being at the forefront. The book became a best-seller.

MJ: Uh huh.

SB: Why would you marry her if you could have her without the commitment? If you wanted to borrow ten million dollars from the bank manager, and he says, "Here Michael, here's ten million dollars," would you then say, "Oh, by the way, you forgot to ask me for collateral. Here it is"? You wouldn't volunteer it. So, you understand what I'm saying? And they might never get married and these women come in their hundreds to me, crying, writing about how lonely they are. They don't know the power of mystery. They go to bed on the first date; they don't know how to hold back. He never has to win them over. And by the way, that's what happened to Madonna. Madonna overexposed herself. She's still a celebrity but she's not what she was.

MJ: Yeah, I know.

SB: She didn't even overexpose herself, Michael, through TV and music. It wasn't that she gave too many interviews. Rather, she overexposed her body. She was a sex symbol. People wanted to know what her body looked like, and she did that stupid, sleazy, disgusting book, and all you had to do was buy the book. The mystery was permanently gone.

MJ: I know, I know. Exactly right.

SB: There are few people today who understand the power of mystery. You understand it because there is an intuitive spirituality to your nature that is a real gift. Because this understanding of mystery, and your understanding of the power of timing, helps us understand the holy. God only reveals very sporadically and at very choice moments. Mystery and timing are central to revelation.

MJ: I love that. That's one of my favorite things to think about too.

SB: How hidden God is.

MJ: How hidden.

SB: You've got to find him.

MJ: You see all his miracles through him but you don't see his face, himself, you know? You see through the children.

SB: Which makes you more interested in him?

MJ: Yeah.

SB: You want to find him?

MJ: Makes you want to seek him out and find him. Absolutely. I love that. And some people just throw up their hands and go, "What is this all about, this whole universe and where is he? I want to talk to him and what is it?" You know I love that. He's the ultimate. He is. He's the man.

SB: So this is how we stop people from being bored. First of all one more thing before we move on to boredom. So you instinctively knew timing, mystery? You just knew?

MJ: Yeah, it's true, Shmuley.

SB: It's not like a manager pulled you aside and said, "Michael. You can be a big star. Don't overdo it"?

MJ: No. No way.

SB: Did your brothers not understand it?

MJ: No, they don't understand it. They would jump on anything, any second. If anybody said, "I want to interview you tomorrow about Michael's new style of dress, "Sure." 'Cause they just want to be on TV, to be on TV. I think people appreciate you much more when you, you know conserve, just hold. . . you know.

SB: Hold back?

MJ: Hold back and build yourself and give yourself a certain kind of class and make them reach out for you and just. . . I love gates, gates to a house. I love huge big pillars and gates. You don't know what's back there beyond the road. You just see these. . . You know, you go, "God who lives in there?" I love that. You know, you never see them but you see the gates and I love that.

SB: But the gates to Neverland are so simple?

MJ: So simple, that's how I wanted them. Because I don't want the gate to represent, you know, it's an act of almost psychology. I was gonna make them so, kind of, almost. . . what's the word? Umm, I can't think of the word I'm looking for. I was gonna have people swing them open and really kind of have them funky and tattered, just so psychologically you really feel like you're coming to a ranch, so that when you go around the bend I want it to change to Technicolor, like the Wizard of Oz does in black and white.

SB: That's exactly what happened with us. First thing we said when we got to Neverland was, 'This can't be his ranch, what are those simple doors?' Then you drive through and you see the sign, "Welcome to Neverland" and then, kaboom.

MJ: Yeah.

SB: It just hits you.

MJ: That, see, that's important to understand in show business. If you open with too much of a bang, where do you go from there? You crescendo too big, you have nowhere to go. You can't do that. That's why I always say, in amusement parks, the guy who creates the roller coaster, the dips, you're going up at first, way up and you go, "Oh my God, why did I do this?" Then it takes you straight down and it takes you up a little bit, then down, and he's the real showman, the guy who creates the dips. You know the peaks and the valleys, then he takes you straight real fast and up and upside down. He's a showman. That guy's a real showman because he understands syncopation and rhythm and structure and that's important. That's real important as an artist of show business and most of your artists today know nothing about it.

SB: They all overexpose themselves.

MJ: At all. At all.

SB: Is that your professional greatest blessing, that you were born with that rhythm? You just had that natural timing and you understood it?

MJ: Yeah, yeah. I think

SB: Is it part of your love for God and his hiddeness and all that, that it's all one, that you sort of tapped into that divine mystery and you know the power of mystery?

MJ: Yeah, I think, yeah, like you say, it's just something. . . like the way you speak. That's the power of God in you Shmuley. You do, I've never heard anybody speak like you, it's amazing. It's like God is working right through you. I mean it's like that, when I'm on stage it's the same way. I don't think about what I'm gonna do, I don't know what I'm gonna do.

SB: You just get into the zone, the timing.

MJ: You get into it, man. You become one with what God gave you. It's like talking, it's spiritual. It's between you and God and the audience is right there with you. How do you describe it, I mean, how do you dissect it, how do you analyze it? You really can't. People say how do you do it? "Well I work out and I train." Well, you don't.

Advice on Fame

Shmuley Boteach: So yesterday, 'N Sync came to see you. The lead singer Justin Timberlake, and I don't know who the other guy was. What's his name?

Michael had invited me to his hotel suite to meet Britney Spears and Justin Timberlake, who had flown in to see him the day after they had jointly hosted the American Music Awards. I was, at that time, not at all enamored of Britney Spears for her sexualization of teenage girls in America. Still, I behaved myself and spoke to them briefly about our efforts to get parents to prioritize their children. Neither of them seemed particularly interested and we didn't really click. Justin said something about contacting his manager or agent. They were there to meet the superstar. I don't mean to be insulting, but I found them unimpressive and forgettable. With all of Michael's myriad flaws, he had infinitely more class. Michael Jackson at least knew how to treat people with dignity and make them feel important, something for which the new generation of stars could use some tutoring.

Michael Jackson: Wade is a choreographer for. . .
SB: Oh, he wasn't from 'N Sync, Wade?
MJ: No, he's a choreographer for Britney Spears and 'N Sync. See I taught Wade.
SB: Really?
MJ: Yeah, I taught Wade. All the stuff you see Britney Spears and 'N Sync doing, that whole style came from me 'cause I taught Wade. Wade's from Australia and I brought him to America.
SB: So he's their choreographer?
MJ: Yeah, and he does music. He was on my record label. We signed him to MJJ. He raps, he does everything.

SB: So he was here with Britney Spears, one of the biggest stars in the world right now, and that lead singer of 'N Sync, and they're boyfriend and girlfriend. When you look at them, and you had a long conversation with them, what would you tell them, based on this idea we're trying to speak about in this book, childlike qualities? Would you warn them against anything that might happen in their careers? Would you tell them, "You know, when I was your age I thought X, Y, and Z and now I've changed my view"? Is there any advice you would give them?

MJ: Just try to stay a child as long as you can. Don't force into adulthood. Don't force it, don't push it. Don't try to be cool and. . . go to Disney, hang out, enjoy your youth, 'cause you'll be old for, I mean you know, just keep your innocence. Have some fun and really be yourself.

This advice from Michael was sorely disappointing. I see Britney Spears, in particular, as a woman in serious need of guidance and counseling. It took Michael several decades to become a train wreck. Britney has done it in her early twenties. But Michael seemed incapable of summoning lessons from his own life to thwart her decline.

SB: So what would you say to these people that are successful in the arts who are younger than you? The 'N Syncs? You would just tell them to be playful as well, don't take it too seriously? Would you tell them anything else? Don't take yourself too seriously or something?

MJ: No, I would tell them always perfect your craft, always. I'm a very strong believer in working hard. But enjoy it, you know? Like be mild-spirited, playful, have some fun. You've got to have some fun, too.

SB: What about, you always say to me how proud you are that your show is a family show, that your concerts are appropriate for children.

MJ: Oh yeah.

SB: Britney Spears was heavily criticized by some in the last MTV awards, like she almost did a striptease on stage.

MJ: Oh. . . yeah, yeah, yeah.

SB: She took this off and that off and just threw off. . . Do you think she needs to use that much sexuality to get out her message? Or, if she's really talented she may not need that? Would you give her any advice on that? Or it's a part of the show and no big deal?

MJ: Umm, I don't want to condemn her for it 'cause it's a show. But she has to realize she has, you know, kids out there who want to be like her and they'll do whatever she does. I don't know, sometimes artists don't realize the danger of what they're doing. If I took a picture of me with a cigarette, how many kids would start smoking that very day? You know, you have to think about all that. And I understand, well, it's just a video, I'm just acting a part, but you're like their god. I mean. . .

SB: You've always felt that sense of responsibility?

MJ: Uh huh.

SB: You've always known how the picture of you appears, people are going to emulate that?

MJ: Yeah, and I understand why some artists may be a little controversial at times. I understand it. You know, if the press start talking too much about her coming from the Mickey Mouse Club and being, you know, cutie Britney, she might think, "I want to give them some edge so I can strip this. I'm edgier, I'm tougher, I'm. . ." You know? So I understand. I think deep inside she's just a sweet person, you know?

SB: So you would say to her, keep your clothes on, keep it in balance here, 'cause there are kids who want to be like you and you have a responsibility?

MJ: Yeah, 'cause I like edge.

SB: You always understood the importance of that responsibility, when you became famous? You knew you had a huge responsibility as an icon and as a trend-setter?

MJ: Yeah, 'cause I don't think, I don't think I've ever done anything offensive on stage. . . ever. Like some of these acts, you talk about how Bobby Brown would get a girl up there and he starts grinding her, you know, right on in front of everybody and police arrested him several times. Like having sex right on stage and all these kids in the audience. My show it's just totally different.

On another occasion I asked Michael why he grabs his crotch, and isn't that a contradiction to his claim of acting responsibly on stage. He told me he is not even conscious of it. It's reflexive and not meant to be sexual.

Sexuality and Modesty

SB: In trying to preserve childlike qualities in your life Michael, you have shied away from talking about overt sexuality. Like when Oprah asked you about your sex life, you responded something to the effect that, "I'm a gentleman and I don't talk about that." Do you feel that we should be more respectful of the sexual side of our lives? Has it all become too overt? I mean you're naturally shy about this.

MJ: Yeah, I'm just naturally, um, 'cause I think that's. . .

SB: Private?

MJ: Yeah, that's my personal opinion. Other people who are exhibitionist, you know naturists, who go out nude and they feel different about it. Um, I don't know, I'm just different in that way.

SB: We don't have to misuse our sexuality to increase ticket sales and record sales?

MJ: No, that's crazy, like some of these singers who put bulges in their pants, that's crazy. I don't understand that. That's like disgusting to me when they do stuff like that. That's embarrassing. I don't want nobody to even look at me down. . . like looking for that. That would just embarrass me so bad, oh God.

SB: Isn't that just a sign of insecurity though? They think that maybe their dancing isn't good enough and they need to highlight that other stuff.

MJ: Yeah.

SB: Would your message to someone like Britney Spears be, "Look, you're pretty and talented. You don't need the sleaze. You're so talented without pulling everything off so that people will look at you. Like Madonna, who's often been criticized for taking advantage of the male sexual drive to sort of get all these guys hunkering after her to make her popular.

MJ: Yeah, uh huh. Aha.

Fears

Shmuley Boteach: Do you live with fears? You know people are going to shoot you down, metaphorically speaking. Does that make you afraid?

Michael Jackson: Not as an artist. I am like a lion. Nothing can hurt me. No one can harm me without my permission. I wouldn't let it bother me, even though I have been hurt and I have felt pain in the past, of course, I have been saved by a lot of that.

This is quite a contradiction to Michael's extreme vulnerability where he told me that everything he had done as an artist was to obtain love. I contrasted the two quotes in the epigraph.

SB: You don't live in fear now?

MJ: No.

SB: Do you think children teach us not to be afraid? On the one hand they are afraid, they are afraid of dogs, they are afraid of the dark, and so many other things. On the other hand they are not afraid to love and not afraid to need.

MJ: We listen, we watch, we learn. We open our hearts and we open our minds, open our souls. Yes, we can learn but you have to realize that. . .

SB: Adults live with more fear than children.

MJ: Absolutely. . . nervous breakdowns. And they have created their own circumstances in a lot of ways. To worry about something until it destroys your health. If there is something they want very badly, kids will keep on saying it until they get it because they have no other way of getting it. Until you give in, which is really sweet, it's adorable. I always say to them, "If that's the most important thing for you to worry about in life then you are a lucky person. If that's your biggest issue then you are lucky." You realize in the future. . . for them it's important at the time, which is sweet. It can be the simplest little thing, too. Sweet.

SB: So, the point I was trying to make was that on the one hand there are things that frighten you [Michael had told me about his fear of dogs], and they are classic childhood fears. And, by the way your love of fear is very similar to that of Adam and Eve. They love danger, you know. God said to them "there is this fruit and it's very dangerous," and that's when they want to eat it. On the one hand, you're afraid of nasty dogs.

MJ: Yeah, I don't like that kind of thing. That frightens me. Or if you cornered a mother cougar among her babies. . . I don't know if they call them cubs or what. . . and she's cornered and she's very territorial, you don't go there. You don't cross that line. I don't understand when people take the gun and they shoot the mother. . . and the baby elephants they do the same dance every time. They let off this screech and they turn in circles of confusion and the mother's lying there dead, they spin in circles like they're going crazy. And I don't understand how man can do that. That hurts me so much. It's so sad.

SB: Did you do safaris when you were in Africa?

MJ: Yeah, yeah.

SB: You got close to some of the dangerous animals?

MJ: Yeah.

SB: And you weren't afraid. . . ?

MJ: No. No I love safaris. I love them so much.

SB: So you see the contradiction of this fear. You're afraid of things like spiders, things that children would be afraid of, but you're not afraid of a lion.

MJ: No, no. I'm fascinated by it.

SB: I mean, in Neverland I saw you get within like a foot of a cobra. Remember that?

MJ: Yeah, yeah. And the rattlesnakes. I mean, we stroked the rattlesnakes. And they're very, highly, highly. . . I mean, they could kill you.

SB: And you're not afraid of anything like that?

MJ: I'm fascinated by things that are dangerous to men and to just look at a shark. Why are we so fascinated by sharks? Because they can kill you. And you yell "Shark!" and everybody goes "where? What? Who?" You know, you say, "barracuda" and nobody cares, you say, "shrimp." It's about the danger and the legend of it, it's about the folklore of it. And I love all that. . . I think I like what PT Barnum liked about it. You know, things that interest people, I love that kinda. . . that's what I love about magic, and Howard Hughes. I love all that.

SB: What are your biggest fears though? I know you're afraid of mean people. You don't like mean people.

MJ: I don't like big, mean, tall guys that are like aggressive. And that's what turned me off about you know who. That hurt me when he asked me, I didn't like it at all. How could a human being have that in him to be that harsh? If that's how he felt, keep it to himself, you don't say it.

SB: You don't like tall, angry, aggressive men. . . ?

MJ: No. In my life, they've been mean. Even though there have been some gentle giants. The tall ones have been turned off of me.

SB: But your bodyguards are tall. . .

MJ: They are tall. . .

SB: But they're all nice. . .

MJ: I make sure they're nice. They have to be gentlemen. And they all know, if a child comes up, you don't turn the child away. If a child comes up and asks for an autograph, you roll out the red carpet of courtesy to 'em. They all know that. Very important. I mean, Brando won't sign autographs for anyone unless they're children. Unless they're a little kid, he don't sign. I think that's so sweet, you know?

SB: What other fears do you have?

MJ: What other fears? Um. . . .

SB: Dogs. I don't understand why children have certain fears. The other night we put on a DVD for kids and there was a monster and Baba started screaming and crying and she ran out of the room and she always pushes her bed time, but she said, "I want to go to bed." And she went to sleep. She just hated it.

MJ: What show was it?

SB: I think it was *Men in Black* or something.

MJ: Ohhh. On DVD? But the other kids were fine with it? They knew it was movie stuff and not real?

SB: Yeah. I don't really let them see stuff like that but they got it and I was watching it with them, so. . . Baba saw the first guy and. . .

MJ: Yeah, it's not for Baba. It's not for her. Prince and Paris love Jurassic Park, even though there can be violence and guns. But I want him to see great movies if they're great. Not too many but great, great art.

Life in a Fishbowl

Shmuley Boteach: What about celebrity? What about the negative things associated with celebrity? What are the negatives of celebrity? What do you dislike about being as famous as you are?

Michael Jackson: I dislike when you become an icon, being a celebrity and then becoming an icon, an international phenomenon which has happened to me—and I am not ashamed to say it—and the jealousy that is involved. I have seen some serious jealousy.

SB: Do you feel it around some other celebrities, and it is palpable, or do you feel it from a distance?

MJ: I have seen it but once they meet me face to face they always, always change. They see I am nothing like that guy. I have had people really start to cry in front of me after meeting me. There have been fans, and there are two kinds of fans. There is the fan who goes, "Oh my God! Oh my God! Oh my God!" And they faint and you have to hold them. Then there's the other fan, who say an abrupt, "Hi." I go "Hi, nice to meet you. What's your name?" They give you their name, but they have got an attitude. I am just as simple and warm with them and then I see them start to cry. I say, "Why are you crying?" And they say, "Because I didn't think you would be this nice." And they go away a different person. I go,

"Well, what did you think I was like?" and they'd go, "I thought you would be stuck up and arrogant." I say, "Please never judge a person. I am nothing like that." They have been so impressed. I'm sure they go away loving you tenfold, a thousand times more. Nothing beats kindness and love I think. Just simplicity.

SB: Have you always been able to melt a hard heart with kindness and love?

MJ: Yes.

SB: What about jealousy from other stars. Is there a lot of jealousy in your profession?

MJ: Absolutely. They admire you and know you are wonderful and great because they are jealous, because they wish they were in your shoes. And "M" is one of them. Madonna is one of them. She is jealous. She is a girl, a woman and I think that's what bothers her. I think women don't scream for other women. Men are too cool to scream for women. I get the fainting and adulation and she doesn't.

SB: Does jealousy have no role? Were you never jealous of someone in your career who made you work harder?

MJ: Never jealous. Admiration, complete admiration.

SB: So admiration can bring even greater goals than jealousy because it is positive and not negative. So you would look at Fred Astaire and say, "I want to be able to do that."

MJ: Yes, absolutely. Complete inspiration, never jealousy. It's wrong, but people are like that aren't they? It's true? Can't people look at somebody great and get totally jealous of them?

SB: Sure, but you have never felt that?

MJ: I don't understand a person who could do that.

Here again Michael betrays an unfortunate lack of self-knowledge. There were plenty of people who eclipsed Michael of whom he was jealous, as we all might be. Elvis was someone whom he certainly admired, but he also felt competitive with him. However, he was understandably never jealous of people such as Fred Astaire because they were never his competitors.

Indeed, Judaism says that jealousy can be a good thing, as I have explained in several of my books, most notably *Kosher Adultery: Seduce and Sin with Your Spouse*. Jealousy is the righteous desire to safeguard that which is legitimately yours. It is *envy* which is destructive. And more than just being a play on words, envy is the unrighteous lust after that which legitimately belongs to someone else. God help husbands and wives who are not somewhat possessive of each other. I have seen plenty of those marriages and they usually betray a lack of desire.

SB: For you it has always been inspiration? You have been in awe and wonder of those with great talent?

MJ: Can a person become jealous of God?

SB: Sure. Look at Stalin and Hitler. They tried to be God. They wanted to decide life and death.

MJ: Wow.

SB: Because they lose the sense of awe and wonder. God doesn't impress them. He threatens them. They want to be all-powerful, so they can't submit to God's authority. They become enemies of God. [Aside from jealousy] what other things do you dislike about celebrity?

MJ: Being famous.

SB: Do you dislike when you can't walk down the street?

MJ: No, I enjoy when people recognize me and they are nice and say, "Hi," and there is a crowd or something.

SB: When I was with you in that van, and we had left your hotel, Michael, twice we saw a young black kid on a bicycle follow us for about four to five miles on the most treacherous streets in New York City, just to get your autograph. And you stopped the car and made sure he got his autograph. We saw three other kids who, after the dinner with President Clinton, chased us for about a mile on foot until you said to the driver, "Stop." And you gave them your autograph. So you see people do that?

MJ: Oh God, Shmuley, hundreds of them sometimes. It is a trillion times worse than what you have seen. They start breaking things and it turns into a mob scene.

I was with Michael as we exited Carnegie Hall after our presentation on Valentine's Day, 2001. I can vouch for the fact that he was nearly torn limb from limb.

SB: Do you enjoy when people recognize you as long as they are nice?

MJ: I think our job as celebrities, I think anybody who has been blessed by God with any sort of talent—be it the sculptor, the writer, the painter, the singer of songs, to the dancer—is to bring some sense of escapism and enjoyment to the masses of people. That's our job, to bring joy.

SB: Anything else you hate about celebrity? Obviously, you hate the tabloid stories as well?

MJ: Hate them. I hate the jerks for doing that sort of thing. I think racism, jealousy, and just hate—evil—are part of it. They vent out their frustration on people who are trying to do good and it is just sad. If anyone believes it, they are like crazy. I mean I wish there was a way to totally get rid of those kinds of things.

Ambition and Patience, Jealousy and Forgiveness, Anger at the Press

Shmuley Boteach: I see how people will do anything to have a piece of you. They want to ride your coattails to fame. They want to be seen with you, photographed with you. But there are people who have gotten close to you who have harmed you, who have hurt you, who have sued you. Have you got any stories where they come to you and say, "I am really sorry, I used you. I am really sorry?" Do you have any stories about forgiveness?

Michael Jackson: I wish. I wish people were that sweet to admit to their own wrongdoing.

Here is Michael playing his favorite role of victim. Of course, I was silly enough back then to believe that Michael, for the most part, was a victim. I did not realize that he had broken many contracts, alienated many of the people he worked with, abandoned people who had been devoted to him, and earned a reputation as not being the most ethical person to do business with.

SB: Not one. Never? No one ever came to you and said, "Sorry Michael, but at that party the other night I claimed to know you better that I really did. I used your name to get ahead"? Have you heard stories like that, where someone has said, "Oh yes I spoke to this guy. He says he knows you so well. He says he's your best friend. And you have never even heard of the guy?"

MJ: I have that all the time. Sometimes not to break their heart I agree like I know who they are talking about, because I don't want to embarrass the person.

SB: So you'll say, "Yeah, yeah. I know who you are talking about?"

MJ: [When really I am thinking is] I don't know who the heck you are talking about.

SB: No one who has ever hurt you has come and asked for forgiveness? There wasn't a reporter who ever came and said, "I wrote this stuff. I am sorry"? I said to the journalist from that newspaper, "How could you write that President Clinton [at the Angel Ball] was publicly distancing himself from Michael when he mentioned him three times in his speech?" I repeated the speech references to him and he actually said, "I'm sorry, I was given the wrong information." He was a decent guy. He said, "I will correct it tomorrow." But have you never had to forgive anyone in your life, Michael? Have you ever forgiven anyone without them asking? Have you forgiven the people who have hurt you?

MJ: To their face?

SB: In your heart.

MJ: Of course.

SB: You have seen someone being mean and you have forgiven them anyway.

MJ: Yes, because I was taught to be Biblical: "Forgive them for they know not what they do." And you do it.

SB: Do you think you are a better person for it?

MJ: Yeah.

SB: So you have no anger in your heart at anyone today?

MJ: I have anger for the press. I am very bitter, mad and angry with them and I am angry at those who deliberately inflict pain upon a child to hurt them. The stories about what they are doing in the wars to the kids. I always try and figure out a way to try and do something about that.

SB: What about forgiveness? There are people who have hurt you. Children do fight, but they don't bear grudges. Can you forgive people with your whole heart, people who have hurt you?

MJ: Yes.

SB: Even I didn't realize this. But when I mentioned Roseanne Barr to you, because I do her television show often as a guest, I later saw that she had made a negative comment about you for no apparent reason.

MJ: She has been mean with me. That was why I was hesitant.

Roseanne is a friend of mine and I served as her daughters' real-life matchmaker on her syndicated talk show. Roseanne, who is Jewish, wanted her daughters to marry Jewish husbands. Since she is a very devoted mother, I was looking to get her involved in our child prioritization initiative. When I mentioned it to Michael, he went silent. It was a mark of his gentlemanliness that he did not badmouth my friend to me. Later someone shared with me the reason for Michael's hesitation because apparently Roseanne once made a negative comment about Michael. But then, I know Roseanne and it could be she made the comment facetiously.

SB: You could tell me that.

MJ: I didn't maliciously attack her.

SB: I saw that. Can you forgive them? There is no malice in their heart.

MJ: You know, "They know not what they do." Words of Jesus. They don't even know me. It has no foundation what they are doing. How can they say it. . . they don't even know me? Do you believe something you have read?

SB: So it is total forgiveness?

MJ: Yes, because Roseanne came to me later on, like a puppy backstage, praising, feeling bad about all of that.

SB: Have you got other examples?

MJ: Madonna has never apologized. She is jealous.

SB: She wants to be the biggest star in the world?

MJ: Yes, she is jealous.

SB: You can't understand that. You would say, "What are you jealous for? You do your thing. I do my thing. . . ."

MJ: But at the same time she will come to my concert and cry. She comes there and tears rolling down her face for the song and the presentation of the song. There are some good qualities in her.

SB: There are good qualities in her. But you're saying she allows her jealousy to mask them at times. But if someone does that, they don't even have to ask for forgiveness because you will just forgive them?

MJ: Yes.

SB: I saw that you made an overture to Jay Leno. You went to a charity benefit with Elizabeth Taylor and you were wearing a red suit.

MJ: Brown suit.

SB: So you saw Jay Leno and. . . ?

MJ: He was sitting at my table with President Ford, Sylvester Stallone, Elizabeth Taylor, Sydney Poitier. When he came to sit down I just walked over to him and started like playfully choking him [because he always makes negative jokes about Michael] and he was like, "Urgghh. Urrrggghh." And then Elizabeth said, "Have you been saying mean things about Michael?" And he went, "Huh?" Later on in the evening he shook my hand with a warm expression in his eyes and the next day he sends a letter to the office saying, "Michael said he would come on the show. Can you set it up so that we can have him on the show?" I never said that. So I don't know how to take it from here. But instead of taking him to one side and saying something nasty back to him, I wouldn't do that. I couldn't help doing what I did to him [Laughs].

SB: That's cute. Everyone saw?

MJ: Yeah, they saw it. He has a big neck too. I couldn't get my hands round.

SB: What is it about Elizabeth Taylor that is so endearing to you? She is like your closest friend for many years. What is it about her, in the context of these childlike qualities?

MJ: We are both from the same place. . . .

SB: She's loyal, right.

MJ: She's loyal. We are from the same place. She can relate to the world I have come from. She's curious. You just look in her eyes and you know. It is like speaking telepathically. You can feel it, it's true, without saying a word and I felt that seeing her the very first time. It's like that with Shirley Temple [Black]. We are from the same world.

Michael and His Fans' Love: A Two-Way Street

Shmuley Boteach: Let me ask you this. Given that you were somewhat disadvantaged as a child, not being given the love that you needed, how do you overcome what you weren't given? How did you learn to make up for the basic tools that you were deprived of?

Michael Jackson: I think music and dance helped me a lot, like therapy. To be able to express your feelings through songs and your emotions on stage and getting all that love back a thousandfold through the fans.

SB: That compensated for what you didn't get?

MJ: Yeah, 'cause when a fan walks up, I mean honestly when somebody walks up to you and says, "I love you so much," it makes my heart feel so good. I could never get tired of it.

SB: Really? Do you not sometimes feel that a sicko fan, a stalker, takes it too far?

MJ: No, nope. I just love it. I just love my fans. I love them to pieces and what makes my heart happy is when I see they support my beliefs about family and children. They have these big billboards of children and babies and they're with me, they get it, you know? They get what I'm saying.

SB: So what you didn't get from your parents you get from your fans, but there's one big difference. Parents are supposed to give you unconditional love, even if you don't deserve it. Bill Clinton's mother, Virginia Kelly, was once asked which son she loved more. Bill, who made her real proud as president of the United

FAME IN ADULTHOOD | 165

States, or Roger, who had drug issues and was accused of being
a deadbeat dad.

MJ: One of her kids?

SB: Roger, Bill Clinton's brother.

MJ: Has a drug addiction?

SB: Sure, I'm almost positive he was in prison for selling drugs.

MJ: Really?

SB: And he was a deadbeat dad, didn't pay alimony and stuff like
that. And she was asked, "One son is kind of a bum and the other
is president, do you love Bill more?" And she said, "What? Are
you crazy? I love both my children, I love them equally." So there's
got to be a difference, Michael, between how the fans love you,
and how your family does. Parents love you unconditionally, but
the fans love you because you can sing and because you can dance,
or do you feel unconditional love from your fans?

MJ: That's hard, 'cause I'm not in their skin. Umm, I think after dis-
covering who I am and how I see them and make them feel good
about themselves, they love me unconditionally. I know they
do. . . I feel it, I see it. You go with me sometime and we go out and
you're gonna run into the diehard fans, you're going to see something. It's unbelievable, it's like a religious experience. They sleep
on the street, hold up candlelight and they have their families out
there, it's just so beautiful. I love seeing the children come, that
makes my heart so happy.

SB: So it's the case of originally they loved you because of song and
dance, but then they went beyond that point.

MJ: Yeah, they discovered what I'm about, what I'm trying to
say. . . There's a message in the music that's more than just a beat
and a rhythm. There's some real depth.

SB: Why do you have such fanatical fans? Can I tell you how fanatical they are? I haven't even shown you, but that one article I published about you, after Neverland and your birthday, has generated
so many hundreds of letters by email to us. You've got to see it.
Half of these people run their own Michael Jackson website.
There's something like hundreds upon hundreds of Michael Jackson websites.

MJ: Yeah, yeah.

SB: How do you account for that? I mean everyone has fans. It's like when we talked about the Spice Girls the other day. Sure they had fans, but where are the fans now? Why are yours such diehard fans?

MJ: I think 'cause they, I've been given the gift that God has given me and I haven't been a "here today gone tomorrow" artist and it allows people, the public, to grow up with me. When they grow with me it's more an emotional contact and they feel attached to me like I'm their brother. I have people walk up to me [and say] "Michael!" start talking, grabbing me just like they're my brother or sister. I play as if, you know, you've got to go along with it. They really feel that you belong to them.

SB: You've known them for their entire life?

MJ: Yeah, all my life and I have to go right along with it. 'Cause I'm on their wall, they hear me every morning, and pictures are everywhere. It is like a shrine and some religions say it's idol worship but I don't believe it's idol worship.

SB: Okay, why isn't it idol worship?

MJ: I have never written once, nor have I heard, [the fans claiming that I'm a god.] Perhaps there were some banners that say, "You are God." We do have footage like that but we don't show it on television. We have banners that say that. I don't think it's anything bad 'cause what I'm talking about is love, let's restore the family. . .

This is shocking stuff coming from Michael's mouth, and truly captures the very essence of how his life went off the rails. Arrogance is at the heart of all human corruption, and it doesn't get much more arrogant than this. Here you have a man who was once a devout Jehovah's Witness, with all their emphasis on purging even an iota of idolatrous conduct from one's life, saying that it's no big deal that his fans have banners declaring that he's God. And I understand that they don't mean it literally. But Michael should have been at the forefront saying, "Everything I have, every talent of which I am possessed, comes only from God and to him belongs the glory."

Instead, we had a sad spectacle of a man allowing himself to be worshipped by a bunch of lost souls who sleep outside his hotel room, desperate for an object of veneration to fill their inner emptiness. Michael should have been the first to tell them to go home and find something truly worth worshipping, to stop obsessing over a rock star and cultivate their own lives and real relationships. Instead, like so many other men and woman who have fallen in love with their own graven image, he became addicted to the adulation until he felt the need to play the role and act as if he were indeed a god.

Michael and I are both students of the Hebrew Bible (what Christians call the Old Testament) and I often told him that the Bible can be distilled into one short sentence. There is only one God, and it isn't you, so make room in your life for the real Creator. I told Michael many times, "Michael, in life we all end up humble. In that there is no choice. One way or another, we will end up with our arrogance deflated. Rather, the choice lies only in how it will come about. Either we humble ourselves, Michael, or God will humble us." How tragic for Michael that he could not humble himself before it was done for him.

> SB: So it's not idol worship because you yourself have subordinated yourself to the higher value saying that I represent this?
> MJ: I'm representing the higher being. I'm not saying I'm God, but I'm saying heal the planet, heal the world, save our children, save the forest. There's nothing wrong with that. Right?
> SB: Idol worship is where it's about me.

Yes, I know. I could have been much more forceful at the time in telling Michael that his words were abhorrent. But I justified holding my tongue in the belief that I had to first build trust before I could really be tough on him, as I increasingly became. I regret my cowardice and my fear that I would lose my intimate relationship with my friend, the superstar. I did, however, correct it a few months later as I increasingly lectured Michael on how his need to be worshipped was ruining his life and alienating him from God. As I predicted, it led to the demise of our relationship. Ordinary mortals do not criticize deities. At least I wasn't burned at the stake.

MJ: Yeah, no that's not what I'm about.

SB: The opposite is "I may be a hero, but I'm a hero for a higher cause."

MJ: If you saw my show you would see it's totally not about me. Big giant screens show them cutting down the rainforest and hungry children reaching out. It's just so beautiful. People start to cry and get emotional. It's so wonderful.

PART 4

THE KATHERINE JACKSON INTERVIEW

Michael mentioned to me that he wanted me to interview his mother for this book. I wanted to discover her impressions on who Michael was, what made him unique, and what was the source of his pain. But more than anything else, knowing what a devout Jehovah's Witness and deeply religious woman Katherine Jackson was, I wanted to know how she felt about Michael leaving the Jehovah's Witnesses Church. It always seemed to me that the church had a salient effect on Michael. It kept him humble and grounded even after he became the biggest star in the world. Having God as part of his life reminded Michael that he was not a deity. He was a mortal man, flawed and incomplete. In the years after he abandoned the church, Michael began to exhibit unhealthy signs of a Messiah complex. He saw himself as the children's redeemer when in truth it was their parents who had to be their redeemers. The trouble with anyone who sees themselves in a superhuman light is that they are above criticism. And the refusal to accept guidance and criticism would later prove fatal for Michael.

Katherine Jackson was visiting New York City, and I met her in her suite in the Four Seasons Hotel. When I walked in, she was reading the Bible. In fact, on both occasions that I met with Mrs. Jackson she was reading the Bible as I entered. A religious and pious woman, she exuded a grace and nobility of spirit that was noticeable and impressive.

On Her Children's Fame and Talent

Shmuley Boteach: So I just want this to be more of a conversation. First of all, I wanted to meet you and it's a great pleasure. I'm friendly with Michael. He always talks about you. In fact, you're one of the central figures in the book.

Katherine Jackson: Oh really?

SB: Oh he adores you. When we went to visit Neverland we saw the Katherine Train and Mount Katherine. And when he talks about you his eyes close and he almost goes into some rapturous ecstasy.

KJ: [Laughing] He is such a good son. He really is a good son.

SB: Oh he worships you. I mean you are one of the great matriarchs in America. I mean, who can claim to have had a family that has achieved the things your family has achieved? You must be very proud of your children.

KJ: I am. I am very proud of them. But, you know, you have to pay the price.

SB: If you ever want me to turn this tape recorder off, I'm happy to.

KJ: You mean whenever I want to?

SB: If you ever want me to turn it off, I'll turn it off.

KJ: That's all right. Just whatever you want to ask me, I'm ready.

SB: You mean pay the price in terms of fame?

KJ: Yeah. When it comes to fame, you know, you pay the price. Some is good and some is bad. People like to hear bad things. People make up things about you and it hurts in a way because you find a lot of people. . . they get on television and they say a lot of things about you they don't even know about. And it's not true and this is what happens. So you have to be strong to get through this.

SB: How do you account for the extraordinary musical talent in your family?

KJ: Well, I've always loved music. My husband did too. My sister and I when we were young we used to sing together all the time and now the funny thing about it, my father, coming from Indiana. . . East Chicago, Indiana. That's where I was raised. My father used to keep the radio station—we didn't have television in those days—used to keep the radio station on a station called, "Supper Time Frolic." And every night it would come on and it was all country western.

He [her father] gave my son Tito a guitar. After I got married and I moved to Gary, my father brought a guitar over for Tito as a gift. And the boys what they did, after they got television, they used to watch, whenever Temptations, you know they would come on, that was back in the sixties. It really started when I used to sing with them.

SB: That I haven't read. You used to sing with them?

KJ: You haven't read that? Yes. No, no, not professionally.

SB: No, I understand. At the house. . .

KJ: When they were little, when they were very young. I don't even think Michael was born at the time and whenever. . . We had [to pay] for a month of TV. And you know, how you get that and then you pay so much a month. And our TV broke down and it was snowing and cold and we didn't have. . . the kids didn't have anything to do. So we would sing songs. They were songs like "Old Cotton Field Back Home." I don't know if you're familiar with those songs, folk songs really. And even before then when my husband and I first married we used to sing together just around the house doing nothing, harmonizing, and we always loved music and my husband's family was musical. He plays the harmonica, he used to, and the guitar and his brother played the saxophone and the other brother played the trombone and my father played guitar. So we just love music and I guess that's where it stemmed from.

SB: So you don't see it as something genetic?

KJ: Well it could be because my. . .

SB: There's no real family that has this record of. . .

KJ: My grandfather or great-grandfather, I would say grandfather, my mother used to tell me stories about how they would keep old wooden windows where they used to throw the windows open, you know, and they would sing and you could hear their voices echoing across the countryside and there was nothing else to do. That was the cheapest thing you could do was entertain and entertain yourself and your family because there was not much money in the black families at that time so they entertained themselves with music. Guitars and harmonicas.

SB: So do you think those families were happier than the families today with money?

KJ: Oh yeah, I think so. I really believe that. Because even when I was in Gary I think I was much happier, in a way. I'm happy today but . . . the families are closer and I think that every family feels that when they're poor, they're closer.

SB: Some of the questions that I have. . . Let's first begin with Michael. He wanted me to meet you because he said many times that you can tell me the kind of stories that he may have forgotten. For example, what made him who he is? And I don't mean the musical side. Most Hollywood stars who have made a lot of money and who are world-famous are arrogant and self-centered. They're not interested in kids. That's the last thing they're interested in. They're interested in themselves. First of all Michael lived at home until he was about twenty-seven years old, which is amazing. I mean who's ever heard of. . . Macaulay Culkin moved out when he was like eleven [I was exaggerating]. How do you account for his softness, his gentility, his love of animals, his love of children, his sensitivity to life? He's like a boy, things surprise him and startle him. How do you account for all of that?

KJ: You know all those questions you ask it's hard to answer in a way. But, they used to own a cat each and I said, "You can have a cat but you can't bring them in," and things like that for years before we came to California.

SB: So here he was already demonstrating this from the earliest age.

KJ: The love of animals from an early stage and Janet was another one that loved animals even when she was [young]. We don't have a law but you had to keep your animals out there. Animals just run stray. Animals everywhere.

After we came to California he was able to get animals, so they had snakes and he had sheep. Here in Encino we had a little zoo. We had a giraffe.

He loved those things. You know I think it's because. . . I'll tell you what I believe. That it was because when we were back in Indiana, it was really a bad place. Gary, Indiana, was really a bad place. And my husband, he wouldn't let the kids go out and be with. . . the neighborhood kids.

SB: Why didn't any of this go to Michael's head? Why did he stay at home? He said to me, "I'm old fashioned, you stay home until you get married." Did you raise the values with him? Was it the religious faith he was raised with? Michael is a fundamentally soft, sensitive person. Where does that come from?

KJ: I'd hate to say it.

SB: Are all your kids like that?

KJ: Most of them, yes. I'd say that—and I hate to say it. I used to tell him all the time that he was too much like me and I didn't want him to be that way.

SB: That's exactly what he says.

KJ: [laughs] I used to tell him, "I don't want you to be that way. You're a man. You have to be strong. You know. But he's gentle. He's just a gentle person.

SB: So what you're saying is that his softness comes from you. He was much more attached to you than he was to his father.

KJ: Oh yeah.

SB: So he took after your example.

KJ: Oh yeah.

SB: And he actually believes in being soft and he'd rather be hurt than inflict pain.

KJ: Nothing bad.

Religion in Katherine's and Her Children's Lives

Shmuley Boteach: And are you "soft" like that because of your religious faith? Michael talks about your religious faith all the time.

Katherine Jackson: No, I've been like that all the time. I wasn't a Jehovah's Witness all the time.

SB: You were a Jehovah's Witness when you were young?

KJ: I was not. I used to be Baptist. My mother raised us going to church school every Sunday and being in the Junior choir.

SB: So you were raised Baptist?

KJ: Yes.

SB: And did you go to church? Were you a religious Baptist?

KJ: Yes, I went to church but I didn't like what I saw in the Baptist church. And so after I got to judge religion by the way the people act and they were doing it and that's why I got out of it.

SB: And where was this?

KJ: In East Chicago, Indiana.

SB: 'Cause you saw things that turned you off and you decided to seek a better religion at the age of what. . . Twelve? Thirteen?

KJ: Yeah. Twelve, thirteen. My sister and I were studying to be a Jehovah's. . . Well, we were just studying with the people next door who were. 'Cause Jehovah's Witnesses come around and they teach the Bible to people. My mother found it and she got angry with us and made us stop. So after I got older, and I got married, and moved away, I remembered that. And that's when I started to study.

SB: Were you married?

KJ: I was already married.

SB: So you were exposed to the Jehovah's Witnesses when you were a teenager.

KJ: Yes.

SB: But your parents felt this was something they didn't want.

KJ: Right.

SB: So they dissuaded you. But it stayed with you internally. So when you had more independence and freedom, you got married young?

KJ: Nineteen.

SB: Nineteen? My wife got married at nineteen. My mother got married at nineteen. It's like a number in the family.

KJ: Mmmm.

SB: So you got married at nineteen and you moved with your husband to Indiana straight away?

KJ: To Gary, Indiana? No, when we first got married we stayed and two months later we moved to Gary, Indiana.

SB: So it was at that time that you went to find the Jehovah's Witnesses again?

KJ: Yes, but it was, I guess, about ten or twelve years later.

SB: And what was the appeal for you? I know a little about it that I've read. Did you feel you found greater sincerity?

KJ: Well, what it is about Jehovah's Witnesses is it's a religion that goes strictly by the Bible and they believe in doing right. Like, if you commit adultery or anything like that, you get disfellowshipped. If you're married and you commit adultery, which is wrong, then you get disfellowshipped from the religion. A lot of things make me believe in it. I believe in it because I believe it's a true religion. I do. There's a Creator who cares about you and then we have examining the scriptures daily.

SB: Every day you have something to read?

KJ: Aha.

SB: Old and New Testament?

KJ: Aha.

SB: And you take these books wherever you go?

KJ: Well, not that one [she points to a book]. But these are just testimonies by people about what they went through.

SB: You feel it's based on the Bible so it's very authentic. Therefore, it's a true religion, so it really spoke to you. And you then formally converted?

KJ: No, I studied. You have to study the Bible.

SB: Did your husband walk this path with you?

KJ: He studied also but he didn't become one. He thought it was too strict for him. My oldest daughter was baptized. Michael was at one time.

SB: No other kids?

KJ: No. No others.

SB: And why was that? Why some and not others?

KJ: I guess they did but I never forced anything on them. It was up to their own free will if they wanted to be.

SB: So at a certain age you spoke to Michael about the religion and he took to it?

KJ: No but, I guess he wanted to and he went with me to the Kingdom Hall.

SB: Were you proud of the fact that he became a Jehovah's Witness?

KJ: I was very proud that he became a Jehovah's Witness.

SB: And by this time was he already famous? Or he was just a boy?

KJ: He was already famous, in a way. Yes, he was famous because The Jackson 5 was very famous at first.

SB: Right, so this was that age already with The Jackson 5.

KJ: Right, right.

SB: But he was the only one of The Jackson 5 who was baptized?

KJ: He was the only one.

SB: And he used to go with you on Sundays to church?

KJ: Oh yes, aha. And he used to go on his own.

SB: I asked Frank to show you this beautiful article that Michael and I wrote about Pioneering and the Sabbath. A beautiful article. [It was published on the well-known spirituality website Beliefnet.com.]

KJ: Oh, really?

SB: Oh, it was covered everywhere.

KJ: Oh, really?

SB: Oh, it was huge. It's a shame he doesn't show you these things. It was a beautiful article.

KJ: Oh why didn't he show it to me?

SB: It's a beautiful article about how he loved the Sabbath.

KJ: Mhmm.

SB: So he would go with you. He told me that what he liked about them was that they never treated him differently. That although he was now a star, they would call him Brother Jackson.

KJ: Aha.

SB: They would go out of their way not to treat him differently, not less than, but not more, than any other.

KJ: Yes.

SB: Did you see that as well?

KJ: Yes, they did. That's how they think. There's a lot of entertainers that are Jehovah's Witnesses. I can't think of the name of the group, you know, Benson, Ronnie Loss. Just, I can go on and on with a lot of entertainers that are Jehovah's Witness. And they treat them the same. They don't treat them any different. Just like one of them.

SB: Did Michael like that? That he could just finally be himself?

KJ: Yes, I think so.

SB: He also told me that they were very good. That if reporters fol-lowed him to church they didn't make a big deal about it. [laughing] In the article, we write jokingly "even reporters are children of God."

KJ: [laughing] That's true.

SB: Okay, so you have all these children, a few of them took to the religion and Michael was one of them, even though he was a big star. It has always seemed to me in our conversations that Michael has a natural spirituality, that he has a natural closeness to God.

KJ: Yes, aha.

SB: Could you comment on that at all? Did you see that from an early age?

KJ: Aha.

SB: Did he pray before he went to sleep at night?

KJ: Yes, I believe he has. Like I have some children. . . I don't know if they even, I don't know, I can't say because. . .

SB: Are you comfortable with talking about this?

KJ: I'm fine. But I know Michael is [spiritual]. He's always been a quiet, loving child. And he just loved people, loved children. And we'd sit there and both of us, we'd just sit and cry when we saw. . . because it's very sad and I knew then, you know. . . and he used to always tell me, "I know I can't heal the whole world, Mother, but I can at least. . . I can make a start."

SB: I was discussing this with Michael yesterday. Jehovah's Witnesses do not celebrate birthdays.

KJ: No.

SB: And is there a reason for that?

KJ: Yes. . . Jesus' death is . . . the only holiday that. . .

SB: Okay, so there's Easter. Do you call it Easter or do you call it something else?

KJ: Uh, we don't call it. . . we don't celebrate Easter.

SB: That's the resurrection. You celebrate the actual day that he died.

KJ: Yes.

SB: Right, okay. Good Friday.

KJ: And that's the only day he said to keep. Not the resurrection, he said.

SB: Do you read the Bible every day?

KJ: Yes.

SB: So this is. . . this is your life, your religion. It's absolutely central to who you are.

KJ: Well, yes, in all the Kingdom Halls [I attend five meetings a week].

SB: Five meetings a week?

KJ: But you don't have to meet. We have a meeting on Sunday night, which is where we go and they teach and we learn, things like that. You never stop learning the Bible.

SB: Right.

KJ: Do Jewish people read it all the time too?

SB: Absolutely. Oh absolutely, we read it. . .

KJ: After reading it day and night. I know you know all about that.

SB: We read the bible every single day.

KJ: Aha.

SB: I mean, by this age already, I'm thirty-four years old, I've studied it my whole life. I know, I mean, I'm not trying to brag, but just from reading it I know a lot of it by heart by now.

KJ: Oh.

SB: At least the five Books of Moses, that is.

KJ: Aha.

SB: Which is what we focus on more than anything. More than Psalms or the prophets.

KJ: Right.

When Michael Left the Jehovah's Witnesses

Shmuley Boteach: How did you feel when Michael began to feel distanced from the Jehovah's Witnesses?

Katherine Jackson: I felt really bad because it bothered me so much. I cried about it, I prayed about it. And I really felt bad about when he disfellowshipped himself from the religion. They didn't disfellowship him. And he thought that would be better because he thought that he would be doing things and. . .

SB: But what was their exact objection? That he was a pop star and didn't fit in anymore?

KJ: He would've fit in. But I guess, I really don't know why he decided to disfellowship himself.

SB: He disfellowshipped himself.

KJ: Right.

SB: Up until that time he was still going with you to church on Sundays?

KJ: Yes.

SB: So he disfellowshipped himself and did he discuss it with you before he did that?

KJ: No. I heard that later. No, that's what hurt so bad. Not that he was. . . I just didn't want to see him disfellowship himself from the religion.

SB: He felt that would give him greater artistic freedom, probably.

KJ: Probably so.

SB: Like with "Thriller" he had to do that thing at the beginning.

KJ: Aha.

As I related earlier, at the beginning of the "Thriller" music video there is a disclaimer which states that nothing portrayed in the video is an endorsement of the occult. As Michael explained it to me, he inserted the disclaimer at the insistence of the church.

SB: Did you call him and say, you know, you should think about this?

KJ: No. No, I didn't because he disfellowshipped himself before I knew it and it was too late then.

SB: But do you still feel that he. . . It seems to me that he still has a very spiritual core, I mean like he talks about God with me all the time.

KJ: Yes, yes. He really is. And I wish he would come back.

SB: Do you talk to him about raising Prince and Paris with some of the spiritual tradition?

KJ: Well, I bring the literature to Grace [the children's nanny].

SB: Right.

KJ: And I bring the little. . . we have a book of Bible stories for children and I brought both of them one and she has them and she reads it to them. And I don't think he has anything against her teaching them or reading to them.

SB: Right. As Michael became more famous, did you see any changes at all, away from the. . .

KJ: The religion?

SB: Yeah.

KJ: No, I didn't see anything against. . . No, I didn't. The only thing he was doing was the way he was dancing at the time when he did "Billie Jean." They always said the way he had. . . he was grabbing his crotch, and things like that.

SB: Right, well he always jokes with me about that. He laughs at it.

KJ: I know [laughing].

When I had asked Michael why he had grabbed his crotch so much during performances, he laughed and told me that it wasn't intentional. He didn't do it to shock. It was impulsive, an intuitive artistic impression. He made it seem like he barely noticed doing it, hence the laughter.

Providing a Sense of Safety

Shmuley Boteach: Okay. Did you feel extra protective over him because he was very soft? Did you feel the need to look after him more?

Katherine Jackson: Yes. He was pretty strong in the way of taking care of himself in so many ways but I guess that's what made me feel close to him because I feel that he's soft. Like, when they were talking about him like with the child molestation thing and everybody was telling me. "Don't say anything, you're gonna make it worse." And Michael's office would say, "Don't say anything. You're gonna make it worse." And I said, "It can't get any worse than what it is. I don't care what you say, I'm going on television." And I did, because he needed someone to help him, to protect him from this stuff. Not that I could protect him, but at least I could try to set matters straight. Even though they didn't believe me, I had spoken. But they all came out for money. They knew they were lying, and I went on television again and I said, "These people work for me, not for Michael." People try to make money any kind of way they can.

SB: And when he was younger, did you also feel the need to protect him? Did you immediately see that of all your nine children that he was softer than the others, that he was more sensitive than the others, that he was gentler than the others?

KJ: You know, I see him more sensitive than the others but. . . I think he's kind of strong when you have to be. Don't you see that? Or do you?

SB: Oh, absolutely, I saw it yesterday. I told you. Michael and Frank had this whole clash about how much he should do tomorrow night at Carnegie Hall. Absolutely, yeah, he is very strong when he has to be.

KJ: Aha, that's how he is.

SB: So you saw that as well. You saw there was a softness, but a strong core.

KJ: A softness, but strong too in a way. And he can be hurt very easily, you know, because people think a certain way or say certain things about him. But I think he's kind of hard now because he's had so many things thrown upon him.

SB: Absolutely.

KJ: He's got a hard shell.

SB: He had to endure a lot. Absolutely. When he chose to stay at home. . . he was now big, even after *Thriller*, he was now one of the biggest stars in the world.

KJ: Aha.

SB: Can you talk about that? About that at all? Did you. . . I mean, I find that very moving that in this day and age when people go to college at like seventeen and they're not close to their parents anymore. . . And here was this guy who could obviously afford to live anywhere he wanted. But he wanted to live at home. Um, so we were just talking about Michael staying at home. As your children. . . your children got married young, most of them, I mean the older boys.

KJ: Yes they did.

SB: Michael didn't.

KJ: No.

SB: And were you happy to have him at home?

KJ: Yes. In fact, I didn't want to see any of my children leave home, but that's how mothers are.

SB: Right.

KJ: You know, but they have to leave and go away.

SB: Well did you say to him, "That's good that you're staying home. You're right, this is the correct decision. Stay here until you get married"?

KJ: No.

SB: Or did you say to him "You're a superstar, you really should be. . . "

KJ: No, no. I never believed in pushing children out or you know, like the mother bird. . . you know, push them out and say fly? But I did believe in them being strong and being able to go, but whenever they got ready. . . twenty-four. . . twenty-five.

SB: He always felt very protective about you?

KJ: He said, "I'm gonna buy you a house."

Being Michael's Mother

Shmuley Boteach: There are a lot of stories he tells me about when he was a boy, about you. Like for example, he said that he always used to dance. . .

Katherine Jackson: Aha.

SB: And he would leave scuff marks.

KJ: Mhmm [laughing].

SB: And everyone would say, "Michael stop dancing." Or, "You're making too much noise." And you used to always say, "No, let him dance."

KJ: Yes.

SB: He sort of credits you with bringing out his musical talent more than anyone else because you. . .

KJ: Oh, really?

SB: Yeah, he always tells me. One of the stories that we have in the book is that he always used to dance and leave marks and be making noise and you would always say, "No, let Michael dance. Always let Michael dance."

KJ: Yes.

SB: Do you remember that?

KJ: Yes, yes. I think Michael was born with it because even when he was a little kid, three years old, and the kids used to sing and he would be. . . that's what made me notice that he was a singer. He was over in the corner, and they were singing and perfect harmony came from him and I thought, "My God where did he get this from?" And then when he was about five years old, they would be wondering, "Now what move can we put with [this song]?" You know how they do the choreography. And he was doing that. He would tell them, "No, let's do this and let's do that."

SB: Almost like he had it inside him?

KJ: He did. He had it inside him. I don't know where it came from and it startled me. Just like some things you see in Prince now and you just don't believe it. And that's how it was with him.

SB: There was something just last week saying that Michael's chin was surgically implanted, and that's how ridiculous it gets. How do you feel about all that stuff as his mother?

KJ: People saying things about him?

SB: When you read this stuff. . . anything. . .

KJ: Oh it upsets me. It makes me angry.

SB: But do you also say to yourself at that time "I believe in God and I believe that everything is done for a reason?" Do you find strength in your spiritual faith that ultimately none of this will matter, that God's will will be done?

KJ: I do feel that way. If it wasn't for my faith, my spirit and my belief in God, I don't think I could've made it with all the stuff that goes on about my family and about Michael. It really hurts. But you have to pray about it. That's the only way that you can. . .

SB: So that's what's gotten you through it?

KJ: Yes.

SB: And did you say to Michael in 1993 or in any of those times, "You have to be close to God. You need that faith. This is what's gonna get you through it"? That it's not the money or the success or the fans. That it's a strong relationship with God?

KJ: Right, right, it is. And I feel that and I feel that. Uh [sigh], well, I can't say it.

SB: Well, for most people, as they become more successful, they become less religious. It's a trend. With you it seems that the more successful the family became, you became more religious. You held on tighter.

KJ: Aha. Yes. There's nothing else out there to me. I'm proud of my children, proud of what they're doing, and they have a talent for it. But as far as anything else out there in the world, there's nothing. Because Satan is. . . and you might not believe me. . .

SB: Oh, please speak openly. . .

KJ: Mhmm.

SB: There are things in my faith that you wouldn't agree with.

[Both laugh.]

SB: But we're both people of faith.

KJ: Well, I believe that Satan is the god of the system. The reason I say that is because. . . all the news you hear, bad news. . . all the people are doing crazy things. And the Bible speaks of children, these last days, of children how they are disrespectful, lovers of money rather than lovers of God and, how children are disrespectful to their parents and parents are disrespectful to their children. And that's what's happening. Don't you think so?

SB: Absolutely. Well, that's why you should come tomorrow night [to the joint lecture Michael and I were going to deliver at Carnegie Hall]. It's going to be a big blow against the side of Satan. You should really come. I couldn't agree more. What drew me to Michael, and you should see the speech he's giving tomorrow, is how he speaks so movingly about how nobody eats dinner with their kids anymore and how no one reads their children bedtime stories. And every time there would be a shooting in the schools, he'd call me up at home when he was in California and I was in

New Jersey. And he'd say, "Did you hear? Another kid got shot." Now in America, it's "Oh, another kid got shot." And you'd turn the page to another story. But Michael cried.

KJ: Mhmm, mhmm. That's Michael.

SB: On my birthday, we brought the national leukemia poster child. Michael came to my birthday party and she sat next to him, this little girl seven years old. And when the mother told him her story, Michael cried like a little baby. It was unbelievable. Do you do that as well?

KJ: Yes, I do.

SB: So he really is most like you. I mean, if I want to understand him, I have to understand you.

KJ: Aha, mhmm. And I hate that about myself and Janet does it too. [Laughing]

SB: Michael told me about you—you can't say no to anybody. People will ask you for things and you can't say no. [Laughing]

KJ: Mhmm, it's hard. And he's the same way and I told him you have to learn to say no.

SB: Now does that come from your parents? Were they very kind people?

KJ: Mhmm, yes. Especially my mother. My father was too.

SB: So you transmitted this tradition of kindness to your children. Kindness was the most important thing.

KJ: That's how I felt. Sometimes when you're poor and you have nothing else to give, give your love, give of yourself. And whatever you had, like poor people always do. When I was raised up, they would always invite people in to eat, that's all they had, you know.

SB: Are you treated differently in the church as the mother of the Jacksons?

KJ: Oh no, no, no, no, no, no.

SB: And do you like the fact that you can just be yourself there?

KJ: Yes. I like that fact. I could be myself. And we have the girl that's in our congregation too that always sits next to me and my friend and all the time who was on tour with Diana Ross. And uh she's. . . [pause in tape] her name is Linda Lawrence and you know they had to quit their tour but she went on tour with Diana, took Mary's place. And she's been traveling as a Supreme. You know, they have a lot before Diana and she's treated the same way. And my daughter's in the congregation, and she's treated the same way.

SB: Which one? Rebbie?

KJ: Rebbie.

SB: She lives also. . . she lives near you?

KJ: She used to. She lives in Las Vegas.

SB: I want to ask this question as well. . . I can turn this off, or not. But Michael has had a tortured, he's had a tortured relationship with his father. I'm not saying anything new. I mean, this has come out, as you know, in interviews and things like that.

KJ: Aha.

SB: You probably know that there's uh. . . I don't know how much he spoke about his father in public but one of the famous things that he said publicly was that once his father walked into the room, he felt like throwing up 'cause he was so afraid of him. Do you remember that?

KJ: I know! Yeah, I remember him saying that. He used to tell me and when I used to go on the road he always said, "Don't bring Joseph." I'd say, "Why?" and he said, "I literally. . . "

SB: I could turn this off if you want me to.

KJ: Yes. Could you, please?

SB: Of course.

We spoke for another half hour and I departed. I would later see Michael's mother again at her home in Encino when she invited me to meet her husband Joe to speak to him about reconnecting with Michael some months after my relationship with him was over.

PART 5

DOES AN IDEAL WOMAN EXIST?

Relationships and Wannabe Girlfriends

People seem obsessed with the question of Michael and women. Was he heterosexual? Were his marriages real? Were they consummated? I would never have dared ask him any of these questions. Nor would I ask them of anyone else. Everyone deserves some privacy. Indeed, in our relationship I limited my questions to areas where I thought I could bring improvement. Michael and I many times discussed his marriage to Debbie Rowe because I thought it horrible, not to mention untenable, that she should have no interaction with Paris and Prince, her two children. This was a permanent sore point between Michael and me. He basically told me that I did not understand the nature of his relationship with Debbie, and that it was better for Prince and Paris not to have a relationship with a mother they have never known. (For their part, when asked, Prince and Paris simply replied that they had no mother.) I responded that a relationship with one's mother is not a luxury that one could do without. It was an absolute necessity.

I further told Michael that time was running out for him, because once the children grew older, they would judge both him and Debbie harshly for not having had their mother in their life, especially when she lived just a few hours away. The kids would know they weren't hatched or delivered by a stork. They were going to ask for their mother. Of course, I never would have revealed any of this had Debbie Rowe herself not gone on television, in that strange Michael Jackson response video to Martin Bashir's documentary, and basically said that she had her children for Michael and that her decision to be excised from her children's life is nobody's business. One could make the argument that the well-being of children is everyone's business and she should be strongly encouraged to involve herself in her beautiful children's life, no matter what kind of arrangement she had with Michael.

On the subject of romance and dating, I pushed Michael constantly to be in a relationship, telling him how essential it was that he have a woman in his life. I told him that a good woman would ground him, balance him, and anchor him. Interestingly, he never pulled me off the subject but rather said that it would have to be the right one. I related earlier that when I brought Katie Couric, whom I knew through appearances on the *Today Show* for my books, to meet Michael, he was so impressed that when she left he actually said to me, "You're always bugging me about dating. Now there's the kind of woman I would like to take out." Well, the gauntlet had been thrown.

I have written in my books that the highest kindness one can perform for another is to end their loneliness. Even God served as matchmaker to Adam and Eve. So, while knowing that it might sound ridiculous, I called Katie at her home. "I know this is going to sound nuts to you," I said, "but you did mention to me that you had been widowed, for which I am very sorry. At that meeting you had with Michael, well, he wants to know if you'd like to go out with him for coffee." Katie laughed and said, "Well, Shmuley, I see you don't read the tabloids. I actually have a nice man in my life." I became embarrassed. "Okay, Katie, well, as I take the foot out of my mouth, let me just tell you how happy I am for you that you have a good guy, and why don't we instead do this as a fivesome. You and your boyfriend, me and my wife, Debbie, and Michael, can all go out for coffee." Katie said that would be wonderful and that was that.

But for those who wonder whether Michael has a real interest in women, all I can say is that when we discussed his need to marry, he certainly never said, "Stop being ridiculous." If anything, he told me constantly that his concern was that women only wanted his money and that the ones he met were not very ladylike. Indeed, when Michael spoke at Carnegie Hall at an event we organized to promote parents spending time with children, he even remarked as part of his speech, "Shmuley has been trying to marry me off for some time now." But while most of the conversations I had with Michael on the subject of romance were off the record, there was one evening where he answered my questions on the subject for the purpose of this book.

Shmuley Boteach: You know how children are always making mock weddings. They tell you they have a crush on someone in their class. Children seem naturally romantic. Have you always been romantic?

Michael Jackson: Not on purpose, but not unromantic, I don't think so. You just be yourself.

SB: Children always have this puppy love thing going on, and they have crushes on each other. They're always passing notes in class.

MJ: I think that is so sweet and cute.

SB: Do you like creating romance? Are you a matchmaking kind of person?

MJ: No, I don't do that. I am too shy to do all that stuff. I am a lot like my mother. We used to ask my mother, "Do you kiss Joseph?" She goes, "Don't ask me those questions." We go, "Mother, do you kiss him?" She goes, "I don't want to talk about it." We go, "Well, how did you meet him? Who asked who to get married?" She says, "I don't want to talk about it."

SB: So you were bought up to be shy and modest about things pertaining to love and romance?

MJ: Yes, we don't talk about it.

SB: You have been married twice, Michael. Do you still believe in romance, or have you had some negative experiences and it is therefore more difficult to believe?

MJ: No, I believe in it, but I am shy about it. None of us have invited our parents to our weddings. We don't believe in it. We are too shy. I wouldn't dare in a million years to have my mother at a wedding of mine. I can't have myself walking down the aisle and my mother sitting there. That's why we all ran off and got married secretly and my mother reads it in the paper and she doesn't mind. Because we are just like her. She would have done the same thing.

SB: So love has to be something hidden and concealed?

MJ: It's like private, like mushy stuff.

SB: And mushy stuff is always private?

MJ: Yeah.

SB: Well, I also believe that romantic love thrives through mystery and concealment. But we can't overdo it. Your parents should definitely be at your wedding. So romance is something you believe in but you have been taught to be shy about it?

MJ: I am shy. I don't know how good I am at it because I am shy. I am very different in that way. I have heard guys be really poetic with girls and, "Oh baby, this and that." I am not like that. I am like straight to the point and say it simply.

SB: So what do you do in things like music videos when you're expected to portray romance and do love scenes and things like that?

MJ: That's why it is my job to cast the girl, because it is my job to think they are cute. So I can do it if I really like them, like some of the girls you see in my videos. I have cast them because I really like them and it caused a problem afterwards because they start to really like me, and I don't want to get that serious, and it becomes a problem sometimes.

SB: You probably face this all the time because not only are you famous, but you are the kind of guy who women want to be around—soft, gentle, not afraid to express his emotions. [This was obviously said before Michael's arrest and the torrent of allegations about him that later come out.] Women die for guys who aren't afraid to show vulnerability and softness, whereas a lot of the guys in Hollywood are stereotypically self-absorbed, self-obsessed, and can't commit. So do you often find that this happens, that women get clingy?

MJ: What do you mean?

SB: Like you said, it is supposed to be a professional thing. You just film something with a female costar, but afterwards they become attached.

MJ: Yes, it happens.

SB: How do you break the news to them that you don't reciprocate?

MJ: When they see me running the other way. Yeah. Some of them follow me around the world and it is so hard.

SB: That probably makes them chase you even more because they probably are drawn to that boyish shyness. To be sure, many women like "bad" boys. But for the same reason, a lot like shy guys. In the same way they believe that they can redeem the bad boy and polish up this coarse diamond, they believe the same thing about the shy guy. They think, "Only I can bring him out of his shell." But I guess after a while, with you running halfway around the world from them, they get the message. But you never tell them directly?

MJ: No, because it would hurt them too much.

Crushes and Puppy Love

The morning after I had taken Michael with me to songwriter Denise Rich's semiannual Angel Ball, a black-tie benefit for cancer research, where Michael was the cynosure of all eyes, we sat down to continue our conversation in his hotel suite.

Shmuley Boteach: What did Cindy Crawford want from you last night?

Michael Jackson: I have seen Cindy from afar several times, and she was with other guys, and we have met up at other functions . . . from afar. I think she felt this was her chance to really meet me. She probably admires me. A lot of the people come over. What you saw was nothing.

SB: You have seen celebrities behave like that, like a pack of dogs, chasing after someone who is more famous than them? It was so degrading.

MJ: Yes! It's worse.

SB: What did she talk to you about?

MJ: [Imitating Crawford] "How are you?" I go, "I'm all right." "Oh, you sure you are okay? Oh, I just love your work, and I love what you do. How long are you in town?" I said, "I am working here. I'm recording."

SB: Do you think there was a romantic interest?

MJ: Yeaaah. I kinda think so.

SB: Was she asking you out?

MJ: Those girls flirt. . . they flirt. She is pretty.

SB: It was blatant. A banker who was with us at the table said to me, "Cindy Crawford, when she is up close, she is just another gal." I said, "But what is she doing here?"

MJ: Did you see Donald Trump come over?

SB: Now he is an interesting man.

MJ: A woman I really liked and respected was Princess Diana.

SB: Why?

MJ: Because she was classy and sincerely cared about people and children and the plight of what was going on in the world. She didn't do it for show. I like the way she made her kids wait in line to get on a ride for something.

I had read the same thing, that Princess Diana made her kids wait in line at Disneyworld. That is pretty amazing. I hate waiting in the lines at Disneyworld and if I could use clout to cut them, I probably would. That is a real sign of character and a sincere desire to raise humble rather than entitled kids.

SB: Can we say that there was an ever so innocent slight romantic attraction? Or do you not want to say that? Do you just want to say that you thought she was a very special woman?

MJ: I thought she was very special.

SB: Was she a feminine kind of woman?

MJ: Very feminine and classy. She was my type for sure, and I don't like most girls. There are very few I like who fit the mold. It takes a very special mold to make me happy and she was one of them. For sure.

SB: Because of her love of kids?

MJ: It takes a lot to find a mirror image, a mirror image. People always say that opposites attract and I think that is true, as well. But I want somebody who is a lot like me, who has the same interests and who wants to help and they gotta go to hospitals with me and care about Gavin [Michael's later accuser]. That's why you saw Lisa Marie and me at those kinds of things. She cared about that stuff, too.

SB: Did you ever think of asking Princess Diana out?

MJ: Absolutely.

SB: So why didn't you have the nerve to ask her?

MJ: I have never asked a girl out in my life. They have to ask me.

SB: Really?

MJ: I can't ask a girl out.

SB: If she would have asked you out?

MJ: Absolutely. I would have gone. Brooke Shields asked me out every time you saw us out together. It was her idea to go out and do it every time. I sincerely liked Brooke Shields too. I liked her a lot.

SB: Does she like kids?

MJ: Yes. My first girlfriend, Tatum O'Neal, she'd won the Academy Award for *Paper Moon*. . . I was sixteen, she was thirteen. And was I naïve. She wanted to do everything and I didn't want to have sex at all, because there were a lot of values associated with being a Jehovah's Witness. I said, "Are you crazy?" One of those was to be kind to everyone. When I held Tatum's hand it was just magic, better than anything, kissing her, anything. Her, Ryan O'Neal, and myself went to this club and were watching a band and underneath the table she was holding my hand and I was melting. It was magical. There was fireworks going on. It was all I needed. But that means nothing to kids today. She grew up too fast. She wasn't into innocence, and I love that.

Now Brooke Shields, she was one of the loves of my life. We dated a lot. Her pictures were all over my walls and mirrors. I was at the Academy Awards with Diana Ross and she just came up to me and said, "Hi, I'm Brooke Shields. Are you going to the after party?" I said, "Yeah, and I just melted." I was about twenty-three. . . during *Off the Wall*. I thought, "Does she know [that photographs of her are] all over my room?" So we get to the party and she says, "Would you dance with me?" And we went on the dance floor. And man, we exchanged numbers and I was up all night, spinning around in my room, just so happy. She was classy. We had one encounter when she got real intimate and I chickened out. And I shouldn't have.

Lisa. . . we're still friendly, but she's running around. She just changed her number and we don't have the new one yet.

SB: Can you immediately tell innocence?

MJ: Right away, although I find it harder to tell with women because they're so smooth. But with men, I can usually tell, because they're more open and like puppies, while girls are more like cats. You know how if you've been on vacation and get home and a puppy is all over you, while with a cat, it's, "Hey, I don't need you. You walk over to me and pick me up." They give you attitude. They'll walk right by you even though they haven't seen you in three months. Women are very smart. Walt Disney always said they're smarter than men, and [he] always hired more women.

Thinking About the Perfect Woman

Shmuley Boteach: The same principle of not being overexposed. Would you advise women in relationships to do the same thing? Would you say to people today who get bored of one another, "You know, fifty percent of marriages end in divorce and so much of it is that husbands and wives just get tired of one another. They get weary and bored. Would you say that if there was more mystery, if they learned to hold back and leave room to discover one another, then there would be more adventure in their relationship?

Michael Jackson: Yeah, yeah. I think going away is good. Like they say, "Absence makes the heart grow fonder." I totally believe in it. Going away is really important. I don't understand how people can be together all day with each other and be totally fine. I think it is sweet and beautiful. . .

SB: Have you seen marriages like that?

MJ: I have seen couples, yes. I don't know how they do it. Because creatively they have to do so many things.

SB: So the women you have dated, the ones who were smart enough not to throw themselves at you, were they the ones that you were more interested in, the ones who weren't always available and you had to chase them a bit?

MJ: The ones who were classy and quiet and not into all the sex and all the craziness because I am not into that.

SB: They are the ones that you are more interested in?

MJ: Aha. I don't understand a lot of things that go on in relationships and I don't know if I ever will. I think that is what has hurt me in my relationships because I don't understand how people do some of the things they do.

SB: Mean things?

MJ: Mean things and vulgar things with their bodies. I don't understand it and it has hurt my relationships.

SB: So for you love is something very pure?

MJ: Very pure. It shocked me some of the things.

SB: What was it about Diana, that kind of a woman, her dignity, that kind of innocence? Do you see that often in people where they have a regal bearing to them?

MJ: No, we don't see it and that's what I love. I think she truly cared about people's feelings and really tried to make the world a better place. I really believe that her heart was out for other people. You could see it in some of the photos where she is touching those little baby's faces and they are sitting on her lap and she would be holding them. That is not faked. You could see it. When you see the queen come out she has got these gloves on and she is waving from a distance, you can see the heart. You can see. You put your money where your mouth is and you go in those huts and go in those ditches and sit with them and sleep there. That's doing it, that's what I do. Remember when you said you saw my picture in China in some hut, some lady's hut. I go in there and I touch the people and I see them.

Michael was reading my mind. When I watched the videos of Princess Diana holding disease-ridden children in her arms, it moved me just as much.

SB: When you are in a meeting, are you able to see who is the hard-nosed businessman, bottom line is everything, he'll manipulate, lie, whatever it takes, and the ones who are pure, more innocent, who you want to do business with? Can you see immediately? Or, on the contrary, do you see with a child's eyes and see goodness in everybody, which is why you have sometimes ended up with people who aren't the nicest people?

MJ: That's true, too. It works both ways, but you can detect it and feel it in another person. There is this man in LA and he works in a vinyl record shop and he has got to be in his fifties and he has the spirit of an eleven-year-old boy. I always stare at him and he stares at me and there is like this telepathy going on. He talks like a kid and the way he moves his eyes. I say to myself, "This is so interesting." I'd like to get to know him better and find out what is this. I mean it. It's amazing. I feel it. I feel it in children right away, of course. I pick up on it like that and children can tell it in you.

SB: It's almost like a relief. Here is someone who understands me?

MJ: Yeah. Their eyes light up when you come over and they want to play and they feel it.

SB: Michael, have you never met a woman like that who loves those same things, who'd play hide and seek with you, who'd love the water fights with you?

MJ: Not yet. The ones I have had are jealous of the children. All of them. They get jealous of their own kids and start competing with them. That rubs me in a bad way.

SB: Theoretically, if you were Adam in the Garden of Eden and you found an Eve like that, would that be your ideal woman?

MJ: Absolutely. I haven't found it [women who want to play]. . . I think more guys are more apt to goof off. Even when they are much older, their thirties, and a woman will come in and say, "What are you doing? Don't do that. Are you crazy?" The guy will go, "What, we are just having fun?"

SB: Women almost feel that it is immature if they behave that way, no?

MJ: Yes, but if you look in history you never see real serial killer women.

SB: Yes, but they don't play the way boys do.

MJ: I know they don't.

SB: Even at a younger age they are playing with dolls and they are marrying Barbie and Ken. In other words, the quintessential thing is that if boys are shooting spit balls at each other, the girls will say, "Stop doing that." Even then they want to be older. It is almost against their gender. Have you ever found girls who like the practical jokes that you like? Have you ever found a woman who collects comics?

MJ: It is a rarity. If I find one I will go nuts. Especially, if she has those qualities and is beautiful inside. It would be a home run for me. That's why guys hang out. Because they can do that.

SB: Thinking about mothers and fathers, mothers are really good at doing homework with their kids and being more nurturing. But the rough playing is what the fathers do. They get on the floor and get dirty, wrestle, build castles with them in a sandpit. Isn't that interesting? It creates an imbalance in the book to an extent. On the contrary, it is the girls in school that are always ridiculing the boys for being immature. "Look at those boys. Look at the way they are behaving." Maybe the women need to be taught the art of playfulness as much as the men.

MJ: Do you not think it's embedded in them biologically? Biologically, as a breed, don't you think women are just a different species?

SB: They are definitely different, but the question is, "Why don't they want to play?" The funny thing is this: when they play, it's when they flirt. In other words, if you chase them round the room and there is something romantic going on, then they will run around with you and laugh and giggle. But it's specifically when it is romantic. They don't do it with each other. You don't see two girls running round the room, playing hide and seek or wrestling each other, the way they're prepared to suddenly when it's a boyfriend. A lot of fans—the women who are interested in you—would do all these things just to make you happy. But you don't know if they were doing it because they are really enjoying it. It seems that it's only romance that makes women playful. But then, sometimes it bothers men, because the women become like a tease and, you know, they have this power over you with these little games they play. I have got to find four or five women who fit into this opening chapter who are very successful but who have retained child-like qualities and, so far, we have come up with one. When you think of Bill Clinton don't you think of a guy as being pretty playful? He goes to McDonald's and he jogs and. . .

MJ: Riding his bike at the White House. Did you see it? He was riding his bike in the White House to get him to the next meeting. A great shot of him in *Vanity Fair*. Can you think of Hillary doing that? Nope, not in a million years. I can think of little girls who would join in with play. Girls who are tomboys.

SB: Okay, when they are tomboys. But when they get older, do they still play to the same extent?

MJ: Do you think it is in their heart that they can just be themselves and be dignified?

SB: What women seem to look forward to more than anything else is falling in love. They don't look forward to the playfulness in the same way. But once they're in love a carefree playful side is released.

MJ: I have to play.

SB: Is there a difference in how your male fans and female fans relate to you?

MJ: Sometimes. But I am finding today, and it is so true, that guys today are really changing and I have watched it happen through my career. Guys scream with the same kind of adulation that girls do in a lot of countries. They are not ashamed. They are shaking, "I love you." We have guys chasing us around.

SB: But the fanatics are the women.

MJ: Yeah, they are loyal, women. They have been loyal. They are activists. They will fight you about me.

Motherly Figures

Shmuley Boteach: Do you find it easier to be closer to motherly figures in your life like Elizabeth Taylor, your own mother, who you always praise, and your sister Janet? Do you find that women are more child-like than men? Are they gentler, are they less competitive, less mean? You have been around some mean women, as well, who behave in a masculine-aggressive way, like Madonna. You told me that she can be mean. Is that a feminine trait or do you feel that she has a real masculine streak in her? Do you find it easier to be closer to women?

Michael Jackson: In some ways, yes, and some ways, not. It depends on the age. I have seen some women who are very bitter and mean and they become ladies later. They come into their own and they become good people. I have seen it in my brothers' ex-wives who were horrible. They were like nightmares when they were young. With time and age they become good people. But they were horrible, just horrible. Then with time they just level out, that's what I like when they become truly good.

SB: But, intuitively, do you find women easier to get along with? Are they softer than men? I mean, I personally find women more naturally nurturing, more refined, possessed of a greater nobility of spirit, I have to tell you.

MJ: I am trying to be real honest with you.

SB: But many of your closest friends seem to be women.

MJ: Women are softer than men. Yeah, that's true.

SB: Do you think that a child star as cute as Shirley Temple, do you think a boy star could be that cute?

MJ: Yeah, but he wouldn't have the same. . . Shirley Temple just had something that was meant to give us bliss and make us smile.

SB: Are you more protective of Paris because she is a little girl?

MJ: Paris can stand [on] her own sometimes much more. Prince won't stand up for himself. People can push him about and he won't stand up. She won't take anything from anybody. She fights. She's tough, very tough. It's true, man. Prince will let people take complete advantage of him and won't say anything.

SB: He is more like his father, like you.

MJ: I was like that. My mother always told me, "Don't let people hurt you. You are too much like me." She would cry, "You are too much like me. I don't want you to be like me. I hurt so much." Because people take advantage.

SB: But you never toughened up. It seems that you would rather be taken advantage of than do the taking advantage of. It hurts to be taken advantage of. But it doesn't hurt as much as being a mean and aggressive person. Mean-spiritedness is a form of internal corruption and it makes it impossible to be happy. Notice that evil people never seem happy. They are miserable and they seek to make other people just as miserable as they are.

MJ: Yeah, I'd rather suffer. I hate to say it because I have suffered a lot. God, have I suffered. But I would rather suffer.

SB: You have seen the ugly side of people.

MJ: I have seen the worst. . . the nightmare of the human condition, the human soul. I would never even think that common man would be capable of behaving in such a way.

Oblivious of his own similar behavior until the bitter end, Michael, unfortunately, could give as good as he got. He ran around in a double-decker bus, specially rented for the occasion, to call his friend Tommy Mattola, the head of Sony music, the devil. Unfortunately, he could be quite blind to his own shortcomings.

SB: Children never did that to you, Michael. You never saw the ugly side of them? Unless they were influenced by their parents.

MJ: Unless you see a bunch of kids together and they are picking on each other and just to impress each other that they had a bad up-bringing. If I were to raise the kids to do some of the things that you hear about in the news, they would be totally different kids. They wouldn't conceive of doing such a thing. If I was raised in Jamaica I would have a different accent. If I was an English kid I wouldn't . . . it is all about environment. But genetics plays a big deal and teaching and holding and touching and looking in your eyes and saying, "I love you, I need you, you're here because I love you. I bought you this because I love you." Like I say to Prince and Paris, "You know why I bought you this?" They say, "Because you love me." I say, "Yes, that's why I bought it." They need to know that. I wish I could have heard that more. My mother is great. She is a saint. She is a real saint.

PART 6

ROMANTIC RELATIONSHIPS AND GETTING HURT

Women and Trust—
Lisa Marie Presley and His Brothers' Wives

Shmuley Boteach: How do you feel about men who are not faithful to their wives?

Michael Jackson: I don't think it is good. But I understand it. I know that is a strange answer.

SB: You find women fall in love with you all the time as this megastar, so you don't judge men who are unfaithful, because sometimes you'll ascribe it to women who make themselves available?

MJ: I don't judge them because women can do some things that make guys very unhappy. I have seen it with my brothers. I have seen my brothers crying, in tears and pulling the grass out of the lawn with frustration because of their wives.

SB: Do you think a lot of their wives were more interested in their success than in them?

MJ: Absolutely. They were after their money. That's why I said to myself that I would never be married. I held out the longest. I stayed at home until I was twenty-seven, twenty-eight.

SB: So was part of the attraction to Lisa Marie that she had her own money and her own fame and you didn't have to be anxious that she was interested in you for the wrong reasons?

MJ: Absolutely, and she didn't take a penny [when we got divorced]. She didn't want anything. She makes about a million dollars a year from Elvis memorabilia and selling all that stuff and she has her own thing. She is not here to take, you know.

Michael always spoke with affection and respect for Lisa Marie Presley, with the one exception when he told me that she had wanted him to get involved with Scientology and got pushy. He had to tell her that he had no interest in becoming a Scientologist. Michael was dismissive of Scientology and spoke of how the practices of Scientologists that he had been exposed to were not sufficiently spiritual or substantive for him.

SB: So that means there was almost like one girl in the whole world that you could marry because even a rich woman would want your name. You needed someone with money *and* a name. You were down to a Presley or a McCartney or something like that.

MJ: I know. Lisa was great. She was a sweet person. But it is hard to tie me down. I can't stay in one place one time so that's why I don't know if I [can] really be completely married all the time.

SB: Did you want to be a father to her kids?

MJ: Yes.

SB: Do you still stay in touch with the children?

MJ: Yes, and with her.

SB: But marriage is too confining?

MJ: Yes. I don't know whether I am disciplined enough because I am such a rolling stone. I have such a life when I am always on the move and women don't like that. They want you to be settled in one place all the time but I have to move. I have been in the same city as where my house is and I'll check into a hotel just to feel like I am going somewhere. My house is right there. I guess I am just moving all the time, moving.

At the entrance to Michael's home in Neverland, there were large suitcases that were permanently packed and always ready to go. In the same way that some people buy two of everything—one for the primary home, and one for the weekend home—Michael had a version of that, only the spare things were permanently in the suitcases. He explained to me that he travels so much that he doesn't see the point in ever packing or unpacking. The things in the suitcases never came out.

SB: You have gotten used to it. That's your lifestyle.

MJ: I love being on the move, love it.

SB: It impresses me that everywhere you go you take your children with you. So you are on the move but it is almost like your household moves with you. Prince and Paris aren't unsettled because of it because their source of security is always with them. But what about the families who don't have the resources for that, and most don't? They don't have enough to be able to fly the kids around here and there. Businessmen who have to travel, they fly economy just to afford their own fare, and they can't possibly bring their kids along every time. Should they not travel?

MJ: I feel bad for their children. I feel bad for their children. I always ask pilots and stewards how do they do it? The children suffer. Absolutely. They suffer.

SB: You wouldn't be doing this if Prince and Paris were going to suffer as a result. You are doing it because you have the resources to bring them where you are.

MJ: I couldn't hurt them like that.

SB: Do you want to find them a Rose Fine kind of figure, a bit of a motherhood figure?

Rose Fine had appeared in our earlier conversations. She was Michael's and his siblings' childhood tutor and surrogate mother.

MJ: That would be nice. That would be sweet. If the person is completely sincere like Miss Fine was, who would read to them and teach them and give them the right values and teach them that there's no difference and that we are all the same people. She used to always rub my face and I never used to understand why. She used to say I had beautiful hands. And I used to say, "Why, don't all hands look alike?" But now I see what she means because now I do it to my kids. I rub their face like that because they are so sweet. [Laughs] I never understood why she did it to me. Then you grow up and you realize that it is an endearing thing to do, to say, "I love you."

In truth Prince and Paris had a surrogate mother in their impressive and devoted governess, Grace, a polished, highly intelligent and very dedicated woman from Rwanda.

Celebrity Relationships Gone Wrong—
Madonna and Others

I asked Michael about his celebrity friends. Why could he connect with them more than noncelebrities?

Michael Jackson: Yeah, but I don't really have Hollywood friends. I have a few.

Shmuley Boteach: Why don't you? Why don't you hang out with more celebrities?

MJ: Because I don't think they are all real people. They love the limelight and I don't have anything in common with them. They want to go clubbing and afterwards they want to sit around and drink hard liquor and do marijuana and do all kinds of crazy things that I wouldn't do. We have nothing in common. Remember the line I told you? Madonna laid the law down to me before we went out. "I am *not* going to Disneyland, okay? That's out." I said, "But I didn't ask you to go to Disneyland." She said, "We are going to the restaurant and afterwards we are going to a strip bar." I said, "I am not going to a strip bar." Guys who cross-dress! Afterwards she wrote some mean things about me in the press and I wrote that she is a nasty witch, after I was so kind to her. I have told you that we were at the table eating and some little kids came up. "Oh my God, Michael Jackson and Madonna. Can we have your autograph?" She said, "Get out of here. Leave us alone." I said, "Don't ever talk to children like that." She said, "Shut up." I said, "You shut up." That's how we were. Then we went out again and went to the Academy Awards and she is not a nice person. I have to say it. She is not a nice person.

SB: Did the people around you feel that it was important to be seen with her?

MJ: They knew nothing about it. This was totally between her and me.

SB: So you gave it a chance and it didn't work?

MJ: Yeah, I gave it a chance like I try and give everything a chance.

SB: You basically saw that your values do not match those of most Hollywood people.

MJ: No, they do lots of crazy things that I am not into and at the time I was with Madonna she was into these books, a whole library of books of women who were tied to walls. She said, "I love spanky books." Why do I want to see that?

SB: I think a lot of it is the image. She once said something to the effect that she would much rather read a good book than have sex. I think the other vulgar stuff is part of the outrageous image she tries to cultivate.

MJ: She's lying [about preferring to read a book]. I can't judge. I don't know if she has changed or if she [is] trying to claim she has changed.

SB: Why does she say mean things?

My own belief is that Madonna had changed. A devotee of Kabbala, she has brought many elements of Judaism into her life, has taken a Hebrew name, and has discarded her raunchy image. She also seems to be a very devoted and loving mother.

MJ: I think she likes shock value and she knows how to push buttons on people. I think she was sincerely in love with me and I was not in love with her. She did a lot of crazy things and that's how that went. I knew we had nothing in common. But I am pretty sure that having a baby has to change you. I don't know how much she has changed. I'm sure she is a better person than before.

SB: She has two children now.

MJ: Yeah, I know. How would you like getting a phone call and she is telling you that she is putting her fingers between her legs. I would say, "Oh Madonna, please." She said, "What I want you to do when I hang up the phone is to rub yourself and think of me." That's the kind of stuff she says. She does. When I see her she says, "This is the finger I used last night." Wild, out of control.

SB: But you were raised that all things romantic should have a certain modesty. . . the values you were raised with are very similar to core Jewish values. That kind of thing that Madonna was saying is only shocking at first. Then it quickly becomes humdrum and boring. That's why she has to push the envelope and become more and more shocking just to sustain our interest in her. When people have their breasts out the whole time then you stop looking. Do you see that as vulgar?

MJ: What she does? Absolutely. She is not sexy at all. I think sexy comes from the heart in the way you present yourself.

SB: Have you ever found women who are a bit more modest to be more attractive for that reason?

MJ: Yeah. I don't like the women who are always saying, "My nails need to be done. I have to do my toes. I need a manicure." I hate all that. I like it when girls are a little bit more tomboyish. If they wrestle, climb a tree. . . I love that. It is sexier to me. I like class, though. Class is everything.

SB: If a woman walks round with all her cleavage showing. . .

MJ: Frank *loves* it.

Michael gestured to Frank Cascio, who was sitting right next to us. We all laughed.

SB: A man might want to have sex with a woman like that. But it doesn't mean he would want to fall in love with a woman like that.

MJ: Of course you want to look. I am in love with innocence and I tell Frank that.

SB: Have you met women who have that innocence or by and large would you say that this generation is cultivating women who are not innocent, who are not encouraged to preserve their innocence?

MJ: I wish they were.

SB: Celebrities are targets for people who marry them for the wrong reasons, their fortune and their name. But don't you know when someone is interested in you for the wrong reason?

MJ: You don't know.

SB: The ancient rabbis said that words that emanate from the heart penetrate the heart. That sincerity cannot be faked. You can't tell when someone is faking it and is full of it?

MJ: It is hard because the women today can do a good job of faking it. I mean a real good job. They are so smooth. Look in the Bible. Women have taken the most powerful men down to nothing because of what is between their legs. Samson, nobody could cut his hair, and he had sex with Delilah.

SB: Monica Lewinsky and Clinton. . . what everyone overlooks is that she went after him, which doesn't excuse Clinton, but she's not off the hook either.

MJ: Didn't I say that the other day? One woman did so much pain to this president. How much can a woman do to try and hurt a president? Look what she caused, and that's why I don't like Barbara Walters because she instigated a lot of it. She made it all on television. She tried to come here today and I cancelled it.

Michael's view of women was shaped by his childhood experiences—which were not childlike at all. I believe this negative image of women has unfortunately remained with Michael and may account for why there were very few women in his inner circle. Michael saw women as catty, fomenting jealousy between men, as he believed his sisters-in-law did between The Jackson 5. Women, to Michael's mind, could be sleazy. They were materialistic and more interested in Michael's money than in him. Of course, this misogynistic view, for which Michael may not be to blame, is wildly offensive. But it speaks volumes of the kind of people—and perhaps the kind of women—Michael had drawn to him in the past and how it had scarred him in the present.

But there is something more. As I noted earlier, there can indeed be a connection between these prurient sexual scenes that Michael witnessed as a small and impressionable child and what many believe to be his adolescent sexual interests. It could well be that at that vulnerable age Michael developed an impression of adult sexuality as manipulative and squalid, and searched, in his own broken way, to find a carnality that was much more innocent. Of course, conjecture in this regard is not always helpful. What is certain, however, is that children are scarred by exposure to adult sexuality that they are not equipped to handle.

MJ: I don't like clubs now, I did all that when I was eleven, eight and going back—nine, eight, seven, six. Fights break out, people throwing up, yelling, screaming, the police sirens. Our father never let us become a part of it other than to perform and leave. But sometimes in having to do that you would get caught up in some of the craziness. I saw it all. The lady who came on right before, when The Jackson's were little, "And now next, The Little Jackson 5," was the lady who took off *all* her clothes. Threw her panties into the audience and the men would grab them and sniff them. I saw all this. Her name was Rose Marie and she put these things on her breasts and moved them around and she showed everything. So when I became sixteen, seventeen and guys would say, "Let's go clubbing," I would go, "Are you crazy?" And the guys would be like, "No, are *you* crazy? We can get girls, we can get liquor." But I had done that. I did that when I was a baby. Now I want to be a part of the world and the life I didn't have. Take me to Disneyland, take me to where the magic is.

Loneliness, Wanting Children, and Lisa Marie Presley's Second Thoughts

Shmuley Boteach: Let me ask you about loneliness. So wherever you travel, you, thank God, have an entourage. People you've been with for a long time, Frank and Skip [Michael's bodyguard at the time, a very pleasant and decent man from New Orleans]. But it's still not like having a wife in your life or something. Do you get lonely? Or is there so much going on in your life that it doesn't really happen?

Michael Jackson: Like lonely for like a wife? For like a mate? Like that?

SB: Yeah.

MJ: I've been through two bad divorces and I just got out of the second one. Even when married to those women that I was married to, I'd go to bed hurting. I was hurting. I was crying last night as I went to sleep and I didn't sleep good last night. And I cry, Shmuley, because I feel this. . . and I'm not trying, I'm telling you the honest truth and if you don't believe me you can ask Frank. Frank knew how I was hurting. I just was feeling all the pain of the children who suffer and I was hurting so much. That's why I was trying to reach any child I knew who had pain, from [Michael mentions a little girl who was battling cancer and whose family he met at our home] to Gavin [Michael's later accuser]. I was trying to like, calling, dialing and I woke up the first thing, the first person I called was [the little girl's] house and she had gone already. It hurts me. But I think that's where my real love comes from, Shmuley. If I can help in that way, I'm fine and I don't need the other [romantic love]. You know if I meet some girl somewhere and I think she's beautiful, which I see a lot of them, that's great. I mean, I'll go on a date or something. Nothing wrong with that. Jennifer Lopez looked awfully good the other day, she did. I was shocked 'cause I never thought. . . She looked good [Michael laughs as he says this].

SB: But have you given up on women understanding you? You tend to think that children will understand you a lot better?

MJ: I'm not easy to live with in that way for a wife. I'm not easy and I know I'm not easy. Because I give all my time to someone else. I give it to children, I give it to somebody sick somewhere, to the music. And women want to be the center. And I remember Lisa Marie would always say to me, "I'm not a piece of furniture, I'm not a piece of furniture. You just can't . . ." I say, "I don't want you to be a piece of furniture," and, you know, there'd be some sick little girls calling on the phone and she'd get mad and hang up on them. And, you know, I feel that's my, that's my mission, Shmuley. I have to do it.

SB: What if you found a woman who was that soft, who was incredibly soft?

MJ: Like a Mother Teresa or a Lady Diana or. . . That would be great. It would be perfect.

SB: Would that be better than having to do it on your own?

MJ: Absolutely, and Lisa was great with going to the hospitals with me, and she was so sweet about that. They would tie the babies to the bed or chain the children down. We'd go unchain. . . we'd go free all these babies. I hated that and she, she discovered a lot of that injustice with me. Countries like Romania and Prague, Czechoslovakia and all that, Russia. You should see what they do to the children in those. . . you'd be shocked. They chain them to the wall like they're animals and they're naked and they slept in their tinkle and their feces too. It's just so sad, it made me sick. So we brought clothes and toys and just love and love. I love them and I went back every day visiting them, hugging them, wanting to take each and every one of them to Neverland.

SB: When you started becoming this childhood star, did you realize that your childhood was slowly slipping away? You won a contest at age eight. In 1964, you were chosen as lead singer for the family band. Did that make you feel excited or were you worried? Did you think to yourself, "Where is all this headed? What's it going to lead to?"

MJ: I didn't think about it. I didn't think about the future. I just took each day as it came. I knew I wanted to be a star. I wanted to do things and make people happy.

SB: Did you know what the cost was going to be in terms of childhood?

MJ: No way. No way.

The phone rings. Michael talks to the president of Sony Records, Tommy Matolla, who has invited Michael to his wedding. Michael says he wants to sit musicians with him so he can throw peanuts at Tommy. I think to myself, "Michael's playfulness never ends."

MJ on phone: Tell the guys to let the music talk to them and not to, like, jump on it right away. Listen to it a couple of times and let the melody create itself. That's the thing, let the music speak to them. Alright? Goodbye.

SB: Is that your dream that one day, like part of the messianic future, as far as you're concerned, that all these kids will come and live in Neverland and live happily ever after?

MJ: Yes.

SB: And if you had the resources truly you would just. . .

MJ: I would do it, Shmuley. I would do it. I would love it.

SB: Lisa Marie was good about at least visiting. So she had no problem going and doing some of the compassionate things of giving these children love and making them feel special?

MJ: She had no problem doing that but her and I had several big arguments 'cause she's very territorial with her children. Her children were [her major concern]. . . and I said, "No, all children are our children," and she never liked that coming from me. She was very angry about that. Plus, she had a fight with me one time when two little boys in London killed this other kid and I was going to visit them 'cause the queen gave them adult sentencing of life. These were like eleven- and ten-year-old boys and I was going to go to the prison and visit them. She said, "You idiot. You're just rewarding them for what they did." I said, "How dare you say that." I said, "I bet if you trace their life you can find they didn't have parents around, they didn't have any love, nobody there to hold them look in their eyes and say, "I love you." They deserve that, even though they're going to get life, I just want to say I love you and hold them." She said, "We'll, you're wrong." I said, "No, you're wrong." Then the information came out that they came from broken families, were never watched as little kids, attended to. Their pacifier was those *Chucky* movies with the stabbings and the killings. And that's how they became conditioned to that.

SB: Did she admit then that you had a point?

MJ: Nope, she thinks I'm rewarding bad kids.

SB: Did she want you to be a father to her children?

MJ: Well that was once asked of her. She was asked that question on TV and she said, "No, they have a father. Their father is Keogh," that other guy. But I was really good to her children. Every day I'd bring them home something and they'd be waiting by the window for me and hug me. I love them. I miss them so much.

SB: Did she get used to living in Neverland or was it too isolated?

MJ: Lisa didn't live at Neverland. We visited Neverland the way. . . I lived at her house in the city and every once in a while we visited Neverland. It'd be like our big fun weekend.

SB: And her children liked it?

MJ: Are you kidding me? They were like in heaven.

SB: And you were happy to show it to them?

MJ: Mm hmm.

SB: Did it have more meaning to you suddenly when you had a family you could show it to?

MJ: Yes, yes. It's just a place to make families, to bring them together, to bring people together through love and playful spirit and nature. It makes families closer, Neverland. It's healing.

SB: Since you idolize the family was it very hard for you when you had to go through that divorce then?

MJ: Which one?

SB: With Lisa.

MJ: Was it hard for me?

SB: Did you see the writing on the wall? That you were different? Meaning my parents divorced when I was eight. So I really, really romanticized marriage.

MJ: Really?

SB: Oh phenomenally. It's what all my books are about, marriage. Because I couldn't deal with. . .

MJ: So you really believe in marriage and all that? You love marriage?

SB: It's what I believe most in the whole world. I believe in family, I really do.

MJ: I do too, Shmuley.

SB: It's what I didn't have. I even wrote about you in one of my books in the context of marriage, even though it was before I ever thought we'd meet. This was the main point, this was the beginning of the book. Chapter one, the very first chapter. How does it start? "At the heart of all our lives is a strong and potent mystery. Michael Jackson steps off an airplane and thirty thousand fans await his arrival. He feels mighty special. They all excitedly shout his name. They've taken off time from their work to greet and cheer his arrival. But then off the same airplane steps Mr. Jones. There aren't thirty thousand people waiting for him to disembark. In fact, there is only one woman, Mrs. Jones, who's been waiting. But while everyone walks by, even when Michael Jackson himself walks by, she ignores them all. To her Mr. Jones is even more important, more thrilling than the world's biggest pop star."

I used you as the ultimate example of how marriage makes one person into a celebrity. In other words to my wife, I'm a celebrity. She waits for me to come home, she has a picture of me up on the wall, you know? You feel special to one person. And in life all you need is one real fan.

MJ: That's right.

SB: And the secret to life is you don't need thirty thousand, a hundred thousand. You have that, Michael. But you can count on one hand the people who have that in the world. But the idea with marriage is you get one fan. One big fan who puts you first. And that's all you need. One sincere and loving fan who loves you for who you are, rather than tens of thousands of people who love you for what you do. That was the first thought in the most important book I ever wrote, *Kosher Sex*.

MJ: It's beautiful, Shmuley. Thank you.

SB: I never knew I'd meet you back then, but I've been talking about this. Your name has come up in every lecture around the world on the subject. In other words, my whole point was, marriage is where you make one person feel like they're a superstar like Michael Jackson.

MJ: That's beautiful.

SB: But I'm a big believer in marriage. So when your relationship with Lisa started to fall apart was it very hard? Your idealism about the family, everything you believed in building the intimate family you always wanted, especially because you knew. . .

MJ: I wanted children and she didn't.

SB: She felt she had her kids.

MJ: Yeah, and she promised me that before we married, that would be the first thing we'd do was have children. So I was brokenhearted and I walked around all the time holding these little baby dolls and I'd be crying, that's how badly I wanted them. So I was determined to have children. It disappointed me that she wouldn't keep her promise to me, you know? After we got divorced she would hang out with my mother all the time. I have all these letters saying, "I'll give you nine children. I'll do whatever you want," and of course the press don't know all these stories and she just tried for months and months and I just became too hard-hearted at that point. I closed my mind on the whole situation.

SB: So she thought maybe you could get back together?

MJ: Uh huh.

SB: But children were a major, major issue?

MJ: Of course.

SB: She had the kids and that was it.

MJ: She had hers and I wanted us to feel like we all were one big family and have more. Just. . . my dream is to have nine or ten children, that's what I want.

SB: You're still very young. Do you think that will happen?

MJ: Yeah.

SB: But then it means getting married again.

MJ: Yeah.

SB: Are you happy to do that?

MJ: Uh huh. . . or adopt.

SB: Is it possible Michael, that you're attracting the wrong kind of girl because of your celebrity?

MJ: It's hard. That's why it's hard, it's hard for me. It is hard. It's not easy for celebrities to be married.

SB: Do you think that you could only really marry celebrities so that they don't need you as much?

MJ: That helps, in my opinion. And they understand what you go through. They've been there.

SB: They help you for the right reasons, then?

MJ: Yeah, they're not after, you know? What you've made [the money] or, you know? [singing] "That's what you are. . . " [He won a Grammy for that.]

SB: Right, right.

PART 7

FRIENDSHIP WITH CHILD STARS

Looking for True Friendship

Michael was adamant that the only people in the world who could understand him were fellow childhood stars. Only they knew what it felt like to be robbed of the most magical period of life. Only they knew the loneliness, isolation—the imprisonment—that stardom brought. He often spoke to me of his dream of creating a museum of childhood stars at Neverland that would chart both their triumphs and their falls.

Shmuley Boteach: Love and fear, as I said, are antithetical. They are like fire and water. The more of the former, the less of the latter. The more valuable you feel, the less you fear your destruction. The more love you have in your life, the less room there is for fear.

Michael Jackson: That's right. I used to walk the street asking for people to be my friend. It's true, in Encino right down there. People would look at me and go, "Michael Jackson!" I just wanted to talk to somebody. I was up there alone in the house and my mother and father were downstairs watching television. And I was up in my old room and all my brothers and stuff had moved out because they were married and stuff, and I was up there all alone and you can't go anywhere. You feel like a prisoner and you feel like you are going to die. And that's it. I am walking and I would just go walking down the street and traffic would get backed up and people would be taking pictures. I knew I looked sad and some people would come up and talk, and they would go, "What are you doing?" I'd go, "I am walking." They'd go, "Why are you walking? Where are all the guards?" I said, "I don't feel like all that. I just want to walk and I am looking for someone to talk to me." So they would talk to me. I've done that many times. I'd ask people to be my friend and they'd say, "Sure." It's true. I'd go to the parks. Then I realized that that could be dangerous too, but I was hurting that much.

SB: Were they intimidated when you asked them to be your friend? Did they say, "I can't be your friend. . . you are Michael Jackson?"

MJ: I would even ask for their phone numbers. Then I realized it is hard to find a friend because they are befriending you as the thing that they see. Are they a *real* friend? So it became difficult.

SB: But you have found some real friends like Elizabeth Taylor.

MJ: Yes.

Michael and Shirley Temple Black: Kindred Spirits

Michael had just gone to meet Shirley Temple Black, for the first time, at her home in San Francisco. He was very excited when he got back, and we discussed what such visits with fellow childhood stars meant to him, which proved to be a sensitive subject.

Shmuley Boteach: We were talking about Shirley Temple Black. She said to you that in you she found a kindred spirit because you were a child star and she was a child star?

Michael Jackson: Absolutely.

SB: So you arranged to go and see her?

MJ: Well, a good friend of hers is a good friend of mine. I have known this guy for twenty-five years, and he is such a nut. [Michael is referring to producer/promoter David Guest, best known, outside Hollywood, for marrying, then divorcing, Liza Minnelli.] But he has become a real powerful person because he produces a lot of shows and does all these celebrity events, and he is a great guy. So I went up there with him. We also went to the Memorabilia Convention a lot because I love movie memorabilia. I was in disguise there every day but I think they knew it was me. But it was fun. I had a great time with Shirley Temple.

SB: How long did you spend with her?

MJ: We spent several hours. I went to her house. I left there feeling baptized, I really did. I didn't know that I would break down crying when I saw her and I just broke down. I said, "You don't know how you've saved my life." She goes, "What do you mean?" I said, "So many times I have been at the end of my rope and I have felt like throwing in the towel and I just look at your picture and I feel there's hope and I can survive this." She said, "Really?" And I said, "Yeah."

I [used to have] a guy who would travel with me. His job was that before I got to every hotel, [he] was to set up the whole hotel room to Shirley Temple. I would do this for many, many years. All her pictures and cut-outs, that was what he did. So that when I walked in I would see her. I would have her taped to my mirror backstage. She was so happy. She said, "I love you, I want us to be closer." She said, "I want you to call me, you understand me?" She looked at me and said, "I'm sorry I grew up." I said, "You are not to apologize, because I know what it is like, I have been there."

There was a time I was in an airport—and I will never forget this as long as I live—and there was this lady who said, "Oh, The Jackson 5. Oh my God! Where's little Michael? Where's little Michael?" I go, "Here I am." She went, "Urhhhg! What happened?" They want you to stay young and little forever. You go through that awkward stage and they want to keep you small. She [Shirley Temple] had it bad because not only did she go through the stage, it was the end of her film career. But I have graduated to other things. Most of the child stars don't make it because they become self-destructive. They destroy themselves because of that pressure.

SB: What's the pressure?

MJ: The pressure is that they were so loved and liked and they reached an age when studios don't want them anymore. The public [doesn't] recognize them anymore. They are a has-been. A lot of them don't make it past eighteen or nineteen, or in their twenties. . . that's the truth—like all the *Our Gang* kids. Bobby Driscoll who played *So Dear to My Heart*, *Song of the South*, died at eighteen. All these people and you trace their lives and it's the same thing, and it's tough.

SB: Did you discuss that with her?

MJ: Yes. We discussed it.

SB: How did she transition from being a huge star to getting older and not being cute anymore?

MJ: She said she was very strong and it was real hard and she cried a lot. And you do cry a lot. I cried a hell of a lot. She was just real strong with it, and it is hard. She is writing another book. She has done one. She is doing another. Her first was called *Child Star*. I haven't read it. I am not ready for it.

SB: Do you feel that she is one of the few people who understand you because you had no childhood and she had no childhood?

MJ: I said to her, "Did you enjoy it?" She said she loved it and I said, "I loved it too." I loved being on stage and I loved performing, but there are those like Judy Garland who were pushed out there, who didn't want to do it, and that got really tough. Elizabeth made it through. She has been to hell and back and she was a child star, and that's why we understand each other so much. We really do.

SB: Are all child stars like you? Do they all love children?

MJ: They all love children, they all do. They have these playful things around them and they act like kids because they never got a chance to be kids. They all have this fun stuff in their house and nobody understands it. There has never been a book written about it because there are very few of us who have made it and can talk about it. It's not easy. . . it's really not easy.

SB: So you feel confident being around her? You said you felt baptized. Do you feel redeemed being in her presence?

MJ: Mmmm, yeah. [He starts crying.] I don't know if you understand.

SB: To be honest I don't completely, but I want to.

MJ: You really don't, do you?

SB: I have been trying. Just explain to me where does the pain come from? Can you explain it, or when you are around Shirley you don't have to. She just understands?

MJ: It's like telepathy. You can feel each other speak and look into one another's eyes and I feel her and she feels me that way. You pick it up and you detect it so fast. It is like communicating silently. It really is and I knew I would feel that way when I saw her, I knew it. It's the same with Elizabeth [Taylor].

SB: What's the source of your pain, Michael? When you break down like that, what is hurting?

MJ: What is hurting is that it all happened so fast and time has gone by so fast. You feel you missed a lot of things. I wouldn't redo any of it. But the pain comes from the fact that you didn't really get the chance to do important simple things and that hurt. Simple little things, like you don't know. . . I never did birthdays or Christmases or sleepovers or none of that simple, fun stuff. Or going into a shopping market and just grabbing something off the counter, you know all those simple things like going out in society and being normal.

SB: So the whole world dreams about being in front of one hundred thousand people at a concert and you're dreaming about the little things that everyone else gets to do?

MJ: That's why when I befriend people it's usually not the celebrities, it's usually the simple normal family somewhere. I want to know what their life is like. That's why I went to that hut in China or going to some of the mud houses in South America. I want to know what it is like. I have slept in crazy places where people say, "Are you nuts?" And I say, "No, I want to know what it's like."

SB: What do you feel that you have missed? Do you feel that you missed out on something essential to life? It is almost like in your childhood you can just be loved without having to prove yourself. Is that what you miss? That you always had to work, to prove yourself, you could never just be? You had to be evaluated, judged, stared at. You were a curiosity item?

MJ: Yes, and you get tired and it just wears me down. You can't go somewhere where they don't manipulate what you do and say, that bothers me so much, and you are nothing like the person that they write about, nothing. To get called "Whacko," that's not nice. People think something is wrong with you because they make it up. I am nothing like that. I am the opposite of that.

SB: Someone once said that the essence of loneliness is to feel that you are not understood. Do you get lonely in the place you're at for that reason?

MJ: Yes, of course.

SB: You are there all by yourself, and you feel moved when you are with someone like Shirley Temple because she is in that same lonely place?

MJ: Yes, she gets it. And you can talk to her. It is hard to make other people understand it because they haven't been there. You have to feel it, you have to touch it, to know what it is really like.

SB: Did Shirley Temple Black retain her child-like qualities the way you have? Is she playful, or did it take you to bring that out in her?

MJ: It was just there, she came to the door with her apron on. She was cooking in the kitchen and after we ate, she kept touching my hand at the table and rubbing it, as if she knows what to do, do you know what I mean? Afterwards we sat at the table and we talked, we just sat and talked. I was looking at these wonderful pictures. She had each movie that she has ever made in picturesque form in this bookcase and they are originals by [George] Hurrell, the great photographer, and you go through these things and it is amazing. She had every dress she has ever worn in the movies. She has everything. I promised her I will do a museum for child stars and she [will] give all her stuff to the museum and I would get other stuff, all the pictures, everything, to honor child stars. People don't know what happened to them. I don't think people know that Bobby Driscoll went missing for about a year and nobody recognized him. His own family didn't know that he was the one in the pauper's grave with a heroin overdose. He was a Disney giant, the voice of Peter Pan. He played in *So Dear to My Heart*. He won an Academy Award for *The Window* and *Song of the South*. I just see those kids and I can relate to them like that.

It would be nice if the people who now own and run Neverland would consider honoring Michael's wish and build the child star museum that he envisioned. Perhaps it would be a valuable lesson to all those parents who push their children into early acting careers.

SB: Are you going to see her again?

MJ: Oh yes. I'm going to invite her to Neverland. She told me to make sure to say hello to Elizabeth. She kept asking about her.

SB: Do they know each other?

MJ: They have seen each other and spent some time together. But I told Elizabeth today and she said, "Ohhh. You must say Hi from me." I told Elizabeth I spent the weekend with her, and she says, "You did?" I said, "Yes." And she was shocked that I went up there. It was great.

SB: What was it about Shirley Temple, her specifically, that touched you so deeply, and do you think that every little girl can have a Shirley Temple inside her?

MJ: Her innocence, how she made me feel good when I was so sad. It wasn't so much her dancing and singing. It was her being. She was given a gift to make people feel good inside. All children have that but, man, she is so angelic to me, and every time I see her, it can be on a film or a picture, I feel so good. I have her pictures all in the room there. It makes me so happy.

SB: Did you see Shirley Temple in Shirley Temple Black when you met here? Was she still the little girl? Was she like you? Did she retain that child-like innocence, or did you bring it out in her?

MJ: It's still there. She is so sweet.

SB: How many people do you meet who are like that? Is it realistic? Do you meet a lot of adults around whom you can be defenseless and who you don't have to have your guard up for, or feel intimidated by?

MJ: Very few.

SB: So very few have achieved this. Is it people like Elizabeth Taylor, specifically childhood stars? People who didn't have a childhood spend their lives trying to regain it and that's what makes them child-like?

MJ: Yeah, and some people just have it naturally. A lot of creative people have it, and they had great childhoods. I have met them and worked with them, like directors and writers, and it's like we are all the same in that way. We all collect the same stuff, are fascinated by the same stuff. I see it. I go to George Lucas's basement and all the stuff he collects is the same stuff I collect. Steven [Spielberg], same stuff I like and collect. We swap notes on collecting things. It's simple things like old bubblegum cards or certain magazines. . . to original Norman Rockwell paintings. I mean I was at Steven Spielberg's house today and he has got the most beautiful original Norman Rockwell painting. It's so big and beautiful.

In New York Michael took me to a dealer whose entire showroom was crowded with original Norman Rockwells. Michael ran from painting to painting, excitedly explaining every detail to me. I have rarely seen him so animated.

Elizabeth Taylor: A Special Bond

Michael Jackson: Elizabeth Taylor is very childlike. There's nothing that you can do when she'll say, "I don't want to do that." When *Bug's Life* came out, she bugged me over and over to fix my schedule so we could see the cartoon. So we had to go to a public theater at about 1:00 o'clock. She makes me go out every Thursday because she says I'm too reclusive. Everybody's at work, so there's no one there and we never pay. . . we come with nothing and they always say, "Oh, my God, Elizabeth Taylor and Michael Jackson." We get free popcorn, everything. She loved *Bug's Life* and loves Neverland. She'll go on the carousel and the Ferris wheel, but not the scary rides.

There are other childlike qualities of Elizabeth Taylor. She was in *Jane Eyre* around eight or nine. Our fathers were very much alike, tough, hard, brutal. She's playful and youthful and happy and finds a way to laugh and giggle even when she's in pain. She's ready to play any game, go swimming. She's very good with children. She loves toys and cartoons. I get to learn so much from her. She'll tell me about James Dean and Clark Gable and Spencer Tracey and Montgomery Clift, because she did movies with all these people. She tells me what they were really like, the ones who were nice people and the ones that weren't.

We were in Singapore—she came on most of the *Dangerous* tour with me—and we decided we wanted to go to the zoo. And we hung out and had our own private tour and we had fun. She's Prince and Paris's godmother and Macaulay's their godfather. She's just retained that little girl quality. That little child you see in *Jane Eyre* and *Lassie Come Home*, that's still in there. It's in her eyes. She has this glow like a child. It's so sweet. But Shirley [Temple Black], too. She says, "You get it, don't you. You're one of us."

[Elizabeth Taylor and I] we're like brother and sister, mother and son, lovers. . . it's a potpourri. . . it's something special. We go through this whining thing on the phone. . . "I need you. . . ." "Oh, I need you, too." We can talk about anything. She's been my most loyal friend. She says she adores me and would do anything for me. She says Hollywood has to write a movie for the two of us. We just have to do something together.

Shmuley Boteach: Do you get jealous when she dates other men? She got married in your backyard.

MJ: Do I get jealous? Yes and no. I know that if we ever did anything romantically, the press would be so mean and nasty and call us "The Odd Couple." It would turn into a circus and that's the pain of it all. You know, I push her in a wheelchair sometimes, when she can't walk. It's none of their business what we have together. I have to be with people like me. Some rappers will say to me, "Let's hang out. Let's go down to a club." And I'll say, "What? Let's hang? I don't think so." That kind of thing's not a party for me.

On that tour [*Dangerous*], she fed me because I wouldn't eat. When I get upset, I stop eating, sometimes until I'm unconscious. [The molestation allegations had just been lodged against Michael while he was on tour in 1993. Hence, the reason for his upset.] She took the spoon and opened my mouth and made me eat. She said she wouldn't let me go without her, and her doctors advised her not to go. She went to Thailand and followed the tour all the way to London. I ended up at Elton John's and he was really sweet hiding me. He's one of the sweetest people you could meet on this planet. He and I took care of Ryan White, all his medical expenses.

Then they started doing it intravenously. I go through these serious food crises when I could go weeks without eating. I take stuff to keep weight on. What turns me off is that I don't like eating anything that used to be alive and now it's dead on my plate. I want to be a strict vegetarian, but my doctors keep trying to throw in chicken and fish.

PART 8

ON CHILDREN AND INNOCENCE

Can Children Teach Us Love?

Many of you reading this are no doubt of the opinion that Michael gravitated toward children for all the wrong reasons. But it is worth hearing his words here. Michael would tell me constantly that he loved innocence. Now, remember. Michael was performing in clubs from the age of five. He shared with me that he used to see strippers and other adult scenes as a small child. As I've consistently maintained, it is very possible that he came to associate sex with something perverted and corrupt. He was seeing things that no child should witness. Hence, his love of innocence. Children were innocent. They provided a refuge from this prurient world into which Michael had been immersed. There is a powerful lesson here for all the parents out there. Be careful of exposing your kids to adult content. It can scar and damage them for life.

Shmuley Boteach: Do you think children can teach us love?

Michael Jackson: Yeah, in a different way because they are so affectionate. They can teach us affection and it is quintessential affection and it is pure innocence. That's why I love them so much. I was telling Frank the other day, "Frank, I am in love with innocence, that's what I'm in love with. That's why I love children so much." Innocence is God. To be that innocent and approach things with such a sweet outlook on life, with truly just sweet. . . Where a kid will walk around the house and you'll go, "What are you doing?" and they answer, "I don't know, playing." It's so sweet. I love that. That's why [in] the painting [on a wall in Michael's house is a picture showing hundreds of children playing at Neverland]. . . one kid is screaming in the wind because he is feeling so good. He is just screaming to be screaming. I *love* that. Romance. Romance.

SB: Almost like they believe in love, they are not afraid to get hurt. People are afraid to love today.

MJ: [Are] love and romance two different things? That's why I am getting confused. I see romance as something that is longed for. You long for that out of a stage.

SB: Do you see romance as contrived by Hollywood movies?

MJ: Yes. Very.

SB: Kids are a bit romantic. They have romances in kindergarten.

MJ: You mean like crushes on other kids?

SB: Yes.

MJ: Yes, they do. They can teach you to be loving and sweet and they teach us in that way that probably. . . They give everybody a chance and I teach Prince and Paris to love everybody.

Why Michael Remained Childlike

Shmuley Boteach: When people use the expression *adult*, it can mean mature, balanced, educated, temperate. It can mean patient. But it also has negative connotations that I want you to comment on. It can connote being cynical, untrusting, scheming, manipulative, corrupt, judgmental, scarred. Tell me some of the negative things that adults learn as they grow older.

Michael Jackson: They just have so many problems, adults. They have been so conditioned by other people's thoughts and feelings. That's why I don't trust most dogs. It's not the dog. It's because people instill what they believe and all their anger and frustration is embedded in that dog and he becomes this vicious, crazy thing. And I don't know what kind of package he is bringing to me when he comes up to me and sniffs me. So it's like another adult. That's why I get afraid.

Indeed, when we met Michael amid having every animal under the sun, including tigers and elephants, he had no family dog. Michael asked me why we didn't have a dog either, and I said that I was concerned the children would not take care of it. Then, just before my daughter Chana's tenth birthday, Michael called from Neverland. "Shmuley, will you be angry if I get the kids a dog, just a real little one?" "Well Michael, that's real nice of you. But as I said, I'm concerned that the kids won't take care of it." A day later, the door bell rang. There was no one there. But on the doorstep was a beautiful toy Maltese puppy. The kids were thrilled. Marshmallow, as the children named her, has been a member of our family ever since. A few weeks later, when Michael came for dinner with his kids, his children played with the dog and begged him for a dog as well, a request that Michael finally granted, telling me that our puppy had helped him get beyond his own fears of dogs. But then, our pet was his gift.

SB: So you want to know what the person's motives are. You want to know if he has a vicious nature or. . .

MJ: *Yesssss.* But that is the perfect representation of what people have let themselves become. Somewhere along the line they have gotten lost and I believe in just staying childlike and innocent and simple. As Jesus said, "The greatest among me is like this little child here. Be like him and you are the greatest in my eyes." When a lot of adults first come to me, they look at me and they are checking out what you are wearing and who you are with. I see it. Then once they speak to me and they see that I am just a simple person who wants to be a friend, their heart melts. I see it.

SB: So children are accepting initially. They don't judge.

MJ: Yes, they let it all hang out. Kids go, "Oh my God, it's Michael Jackson." And I go, "Hi." An adult will smile and go, "Hi." Then, judging it a little bit, they go, "I like your stuff," but they won't let it all come out. [They won't let themselves appear impressed.]

SB: Why won't they? Why do they bottle up their enthusiasm? Are they trying to show, "I'm not going to be won over by you. . . I'm a person, too." Is it insecurity?

MJ: They are having a psychological warfare going on, how to approach me, what to say, what not to say. [But what I want them to know is that they should] just be yourself, be like a child. Be innocent. Be the way you were when you were born.

SB: Maybe what you are saying to them is this: "I am not trying to be bigger than you. I am who I am, and you just be who you are."

It's almost as though you are saying that children are more of your equals than adults are.

MJ: Of course they are. I can relate to them much easier. They don't come with all the baggage or stuff. They just play. They don't want anything from you. You don't want anything from them but love and innocence, and to find true happiness and magic together.

SB: It's also like adults make you into someone you don't want to be. You don't want to be defensive and artificial and you don't want to have stupid small talk. When kids come to you with all this enthusiasm you are Michael. But around adults you come with another agenda. You give the analogy of the dog. You don't know how to react so you get defensive. They make you into someone you don't want to be.

MJ: That's right. That's why I have become. . . not to say that I have let them win the war, but I just don't care to be around them. You can put the message out there. We will change a lot of people [to be more childlike]. We will literally and mentally baptize them with our words and our books, whatever we are doing. But there are so many out there who have shut the door mentally and they don't want to be changed and they refuse to see the light. But we could help a lot of people, a lot of them are just very, very hard. They have been so conditioned. But I believe you can change a lot of people. That's what's so wonderful about it all. You can show them. There are grown-ups who come to Neverland and they say to me, "You know, I haven't done the things I have done here in years. . . you can let your guard down and be a child again." I say, "That's what Neverland is for. To return to your innocence. To have fun."

God Heals Through Children

Shmuley Boteach: All the pain that you have endured with all the attacks, and I have seen it firsthand, and I say to people, so much of the garbage that is said about you is invented and unfair. So why haven't you just become a cynical adult, and thrown in the towel?

Michael Jackson: I'll tell you. Because with the pain, and the arrows that people have shot at me nobody else would have been able to take it. They would have probably committed suicide by now. . . they would have become a drunk. Because they have been very cruel and rude to me. And if they don't think I hear it and see it, I do. I do. It's been the children. I am holding on for them or else I wouldn't have made it. I really wouldn't have made it.

SB: The children have given you the support to continue? Or are you saying you continue because you believe that God gave you a mission to try and care for these neglected children?

MJ: God gave me a mission, I feel, to do something for them and they have given me the support and the belief and the love to hold on, hold on. When I look in the mirror I feel healed all over again. It's like being baptized. It's like God saying, "Michael, everything will be ok," when I look in the eyes of a child.

SB: So as far as you are concerned, you seem to be saying that you have completed every mission apart from your greatest mission and you are hanging on for that great mission and that is that you can bring care to children. Does that mean that you no longer have the same musical ambitions?

MJ: Are you kidding? It is heightened a trillion-fold now, from dancing to music, it inspires me even more now.

SB: But can you show love to adults, do you still trust adults?

MJ: I trust adults. . .

SB: But you are still wary initially. . . you have to be.

MJ: Yes, because they have really betrayed and deceived me in so many different ways and at so many different times. I have had adults with tears coming down their face, saying, "It's a shame what you have been through and I would never ever ever *ever* hurt you or do anything. And they turn around and they hurt me. Honestly, that's the kind of crap I have been through. . . tears rolling down and hugging me. And they end up a year later suing over some ridiculous. . . like a photographer over some pictures, or some person who gets terminated and I didn't terminate them, but I get sued by them and I didn't do it. This is the sort of silliness.

SB: At that moment they probably meant it and that's the problem. A day later emotion can change. But deep down you can still trust. You may have cause to feel betrayed and let down, but you have to overcome the fear you have of people. That is extremely important. I wouldn't be your friend if I didn't believe that. You've taught me more about appreciating my kids, and I want to teach you more about being fearless.

MJ: Ah, that's sweet. I have had so many parents come to me, because when their kids see me, they fall in love with me. They go nuts. They wanna play and climb trees and I do all that with them. They take me aside with tears in their eyes and go, "Michael, I don't know my children. You have taught me to really spend time with my children. I need to learn that." They tell me that all the time.

SB: But children bore most adults, especially if they're not their own.

MJ: But how? Honestly, tell me the truth, do they really bore them?

SB: Yes. First, because children need a phenomenal amount of patience and most adults do not have patience. Second, children ask so many questions, and, the adult thinks, "I want to get on with my work!" Because parents have decided that making a million dollars is important, but the child wanting to know why a cat has four legs is not important. Do you like those questions from children? Do you think that children know what is important even more than adults?

MJ: It depends on value, on what we consider to be truly important. In my true opinion, to be an entrepreneur and climb the corporate ladder and all those other, worldly things that people do, that's worldly to them. I think children worship fun, love, they worship attention. They want a fun-filled day, things that when you experience it with them you have a special place in their heart forever. It changes who they become and what our world becomes, the totality of what happens in this universe becomes. It is the future.

SB: But what if someone says, "Fun isn't serious. We have to work. We have to cure diseases. We have to build houses and find out what the weather forecast is for the weekend. And fun doesn't do any of that. Children have to grow up to know that they have responsibilities, that they have to do work."

MJ: I think we learn through play, through having fun and after having fun I think magic happens. Or during having fun, magic happens. I know for me it does. I wrote one of the prettiest songs I've ever written when I was playing with some children, for this album. It completely came from them and when I had my songs laid out I go, "Ok, this one came from this kid, and this one came from this kid." They inspired it. It came from their being and their presence and their spirit. It's true.

SB: So children are like a swimming pool and the water represents Godliness. And as you get older and grow up the water begins to freeze until it becomes ice. And children are just this reservoir of warm, free water and you can just play, whereas ice is hard and cold and not inviting. So you want to get adults to thaw, as it were, melt the pool again.

MJ: That's why when I direct movies—and I am going to start directing again soon—I see everything through the eyes of a child. All my stories are going to be about issues about children, how they are affected by the world and how they see the world through their eyes, 'cause that's all I can relate to. I can't deal with some court story or murder crime. I don't understand that. I can understand if a kid were involved in a crime and tracing his life and what happened and why it happened and how he is feeling being sentenced to life and what goes on in that little heart that is pounding. I can understand that. I can direct that, I can write about that because I feel that.

SB: How can an adult get that feeling? Is it a gift? Can I acquire it? Being around you I do feel it more.

MJ: That's really sweet.

SB: I love my kids very much, but I don't love other people's kids as much. But when I see Prince, he melts my heart because he is such a warm and loving kid.

MJ: That's how I want them to be. Since they were very little I taught them to love everybody.

SB: How are you going to preserve that as they grow older? You are going to have to protect them, obviously, from that *News of the World* thing.

A rare picture of Michael's children had just appeared in *News of the World*, a British tabloid, a few days earlier. Prince and Paris had gone from Neverland to Los Angeles for a doctor's checkup. In the back of a limousine with tinted windows, Prince was playing with the electric windows, which then opened, and a photographer quickly took his and Paris's picture. Michael was devastated. He called me in the middle of the night from Neverland to see if something could be done to have the picture removed from their website. A day later, a lawyer fired off a letter, but the picture remained. Michael often told me that he is protective of his children's images, and put those silly scarves on their faces when they are in public so that they can't be photographed, to protect them from kidnapping. My own thoughts were that he hated people speculating as to their paternity and whether or not they had a resemblance to him.

Here, Michael was right. It was always grotesquely unfair to two innocent and vulnerable children for the world to speculate as to whether Michael is their true father. It is simply nobody's business. Could you imagine inviting a dinner guest to your home who sat there scrutinizing your children's eyes and hair to determine if they were your biological children or if they were adopted? Could you imagine being asked by your neighbor, "Is this your husband's son, or does he come from a sperm donor?" But Michael's handling of the subject, in particular by veiling the children in public, was typical and unfortunately extreme and weird. To be sure, the children do need to be protected from a prying public. But they also need a normal upbringing and balance must be found.

> MJ: I teach them to love everybody and to be kind and to be good in their heart. But they have that naturally. I didn't have to program it. . . they have it naturally.

I have to say, Prince and Paris did really seem to be extremely gentle and well-mannered children. And exceptionally close to their father.

> MJ: What you don't know about me is how much I love film and art and I want to direct so badly. I could scream, I want to show the world through the eyes of a child because I understand them so

much. Their pain and their joy and their laughter and what hurts them. And I see the world through their eyes and I want to portray that on film. That's my real passion. I love it. It's too much.

SB: So as a director you can give the whole world your view of how children are because they can see it through your eyes, even if you do a movie for adults?

MJ: Yes, and I searched my heart many times and I said, "Can I do a real serious film for adults?" And I know I can. But I don't think I would enjoy it. I don't think I would enjoy it. I know I can do it, but I wouldn't enjoy it.

SB: If there was one movie that you could have directed, which one would it be?

MJ: *ET*, *The Wizard of Oz*, *400 Blows*, which is a great movie by François Truffaut. I love *Shane* and I am crazy about *To Kill a Mockingbird*. That's the story that I see and every time I see it I have a lump in my throat in the same place. Have you seen it? Oh, I can't wait to show it to you. Please see it with me. We'll turn off all the phones and we'll just watch it.

SB: Can the kids watch it?

MJ: Absolutely, they will learn. It's about racism in the South. It's about a man who is put on trial saying that he raped a white woman. There are some hard areas but it is seen through the eyes of children. Man this movie will wear you out. I love it too much. It is definitely one of the best movies. I wish I had directed it. Oh God, it is so sweet.

Do Black People Have Greater Musical Talent than Whites?

Shmuley Boteach: Let me ask you a question. . . Well, but I mean, that's what makes you unique—that you are talented across the board. Do black people have more rhythm than white people? When you speak about dancing and everything. . . I mean, it's like a joke, but it's not just a joke that white people have no rhythm.

244 | THE SOUL OF MICHAEL JACKSON

When you speak about, like, the natural rhythm and everything
and the way these black kids in the ghetto, the way they dance,
you always talk about that. It's like natural. . . you always see it
around here in Manhattan? These kids on the street who busk.
It's amazing!

Michael Jackson: It's amazing, and it is natural. . . they have a natural rhythm that nobody can explain. It's a natural talent.

SB: Do you see white people having that rhythm?

MJ: It's not the same and I'm not saying it out of being. . .

SB: But the sense of timing. . .

MJ: Stan would always tell me, and he would go to all the black
clubs. . . he would sit in the Apollo Theater, he called it Cut-time
rhythm. He said he had to have the black rhythm so he hung out
with the blacks to get that cut-time rhythm [mimicking noises].
You know that's what rappers do now—they do cut-time rhythm.
That's what it's all about, it's that natural rhythm thing.

SB: That reflects their inner rhythm?

MJ: Yeah, yeah. But you take a little black child and they got the
rhythm of a grown-up, like a real dancer. And it's just a natural
ability, you know?

SB: Without trying to penetrate this too deeply, traditionally, Africa
was more childlike than Europe. Europe prided itself on its sophis-
tication, its perfumes, its fancy clothes. Africa was dismissed as
"more primitive" but therefore much more natural, more organic.
They were much closer to the earth. So it could be that they never
detached themselves from those natural rhythms?

MJ: But how does that become genetic?

SB: I don't know.

MJ: Could you take a Scottish or Irish child and put him in that same
situation, let him be born in Africa among those. . .

SB: Well, that's the whole question about Elvis, right?

MJ: Elvis always hung out around blacks.

SB: And he acquired that rhythm, right?

MJ: Yeah, he acquired that rhythm, he wanted to do the steps, and
he talked black and acted black. We knew Elvis very well and Lisa
Marie and myself always talked about how. . .

SB: Had he not been a white man, you don't think he would've been as successful, right?

MJ: Not nearly. Not nearly because it would've been expected of him. Remember the slogan that Philips, who owned Sun Records, he said, "If I could only find a white man with a black man's sound, I could make a million dollars," and in come walks Elvis Presley.

SB: Now, you ask an incredible question: "How does that become innate, you know?" And especially science today doesn't believe in acquired characteristics. You can't transmit characteristics to a child that have been acquired in a lifetime. So, if you have great musical talent, you can give it to Prince. But if someone taught it to you, you can't give it to Prince. He'd have to get it on his own. It's not in the genes.

MJ: Yeah, yeah.

SB: When I was in my preaching competition, the first year, when I came in second, I lost to this Caribbean preacher and we were so close. I lost by like 3 points out of 130 points and everyone said to me, "He had timing, you didn't." He knew like, you wait, you know the way a preacher has to build up. And all my friends said to me, "Shmuley, he had rhythm."

[both laughing]

In 1998 I became the first rabbi to ever become a finalist in the *London Times* Preacher of the Year competition, the world's most prestigious religious speaking competition. I was the favorite to win, and had already won in a preliminary TV playoff. But in the actual finals, I came in a close second to a Seventh-Day Adventist Caribbean preacher named Rev. Ian Sweeney. The following year, just days before the millennium, I won the competition and set a record for most points garnered in the competition. I say this not to brag, but clearly I had learned something about timing that Ian seemed to know naturally. I continue to love public speaking.

MJ: But you're amazing.

SB: No, but I mean he had it. I told you, the black preachers are the best in the world. They're the best speakers. Look at Martin Luther King. There is no other. . .

MJ: I cry when I hear him talk. I get goose bumps.

SB: Or even Jesse Jackson, or some of the preachers here. Reverend Floyd, here in Manhattan, is supposed to be the best in the country. . .

MJ: But you're so eloquent. I mean, you paint pictures with your words and it makes you think. . . You go everywhere. It's brilliant.

SB: But it's about being moved by the spirit and kids are moved.

MJ: But where do you get the words?

SB: You know, I was describing in the book what happened on Friday night when you came to our house for dinner. It was fascinating.

MJ: What happened?

SB: All of us adults started having dinner and you went upstairs to play hide and go seek. And you were like the pied piper, kids came to you immediately. Little by little. . . the adults came to the third floor, the second floor. They really felt like they were missing out, like everyone was having fun and they weren't. They were having their political conversations. It's like the pied piper, and they want to pretend they're only going up there for the kids.

MJ: I loved when your friend attacked you . . . I loved that! I loved when he did that.

My friend Cory Booker, who at the time was a Newark City councilman, ran into the room where Michael and I were playing hide-and-seek with the kids, and tackled me, breaking the bed. It was of course all in jest and we all laughed. Cory was the president of my Oxford University student organization, the L'Chaim Society, when he was a Rhodes scholar there. Today, as mayor of Newark, he is one of America's most admired and successful leaders.

SB: He's very innocent and he's attacked for it as a politician. All his advisors say you need to be more tough.

MJ: No, no. I wish I could've known Edison and Einstein and Michelangelo.

SB: We talk about all of them, by the way, in the book. Edison was so childlike.

MJ: I know, I see it, I saw him. . . laughing, giggling. I saw the footage, I see what he writes about. It's beautiful man, it's great stuff. I love that.

Michael's Relationship with His Accuser and Other Children

For many years Michael was known for all the things he did for children around the world—how he would personally visit them, hug them, and offer love and support for a suffering child, a child with cancer. He was also condemned by many for his love of children with it seen as a sign of his unhealthy and perhaps criminal relationship to children.

Shmuley Boteach: I said to someone today that the attention you give to children with cancer seems very healing to them. I've seen it. You know when you give that kid attention that you can heal them?

Michael Jackson: I love them. I love them.

SB: It's also the fact that you are very famous and suddenly you channel all that attention that you normally get and you stick it onto someone else, and it is like this beam of light. I don't deny that celebrity can have a restorative effect, but it often has a very corrosive effect. Do you try to use your celebrity to help these kids?

MJ: I love them so much. They're my children, too. I remember we were in Australia and we were in this children-with-cancer ward and I started giving out toys. And I'll never forget this one boy who was like eleven and when I got to his bed he said, "It's amazing how just seeing you I feel so much better. I really do." I said, "Well, that's so sweet." That's what he said and I have never forgotten it. It's amazing and that's what we are supposed to do.

SB: Your devotion to Gavin [who would later be Michael Jackson's accuser] is impressive. I have spoken about it in a thousand forums now. That was one of the nicest things I have seen. That you tried to help him and his family.

MJ: He's special.

In my presence, Michael gave Gavin affection and attention, which seemed very curative to the boy. Michael's characterization of the boy in the *60 Minutes* interview, however, as having arrived at Neverland unable to walk, and Michael having to carry him is, as I said earlier, entirely fictitious. Gavin and his siblings ran all over Neverland. They extensively drove and even banged up some of the go-carts, and came with us twice on the quads on thousands of acres of ranch. Still, Michael did give him affection and encouragement in my presence.

On another occasion Michael told me how upset he was after a phone conversation with Gavin in which he communicated how much pain the chemotherapy was causing him:

MJ: I spoke to Gavin [Michael's accuser] last night and he said, "Michael, you don't know how it hurts me, it hurts." He started to cry on the phone and he said, "I know you understand how it feels. It hurts so bad." I said, "Well, how many more do you have?" He said, "Maybe four. But the doctor said maybe more after that." It took his eyelashes away and his eyebrows and his hair. We are so lucky aren't we?

SB: Do you feel that when you speak to people like Gavin, part of the pain goes away for them?

MJ: Absolutely. Because every time I talk to him he is in better spirits. When I spoke to him last night he said, "I need you. When are you coming home?" I said, "I don't know." He said, "I need you Michael." Then he calls me "Dad." I said, "You better ask your Dad if it is ok to call me that." He shouts, "Dad, is it ok if I call Michael, 'Dad?'" and he says, "Yes, no problem, whatever you want." Kids always do that. It makes me feel happy that they feel that comfortable.

SB: Do you feel like a universal father to children, that you have this ability to love them and appreciate them in a way that others don't?

MJ: I always feel that I don't want the parents to get jealous because it always happens and it rubs fathers in a strange way. Not as much as the mothers. I always say to the Dads, "I am not trying to take your place. I am just trying to help and I want to be your friend." The kids just end up falling in love with my personality. Sometimes it gets me into trouble, but I am just there to help.

SB: I asked you what parents can learn from children, and you iden-
tified a few things—love of fun, innocence, joy. What other things
can we learn from children? For example, when you are around
Gavin, what do you learn from him? Are you just there to help a
child who has cancer? What do you get from the experience? Is it
just you showing pity, compassion for a child who is in trouble? Or
do you feel this is the reason you are alive?

MJ: I feel that this is something really, really in my heart that I am
supposed to do, and I feel so loved by giving my love, and I know
that's what they need. I have heard doctors, and *his* doctors, say
that it is a miracle how he is doing better and that's why I know
this magic of love is so important. He got cheated out of his childhood and I think I can reflect on a lot of that because of my past.
When you were ten you weren't thinking about heaven and how
you are going to die and he is thinking about all of that. I had little Ryan White in my dining room telling his mother at the table,
"Mother, when you bury me, I don't want to be in a suit and tie."
He said, "Don't put me in a suit and tie. I want to be in jeans and
a T-shirt." I said, "Excuse me, I have to go to the bathroom." And
I ran to the bathroom and I cried. Imagine a 12-year-old boy telling
his mother how to bury him. That's what I heard him say. How
could your heart not go out to someone like that?

SB: Since you were deprived of that childhood and now you are trying to confer it as a gift to all these children, do you heal yourself
through that?

MJ: Yes. Yes, I do. Yes I do. Because that's everything. I need that to
keep living. Do you see what Gavin wrote in the guest book, about
his hat? It's a sweet story.

Gavin had written that Michael had given him the confidence to
take off his hat and not to be ashamed about the baldness caused by
chemotherapy.

SB: I have told that story all over the world.

MJ: I like giving them that love and that pride to feel that they belong
and they are special. He was hiding and he was ashamed that he

had a bald head and he had cancer. Everybody has made him feel like an outcast and that's how he came here and I want him to let go. He is such a beautiful child, he doesn't need that hat. I told him, "You look just like an angel. Your voice sounds like an angel. As far as I am concerned you are an angel. What are you ashamed of?"

SB: Do you feel that children appreciate you more than adults?

MJ: Oh yeah, of course. Adults appreciate me artistically as a singer and a songwriter and a dancer and a performer. What is he like? Who is he? He's weird and he sleeps in an oxygen chamber and all those crazy horrific stories that people made up that had nothing to do with me.

SB: The children see right through that and they reciprocate your love. I saw that with Gavin.

MJ: They just want to have some fun and to give love and have love and they just want to be loved and held.

SB: Did you fight to hold onto this sense of caring? Was there a time when you said, "I don't care about anybody else. I am going to get a massage now and hang out in the Jacuzzi? The concert is over, so I'm just going to think about myself." Or even then were you thinking about what you could do for kids?

MJ: Truly in my heart, I love them and I care more than anything. I am still taking care of Gavin. He had chemotherapy yesterday and he is weak and not feeling good and it just touches your heart. Your heart goes out to the world. I think I am a lot like my mother. I don't know if it is genetic or environmental. I remember when we were little she would watch the news and even now she has to watch the news with tissues. I'm the same, I start crying when I watch the news about the woman who takes her kids and throws them in the lake, one drowned, the other survived. So I invited the kids over and went to the funeral, paid for the funeral and I don't even know these people, but you hear these things. It's like asking, why aren't there more people like Mother Teresa? Why aren't there more people like Lady Diana?

SB: They are famous for being good, but you are famous *and* you are good, there's a very big difference. Even Diana, Diana was a good woman. I didn't know her. You did. She had many saintly qualities and did a huge amount of good. Still, she loved the glitzy life. But you love children. Why?

MJ: I am not trying to be philosophical but I really think it's my job to help them. I think it is my calling. I don't care if people laugh or what they say. [Children] don't have a mouth to society and I think it is now their time. From here on out it is their time. They need the world's awareness and they need issues to deal with, and this is for them. And if I can be that light, that pedestal just to shine some light on who they are, and the importance of who children are, that's what I want to do. I don't know how God chooses people, or plays chess with people, and he does put you in position and sets you up. Sometimes I feel like that, like this is my place. I think about from Gandhi to Martin Luther King to Kennedy to myself to yourself. Do you think these are self-made men or, from birth, do you think God said, "Aha!" And smiling a little bit. . . . Do you think that just happened on its own by their fathers, or they were supposed to do this? I am asking you this question?

SB: I think it is the confluence of both. Great men and women are born with the potential for greatness. But it usually has to be squeezed out of them through the crisis of an external event. There is greatness in people but external events help them develop it. Greatness is the synthesis of a man or woman's innate potential matched with their ability to rise to a great challenge. And when you don't have an answer to the question of why God gave you such phenomenal success, you start to wither under the burden of fame. You need to have something like a mirror that deflects all that attention, all that light, that is being shined on you, onto a higher cause or you'll be scorched by its intensity.

On the other hand, Michael's attention wasn't consistent, and often didn't measure up to the ideal he set for himself and spoke about publicly.

SB: A little girl I met last night is fourteen and she's an orphan. Her mother died when she was seven, and she never knew who her father was. She came to the *Lion King* last night because she is a friend of

[name withheld] and her great wish was to meet you. So I told her I
would bring her by for a few minutes this week so she can meet you.

MJ: Oh, who is taking care of her?

SB: She lives with her grandmother and she has a godfather who
brought her to the play last night. Her godfather tries to take her
out and see plays and things occasionally.

MJ: Did the kids have fun at the show?

SB: Oh yes they loved it. It was beautiful. This orphan girl's school
is a few blocks away from your hotel. Maybe I'll bring her and let
her take a picture with you.

Michael later agreed to a very short meeting with this girl, but he
took very little interest in her and never asked about her again. Why
Michael seemed to take an interest in some kids, and had little to no
interest in others, is not something that I ever understood. For example, in another instance, a little girl with leukemia whose mother had
gotten in touch with me, asked if she could bring her daughter to meet
Michael. I invited them both to our home, where they met Michael
over dinner. Later, whenever Michael would come to our home for
Sabbath dinner, I would usually invite the little girl, her mother, and
her three siblings. They subsequently became personal friends of my
family, and our friendship has continued in Michael's absence. For
everyone who said that Michael was only interested in little boys, I can
attest that he showed genuine and ongoing concern for this young
girl, and called her mother several times to check on her condition.

Knowing Ryan White and
Other Children Battling Cancer

Shmuley Boteach: Wasn't there was a young boy you were very close
to who got AIDS from a blood transfusion?

Michael Jackson: Ryan White. The hardest for me is. . . I am going to
answer but I don't understand when a child dies. I really don't. I
think there should be a window where there is a chance of dying

but not in this window of time. When a child dies, or if the child is sick, I really don't understand it. But I listen to Ryan White, twelve years old, at my dining room table at Neverland telling his mother how to bury him. He said, "Mom when I die, don't put me in a suit and tie. I don't want to be in a suit and tie. Put me in OshKosh jeans and a T-shirt." I said, "I have to use the bathroom," and I ran to the bathroom and I cried my eyes out. Hearing this little boy telling his mother how to bury him. That hurt me. It was as if he was prepared for it and when he died he was in OshKosh jeans and a T-shirt and a watch that I gave him. And I am sitting alone in this room with him and he is lying there and I felt so bad I just wanted to hold him and kiss him and say that I love him, which I did all those things when he was alive. I took care of him and he stayed at my house. But to see him just lying there . . . I spoke to him and I said, "Ryan, I promised you that I would do something in your honor on my next album. I will create a song for you. I will sing it. I want the world to know who you are." I did *Gone Too Soon*. That was for him.

SB: Do you think he heard you when you said that? Do you feel in touch with the soul of some of the people you love and have lost? Do you still feel close to them?

MJ: Yeah. Yeah. Yeah.

SB: So you had to deal with his death and other people who you were close to?

MJ: That hurt me so much. One other boy came to me and he was as white as snow, literally as white as snow or a white piece of paper. He was dying of cancer and he just loved me and he came in my bedroom and he saw the jackets I wore and the videos and he put them on and he was in heaven. They told me that he wasn't going to live. That any day he could just go and I said, "Look, I am going to be coming to your town." I think he was in Kansas City. "I am going to open my tour in Kansas City in three months. I want you to come to the show. I am going to give you this jacket." He said "You are gonna' *give* it to me?" I said, "Yeah. But I want you to wear it to the show." I was trying to make him hold on. I said, "When you come to the show I want to see you in this jacket and in this glove," and I gave him one of my rhinestone gloves, and I never give the rhinestone gloves away. He was in heaven. When I came to the town he was dead and they buried him in the glove and the jacket. He was 10 years old. God knows, I know that he tried his best to hold on.

SB: Do you feel angry at God for things like that happening?

MJ: No. I just don't understand them. I wish we knew more about the other side. I know it promises everlasting life and being in heaven. But why suffering and why pain before crossing over to the white light, whatever it is? It should just be the most beautiful experience, whatever it is.

MJ: [The story about the boy] was a true story. I wish you could've seen his face, Shmuley, I wish you could've seen it.

SB: And that was a promise story, right? You said to him "I promise if you stay alive. . ." Right?

MJ: Yeah, I was trying to get him to hold on. They said he was gonna die and I said, "I know I can do something about this." You know? And I was trying to get him to look forward, to hold on and I said "Wear this to the show" and he was so happy. When I got to the town, he was dead. Killed me, killed me.

SB: How do you feel, describe the feeling to me for just a minute. How do you feel when you're around [a little girl with cancer whom Michael and I knew]?

MJ: I love her.

SB: You know that you could make a difference with them and you know that just being around you, part of their illness almost goes away. You know the ancient Rabbis said that every time you visit someone sick you take away 1/60th of their illness. But with you, it's almost like you take away fifty percent of their illness, you know? I know you know that.

MJ: Yeah, yeah. I love making people. . . I don't like to see anybody hurt or suffer, especially children.

SB: Do you feel that you have a healing power that was given to you? Or is it because of the celebrity? In other words, being a great celebrity, when you show a child attention, they feel really good. They know how famous you are, they feel like "wow, someone that famous cares about me, I must be special." But is it beyond celebrity? Is it something in you that you had before celebrity?

MJ: I think it's something that I'm supposed to do because I always had this yearning to give and help and make people feel better in that way.

SB: You had this before, when you were Michael Jackson the boy?

MJ: Yes.

Being Dad with Prince and Paris

Michael Jackson: [To Prince, who is with us]: Prince, what makes Daddy laugh?

Prince: *Three Stooges*.

MJ: He's right. I love them. The fat one. . . I scream with laughter. I keep *The Three Stooges* with me wherever I go. It makes me happy. I have watched them all my life.

Shmuley Boteach: What is it about them? Is it the fact that they can like hurt each other and no one gets hurt and everything's funny?

MJ: Yeah, Curly is the killer. Remember Curly—the fat one, right Prince? [Prince starts jumping around, imitating Curly] Yeah, he loves it too. I love them.

SB: That's what makes you laugh out loud?

MJ: Yeah, I scream. I scream, I keep the Three Stooges with me wherever I go. It makes me happy. I love them. I've watched them all my life.

Prince: Daddy. I want to see *Peter Pan*.

MJ: Me too.

Prince: I want to go fishing.

MJ: I'll take you fishing one day as long as we throw the fish back after we catch it.

SB: Do you feel, maybe, based on everything that you have done for children, that God showed you extra kindness by giving you two really outstanding children who are so attached to you. . . that amid the malice and mean-spiritedness of people, God gave you these two incredible gifts in your life?

MJ: That would be a nice thought. I think they are a gift. I think all children are a gift.

SB: Do you love children more after having Prince and Paris?

MJ: I love them as much and more. It's hard for me to say "my children" because I don't see any territoriality. Maybe because I used to get hectored by my ex-wife Lisa about that because all she used to care about was her own and not others.

I know it would make a huge difference in their future if we do what we say we are going to do [with our child-prioritization initiative]. It's that time, that chance to say, "You, you are special to me. This is your day. This is not Christmas. It's not the day we are celebrating for Christ that's about the day he was born. This is about you and me. I am giving you my love." That would make a *big* difference. If I had that day with my father and my mother, that would have made all the difference. And I love my parents. My mother is like a saint. She is. . . she is not of this earth. She is unbelievably wonderful. I don't have a bad thing to say about her. That would be nice, wouldn't it?

SB: So the first thing you want Prince and Paris to know, before they know their ABC's before they know how to dress, you want them to know that their daddy loves them.

MJ: Yeah, yeah. To make them hold their hands and look them in the eyes and tell them, "I love you." That would be remembered forever. I do it to Prince and Paris every day.

SB: That's the one thing that will never be taken away from them. That's the beginning of all knowledge—to know that you are loved.

MJ: Loved, truly loved. . . to touch their hand, because kids go a lot by touch, and they need to be held, and people know those kinds of things. But they don't know the power.

Playfulness

Is it responsible for a grown adult to be playful in a way that other adults would dismiss as immature? Or are the adults who are doing the dismissing being old and crusty?

Shmuley Boteach: Give me some stories about playfulness. Tell me about your water balloon fights.

Michael Jackson: Water balloon fights?

SB: Yes, at Neverland.

MJ: I think the best way to break the ice with someone you don't know is to play. You bond quicker through play than any other way. Through shaking a hand to usually having a conversation is not as easy as play. I think it's the best way and I think breaking ice with a good water balloon fight or running around together, riding bikes, looking at each other, laughing, smiling, it's the best way to really get to know somebody in the beginning. And they realize that you are just fun and simple and your first association with them is through fun. I think that's important, don't you?

SB: Yes. But I want you to describe it. You have this water balloon fort at Neverland, and you organize two different teams. When we stayed with you we didn't have a water-balloon fight, remember, because it was raining?

MJ: We have two teams, the red team and a blue team and you challenge each other. There are water balloons, there are cannons that shoot sixty feet on each side and there are sling shots where you can sling the water balloons and they have these shower buttons. And if the red team can get over to the blue team and push their shower button three times. . . . And the only way for the red team to turn off the blue team's side is for the red team to run back over and turn it off and we get to hit them. When I say shower, it's like a sprinkler and fountains, it is like a shower all over the place and you get flooded with water. If you hit that button three times, whoever does that first is the winner. And then the loser has to sit on this round thing with his clothes on and you throw this ball and he falls in the water. They are soaked and then they have to go to the swimming pool and dive in with their clothes on. So it is a real fun fiasco.

SB: So when you have guests who come to Neverland you often break the ice through the water balloon fights. Children and adults?

MJ: Adults too.

SB: And how do they respond? Do you sometimes see real serious people suddenly melting?

MJ: Oh they love it. They laugh and we videotape it and once everybody has dried off and had dinner, we show it in our movie theater on the big screen and everybody is laughing and screaming and they realize how much fun it was. It is a wonderful thing.

SB: Do you ever do this with big music executives?

MJ: No. . . yes. . . with movie people like Catherine Byrne and Stephen [Spielberg]. . . we have had some big ones.

SB: What about children with cancer, people like that?

MJ: Sometimes we have it in the grass. I like it better in the fort. There's bridges. You run across and it is fun, great fun.

SB: Tell me some more stories like that. Let's say you are in the middle of a big Sony meeting or a big movie meeting with all these crusty corporate American suits. Have you ever been able to break the ice in these serious negotiations because you are more childlike? They are very rigid, everything is about numbers.

MJ: You don't understand. One thing you don't know about me is how silly I am. Every time I get in these meetings and everyone is uptight I laugh through the whole thing and I can't stop giggling and I have to keep apologizing and my lawyer looks at me and says, "I'm sorry. He does this sometimes." Then they start laughing and they all start laughing and so it becomes fun and light-hearted because they look too serious sometimes and I like it to be a little more light-hearted. I can't help it. I really can't help it.

SB: Does that break the ice when you do that? Do people feel closer, does it make tough negotiations easier? Do they feel that they have bonded more when that happens?

MJ: Yes, I think so. I think there is a commonality amongst all of us that we really are all the same. Things can be really humorous and we can laugh at the same things. There's that commonality in mankind. Really, we are all the same. Really.

SB: Laughter is the quickest way we can achieve something in common?

MJ: Everybody's funny bone is the same color, isn't it? We are all the same, really. I have seen that a lot.

SB: What about practical jokes you do, and things like that? Do you remember Michael Steinhardt at the zoo? He was one of the best money managers on Wall Street, but he was famous for having a bucket of water fall on some guy who was too serious, at the biggest meetings. He was a legendary practical joker.

Steinhardt, who is a dear friend, is a world-renowned Jewish philanthropist and co-founder of Birthright Israel. He is a great lover of animals and has his own private zoo. I took Michael and his children, together with mine, for a visit at his home. Michael later visited again on his own so that his kids could see the animals.

MJ: Are you kidding? That's my most favorite thing in the whole world, to prank people. I love doing it, but I am afraid that some people will get mad even though sometimes I don't care. But I do it all the time. I carry stink-bombs and water balloons. After every video, on the last day the whole room stinks like rotten eggs and it all turns to a big mess and everybody knows what I do and everybody knows that's when it's done. And then I walk out. I love it.

SB: Do you see very serious people becoming more childlike in front of your eyes when that happens?

MJ: Yes, and they talk about it and how funny it was. It is fun.

SB: You will remember that on Friday night at my home one of the guests was a woman who is in her early forties and a successful real estate mogul. She has over 100 employees. But at what price? She is not married, she doesn't have children. She said she didn't have time to date. I said, "What about Friday nights?" "Well," she said, "I am ashamed to tell you that I am normally at the office until 11:00–12:00 p.m., even on Friday nights." So, she has given up a lot of her personal life in order to have this big business. What would you say to someone like that?

MJ: I would try and show them some of the wonderful things that they are missing and not to be overly serious and not too much of a workaholic, even though I am a workaholic. But you must stop sometimes and have fun. There is so much fun to be had because once . . . our time can be so limited on the planet and I think real family and great memories and doing things with children are some of the most wonderful treasures. I have had some amazing good times. When I am sad I start reflecting on the good times to make me feel better. I do it in bed at night sometimes when I get down on myself. I put the most wonderful thought in my head, some wonderful experience and I feel a chemical reaction taking over in my body where I am actually there and I love that. I get upset if some idiot, I mean worse than a Stooge, a complete idiot writes something stupid and so untrue and so unlike what happened at the event or something I was at. And I get so angry and I try not to be angry because I am hurting myself. And I start thinking about me flying through the air with the wind in my face. I do it in Africa. I go way up high and I am so happy up there and I am flying. I think it is one of the most wonderful things I have discovered and I love it. It's the freedom. It's bliss. It's quintessential bliss, I think. It's the height of fun.

SB: Do you ever close your eyes and see yourself in front of one hundred thousand adoring fans? Does that help?

MJ: I love the fire and the majesty of all of that, that you can command an audience and the feeling of all of that. I love that a lot. That's another great feeling. But it's not the same as this feeling of flight. Or just looking over a panorama of some beautiful picturesque scenery which is so beautiful you really start to cry. I cry. I say, "Thank you." You see the most beautiful sky where the clouds are hues of orange and purple. God, it's so beautiful. I start to pray. I kinda take a mental picture of it because I want to remember it.

SB: What would your prayer be in moments like that?

MJ: God, this is so beautiful. Thank you for making the heavens and earth such a beautiful place. If other people don't recognize it and appreciate it, I do. Thank you, thank you so much. That's what I do. I have had moments when I have said to another person, "Look at that beautiful sky," and they have said, "Yeah? It's nice." I go, "There must be something wrong with me. Why do I see it and they don't?" Why do I appreciate it and they don't appreciate it? I went to a museum in Paris and I swear to you, my bodyguards are a witness to what happened to me, they had to carry me. I broke down crying and the lady who was showing us round said, "What's wrong with him?" And they said, "He is so moved by what he has seen."

Practical Jokes

Michael described to me his honest love for playfulness, which could be amusingly childlike or annoyingly childish. Michael often could not discern the difference between that which was innocent and affable and that which was obnoxious, with laughs coming at other people's expense.

Shmuley Boteach: Tell me more about your practical jokes.
Michael Jackson: [Once] I took a whole bottle of scotch and I poured it into this glass in this serious meeting with all these people and I started to drink the whole thing in one gulp. And I swallowed it and I started breathing and everyone went silent. I filled it with water. They died laughing. I love doing stuff like that. I had 'em Shmuley. They thought it was vodka.

When Michael told me this story, I was still under the impression that he never drank. Even when he came to our home on Friday nights for the Sabbath dinner, in which it is customary for everyone to have at least a little bit of the Kiddush-benediction wine, he still never drank what he called "Jesus juice." Why he would have gone to such lengths to mislead me and brag to me that he never even had alcohol in the smallest quantities is beyond me. Clearly, I would not have judged him harshly for having a glass of wine. It was a grave disappointment, therefore, to discover in his 2005 trial that he had lied so much about not consuming alcohol, the sin being in the lie rather than in the consumption.

SB: I was visiting my brother's house in LA. Debbie and I were dating at the time. Debbie came to my house because we wanted to get married and we wanted to get my father's blessing and all that and we are very traditional. My father is Middle Eastern and he is looking at Debbie and she was only nineteen and I was twenty-one. I got married very young.

MJ: I wish I had.

SB: I always say better to have married the right person at the wrong time than the wrong person at the right time. Anyway, you know the hottest peppers, the little red ones. My brother, who is a practical joker, said to Debbie, who has this very sweet and trusting nature, "Have those." She said, "Aren't they the hot ones?" He said, "No. They are the sweet ones." Debbie takes two and puts them in her mouth. She turns red, purple, blue, and says, "Oh my God. Water!" My brother says, "Here's some water," and gives it to her and she drinks the whole thing. And it was vodka. Pure vodka. It's the first time she had met my father. Debbie can't drink. She barely even drinks wine. She nearly passed out.

MJ: That's funny.

SB: Debbie is very innocently naive. Tell me more of the practical jokes you have done?

MJ: I love doing rowdy stuff. Tell 'em Frank.

Frank: Shmuley, we went to the south of France getting a music award. We were in a suite overlooking the ocean. It's a beautiful view. Downstairs below are people eating in a restaurant, elegant ties, suits, gorgeous, eating. It was 7:30–8:00 pm and it was still light. We were looking at each other and we had the same idea in mind. We got to the garbage bag and filled it with water and right below us the people are eating. We threw it [the rest is inaudible because Michael and Frank are laughing]. . . the deluge of water is on the table. We laughed so hard that we were dying. It was so mean, the dinner was over. They were standing up going.

That same night, 4 am, people coming in, the sun's coming up. They were singing. We got a bucket of water and waited until they got close enough.

I love stuff like that. They don't know where it came from.

Frank may sound obnoxious from this story, but he was always charming and well-mannered when the three of us spent time to-

gether, which was quite often. Later, Frank would become an unindicted coconspirator in Michael's trial, accused of attempting to
abduct Michael's accuser's family. But Frank was never violent or
threatening in any way, and I found the idea of him harming, or
threatening to harm, Michael's accuser's family utterly inconceivable.
Frank and I clashed somewhat over what Michael should be doing
with his life. Yet today Frank is one of my dearest friends and I have
tried to play the role of something of a mentor to him. When the trial
ended, Frank told me that he had spoken to Michael the day after
the trial and basically reaffirmed to Michael everything that I had
preached four years earlier, namely, the need for Michael to reconnect
with God and his family, to leave Neverland and live in a normal
community, to stop taking medication for every ailment, and to get
serious with his life.

MJ: It was so much fun.

SB: Did you ever get caught?

MJ: No. I had one of my stage managers make me a laser and it was
this long (makes a hand gesture) and it shoots out for several miles.
People could have been walking several blocks away but we made
this red dot go along with them. We do that everywhere. Here in
the Four Seasons. They called the police and knocked on the door.
It was four years ago. We were spying in somebody's room, it was
so much fun. We hid it because I didn't want to lose it. The police
knocked on the door and our security was talking to them and
taking care of it. I don't know what he said. You have got to have
some fun, come on. We love anything with water.

Frank: We were in a hotel once. . .

MJ: South America wasn't it?

Frank: We filled up a garbage can of water and if you tilt it toward
the door when you open it, so when you open it water falls all
over you.

MJ: I love that.

Frank: So we knock on the door and we run. They open the door.
Wham! Water.

SB: This is in a hotel? This is the South American story?

MJ: South America was different. There people go out on their balconies right below you, sunbathing, with no clothes on hanging their dirty laundry that they just cleaned on the rail of the balcony, their panties drying in the sun. Boom! A bunch of water goes over everything. I love that. I love it too much. It gives me great pleasure.

Frank: There was this girl and this guy and the girl has no top on. We lean over, we see them, all of a sudden, whooom!

MJ: [Laughing] When it comes down I love that. When they jump, it kills me.

This is another sign that for all of Michael's protestations that he was never childish but only childlike, that was simply not the case. To be sure, dropping a water balloon on some tourist is not murder or rape, but it sure can ruin your evening if you're the target. And it always puzzled me that Michael, who was scrupulously careful to appear gentlemanly in my presence, could at times behave with such disregard for other people. But to be fair to Michael, certainly from everything I witnessed, he was scrupulously courteous to everyone he met. And, perhaps, these accounts were somewhat exaggerated. As I said, Frank especially was always a gentleman.

SB: You have only ever got caught once with that laser? Where is the laser now?

MJ: It's in storage somewhere in California. I wish I could find it. I would take it all over the world. It goes miles. Any of these buildings (Michael points out the window) where you are walking, it is a red dot.

Fall of an Icon

Humpty Dumpty sat on a wall:

Humpty Dumpty had a great fall.

All the King's horses and all the King's men

Couldn't put Humpty Dumpty in his place again.

    —Lewis Carroll

"Humpty Dumpty" is said to have been inspired by England's notorious fifteenth-century monarch, King Richard III. But it might also be applied to the self-styled King of Pop, Michael Jackson, the Humpty Dumpty of our time, who fell off the wall, became tragically disfigured, and crumbled before our very eyes. All the King's horses and all the King's men—the retinue of lawyers who got him out of legal trouble, the cadre of doctors who medicated him into oblivion, the sycophantic brownnosing handlers who catered to his every destructive whim—not only failed to put his life back together again but served as the principal culprits behind his fall.

Off the Wall is, of course, the title of Michael's first solo album as an adult artist, and it seems to capture the public's experience of Michael in the years since we parted ways in 2001. To most people, Michael Jackson had become a weirdo, a freak, arguably the strangest celebrity on earth. His trial on charges of child molestation neatly confirmed for most people the fact that he was beyond redemption.

But from reading these moving and at times heartbreaking transcripts, you may have arrived at a different conclusion, one that I arrived at years ago. The story of Michael Jackson is that of a once decent and humble man who was so desperate for attention that he made himself into an idol to be worshipped, only to be later exposed, like all false gods before him, as an impostor, as a god of tin rather than of gold, as a one-trick deity rather than an all-powerful divinity.

Yes, Michael was once a very special man, a man of deep faith who grew up as a devout Jehovah's Witness, a son of considerable devotion to his parents who despite being the most famous entertainer in the world insisted on living at home until his late twenties. A pop star who eschewed the usual mix of hallucinogenic drugs and promiscuous sex with groupies and, instead, visited hospitals and orphanages. An American icon who announced that his celebrity would be devoted to alleviating the plight of unloved and uncared-for children.

Indeed, there were times in our two-year friendship when I stood in quiet awe at what I saw as this man's deep-seated goodness. That it all came crashing down so thoroughly prior to his death, that Michael became one of the most loathed and reviled public figures of our time, was a tragedy of epic proportions.

The sensitive and introspective Michael Jackson that you have encountered in this book, the man whom I once called my very dear friend, ceased to exist years before his tragic and untimely end. In its place a sad and hollow shell of something that once resembled a man lived on in squalid infamy. His reputation in tatters, he appeared more mannequin than man, more beast than being. Peter Pan had become Peter Porn. The man who expressed his ideas so eloquently in this book might have surprised you with his intelligence, delighted you with his wit, and provoked you with the depth of his insights about life.

Possibility of Redemption

In general, there are only two kinds of people: stars and planets. Those who give off an autonomous, inner light, and those who are forced to reflect a borrowed, exterior light; those who illuminate the lives of others with an intrinsic inner glow and those who are so inwardly dark that they become a black hole, soaking up every last speck of light so that none is left for others to enjoy. The irony of Hollywood is that nearly all our celebrities are planets rather than stars. Lacking an inner radiance, they become dependent on the external spotlight. Soon they become its prisoner and, bereft of a connection with the Source of all Light, they suffer the corrosive effects of celebrity sunburn, which usually manifests itself in the form of moral degeneracy, irredeemable loneliness, and deep unhappiness.

A close friend of mine who is a television producer called me up after Michael died and told me that he was profoundly disappointed in my refusal to get back into Michael's life to try and help him. "It seemed so unlike you, Shmuley, to give up on someone."

What my friend did not understand was that salvation must always involve some act of personal redemption. One cannot rescue someone who is not prepared to exert any effort to rescue themselves. I knew that if I went back into Michael's life it would be me who would end up needing rescuing. Michael would have dragged me back into his orbit and the dysfunction and chaos would have ripped me from my moorings. I would have been one sinking ship trying to save another.

Do you really believe that all the hucksters who surrounded Michael at the end of his life—the publicists who served as apologists for his most reprehensible behavior, the doctor-pushers who fed him his constant supply of drugs, the agents and managers who sucked his blood dry—were all bad people? I assume many or all of them were once quite decent. But they got slowly pulled into the unethical world of supercelebrity until they were compromised by it. A doctor would start by trying to resist Michael's entreaties for more sedatives. But Michael would seduce him by making him feel that he needed him so badly. And it's heady stuff to be needed by a global superstar. It makes you feel important and special and soon you close your eyes to all you know to be righteous. The glow of fame is too bright, the gravitational pull of celebrity too difficult to resist, until you have become nothing but a satellite in its orbit. All resistance has been quelled by the superpowerful narcotic of superstardom.

So, was Michael Jackson beyond redemption? I am loath to answer that question. I am a rabbi, for goodness sake, and with the exception of cold-blooded killers, terrorists, and violent rapists, I believe in the divine spark of every human being. And it was undeniable that Michael had a luminous soul that once shined brightly.

But having said this, I believe that short of the most profound and gut-wrenching intervention, Michael's early death was almost inevitable. The reason: He had lost any real reason to live. Yes, there were his children, and he loved them dearly. But that was all. Other than that, his life had become so riddled with pain, his existence so directionless, his everyday routine so vacuous, that, aside from watching his children grow up, he had nothing to look forward to.

It remains a mystery to me why the precious responsibility of caring for his children was not enough to make him choose life. But what is clear is that everything else that was important to him—being loved by the public, helping the world's children, having relationships that were not mutually exploitative—were, in his mind, out of reach forever. In this sense, dare I say it, Michael was beyond redemption because he could not summon the strength or energy to redeem himself. He was lethargic, burned out, and drugged into a near comatose stupor, all under the watchful eye of people who claimed to care for him.

Destructive Effects of Celebrity

Celebrity, in the parlance of PR gurus, is called "exposure." The term is apt because it connotes a negative that can be either properly exposed or overexposed. If film is not developed in a darkroom, if it is immediately exposed to light, the image is lost. Very early on Michael Jackson began to lose that darkroom, that private haven. Every particle of his being was exposed to the public. There was no place where he could retire for repose and reflection. His very existence belonged to the fans and he was their prisoner. He was exposed from the early stages of childhood and was never afforded a place of peace and solitude where he could regain a sense of self and reconnect with God, a nurturing spiritual presence who gives life higher meaning. The result was an image that, quickly overexposed, slowly faded until it disappeared. To be sure, Michael got a full hour rather than just fifteen minutes of fame. But the overexposure made him wither under the powerful lights until he shriveled and even his undeniable talent could no longer save him.

Celebrities like Michael Jackson have become so accustomed to being rescued by paid lieutenants that they forget that true salvation comes from the inside rather than the outside, through inner transformation rather than transient cosmetic modification. Only Michael Jackson could have rescued Michael Jackson. The conversations in this book serve as a good reminder of what he once was and aspired to be. But more importantly, they are also a morality lesson for a society filled with people who believe that their lives will become meaningful through fortune and fame.

The blessings of renown and resources are ones to which many of us aspire. But if a solid grounding in something wholesome and spiritual is not laid before the journey commences, and is not sustained when the journey is at its peak, there is no telling to what depths one may fall. Without a solid moral and spiritual anchor, we become first a life adrift, then a life that is steadily eroded by the shifting sands of celebrity.

In this sense, the literary figure that Michael came to resemble was J. R. R. Tolkien's Gollum, who is destroyed by the "ring of power," or what Gollum calls his "Precious." As Tolkien so brilliantly portrays in his *Lord of the Rings* trilogy, the ring of power eventually brings out the very worst qualities of its owner.

Gollum, who started life as a decent hobbit, slowly becomes ravaged by the effects of the ring until he is only a grotesque and sinister caricature of his former, wholesome self. In our time, celebrity is that "ring of power." Like the ring itself, fame is shiny and glitzy, precious to behold, and makes ordinary people powerful beyond their wildest dreams. Even someone unknown, like "Joe the Plumber," can try on the ring, become famous for fifteen minutes, and suddenly become the subject of presidential debates, be enveloped by photographers, and bring traffic to a halt by simply walking down the street.

Fame is our modern "Precious," a circular aura that we don to temporarily render us not invisible but invincible. Fame is power. Obscurity is death. We treat life today like the proverbial tree in the forest that falls with no one to hear it. Did it really fall? If you lived your life and no one has heard of you, did you even exist?

But just like the ring, celebrity has a dark and sinister side. While millions crave it, very few have survived its ruinous effects. Like smallpox, fame usually comes in bursts and by the time it passes it leaves hideous scars. Sometimes those scars are the scars of divorce and loneliness. In our conversations, you heard Michael himself talking about how fame nearly always destroys the lives of childhood stars, many of whom never even make it to their adult years. At other times, he rightly notes, fame leaves the scars of deep isolation and unhappiness, which in turn lead to the scars of substance abuse and addiction—anything to dull the pain. Other times, celebrity leaves the scar of damaged children. Most tragically, celebrity often causes the scar of early death.

There is often a tragic correlation between superstardom and early death, as in the cases of Marilyn Monroe, Elvis Presley, James Dean, Janis Joplin, Jimi Hendrix, Jim Morrison, John Belushi—and now Michael Jackson. And yet, for all the tragedy and disaster it causes, like the ring in Tolkien's tale, still we pursue it. Even as it consumes us, chews us up, and spits us out, we worship steadfastly at its altar.

Michael Jackson tragically became the Gollum of the modern age, a desiccated and disfigured incubus. Like Gollum, Michael's voice sounded odd to those who heard it. Like Gollum, Michael evoked the image of a healthy past and a tragic present. Like Gollum, Michael held tenaciously onto his ring, his "Precious," his fame, even as he so eloquently articulated its toxic effects. Strangely oblivious to how it disfigured him, he refused to forsake it.

He was not only proud but obsessed with being the world's best-known entertainer. In many of our conversations, he compared himself to Elvis Presley—"my former father-in-law"—indelicately bragging that he had garnered more number-one hit records than Elvis. Michael seemed oblivious, however, to the other ramifications of the comparison: that he, like Elvis, was slowly mangled by celebrity. Tragically, like Gollum, Michael was oblivious to how the "ring" was killing him. Yes, Michael may have had Deprivan, Demerol, and Oxycodone, but fame was always his drug of choice.

No matter how dedicated Michael was to changing the course of his life during the years of our close relationship, the corrosive nature of his celebrity was always evident. I saw what it did to him, and I saw what it did to the people around him—often bringing out the absolute worst in them.

And here I am not just talking about ordinary people who went berserk around Michael. I am talking about celebrities who become just as sycophantic as the others. I remember once Michael inviting me to his hotel suite in New York to meet Justin Timberlake and talk to him about how he might assist us in promoting parents spending time with children. Justin had just flown in from Las Vegas, where the night before he had hosted the American Music Awards. He did not tell Michael that he was bringing his girlfriend at the time, Britney Spears. So when he came into Michael's suite, he sheepishly said that Britney was waiting in the room with the security guards, afraid of entering without Michael's permission. Michael told him to bring her in. And here I was, face to face with a woman I sadly have come to disrespect for her irresponsible role in over-sexualizing young teens. I spoke with each of them briefly, told them something of the public lectures Michael and I were conducting, and then promptly departed. When I got home, my young daughters asked me what it was like to meet Britney Spears. I responded, "Ordinary. She is absolutely ordinary. There was nothing special about her." Indeed, Britney seemed pretty intimidated by Michael, and Michael was a bit intimidated as well. Which just goes to show that even stars are star-struck.

The game of celebrity one-upmanship is one that can never be won, as Farrah Fawcett found out. She had the tragic misfortune not only to die young from cancer, but on the same day as Michael Jackson. A huge star when I was a boy, she was consigned to oblivion because a super-nova exploded on the day of her death. Most celebrities nurse even worse insecurities than us mortals. Britney, since that meeting four years ago, has degenerated sharply, having largely erased the line that separates the female recording industry from soft porn.

Another case in point was the star-studded Angel Ball, organized by Denise Rich. As mentioned in Part 1, Denise's daughter, Gabrielle, whom I knew at Oxford when she was a student, died of leukemia, and the biannual ball raises money to help fight the disease. Denise asked me to attend and to bring Michael along.

I also invited my friend Elie Wiesel, the Holocaust survivor and Nobel laureate, together with his wife, Marion, to be the guests of honor at our table. When we entered the reception, the room was filled to the rafters with bona fide celebrities, including the guest of honor, Denise's friend President Clinton. But Michael outshined them all. There was a rush from all over the room as people hurried to meet him. His security force could not hold the people back.

Elie Wiesel, one of the most respected men in the world and a recipient of the world's most prestigious award, was literally shoved and pushed by Hollywood's elite as they eagerly raced toward Michael. It was embarrassing and humiliating. Women as well-known as Cindy Crawford were lining up to get their picture taken with Michael. I was trying to keep people from stepping on the Wiesels.

A prominent banker who was sitting next to me at the dinner, and who watched the world's most famous Holocaust survivor being nearly trampled to get to the singer, turned to me and said, "It makes you lose hope for the human race, doesn't it?" (The only ray of hope that evening was when Lance Bass of 'N Sync walked over to one of our retinue. We were all convinced that he too was requesting the opportunity to meet Michael Jackson, but he said to her, "Do you think I can meet Elie Wiesel? That has always been a dream of mine." A classy guy.)

False Idol

Many chart the beginning of the fall of Michael Jackson to the 1993 molestation accusations. I disagree. Yes, Michael settled those allegations, leading many to believe that he was guilty. Still, he survived them and even began to successfully rebuild his career. Aside from the toxicity of childhood exposure that robbed him of a normal life, in his adult life I find a different starting point that marked his accelerated decline. It took place when Sony launched his *HIStory* album in 1995. Accompanying the release were huge statues of Michael placed in cities all over the world, as well as a music video depicting Michael as a gargantuan idol, complete with thousands of soldier-worshippers at his beck and call. I was living in Oxford in 1995 and can well remember the large statue of Michael that was dragged down the Thames in London.

I watched this video with Michael at his Neverland Valley Ranch theater for the first time in August 2000. Michael, sitting about three feet away from me, was nostalgically reliving his earlier success. But seeing a mortal man depicted as an enormous object of worship nearly made me fall off my chair. I can still remember the intense discomfort I felt. Here was a man who had been a devout Jehovah's Witness, with an innate, deep-seated spirituality, setting himself up as a god! Even after *Thriller* came out, Michael continued "witnessing" for his church every Sunday, going from door-to-door selling *Watchtower* and *Awake* magazines.

How could a man with such a deep attachment to God suddenly make *himself* into a deity? Once he set himself up as an idol to be adored, it was but a short step for Michael to create his own rules and live by his own set of laws. The erosion of Michael Jackson from a man of decency and humility to a man who had disfigured his face, given his two sons the same name—Prince I and Prince II (who became known as "Blanket")—and dangled his baby from a balcony in the belief that he need answer to no higher authority, dates from that period.

Right and wrong was now what Michael determined them to be. The world may find sleepovers with another person's kids revolting. But the world be damned. Inhabiting a lower level of consciousness, they just did not understand. The Bible commands that we honor our parents. But Michael reserved the right to condemn his father publicly on many occasions, even when those condemnations served no healing purpose in their relationship.

I would tell Michael he had no right to denounce his father in front of strangers, that he was transgressing the Fifth Commandment. Indeed, the lecture I wrote for him to deliver at Oxford revolved around forgiving, rather than abhorring, his father. It was designed to reestablish the integrity of his relationship with his father. But that was Michael Jackson the innocent boy who was listening to me. Within time he would revert to Michael Jackson the icon who treated me as a well-meaning nuisance who dared question things that are way beyond his understanding.

New Faith of Celebrity

It seems bizarre, therefore, that we single out only Michael for his excesses when so many celebrities are destroying themselves and those around them, even if it is to a lesser extent. And we the public are not completely innocent. Celebrities live in a world not of their own creation but of *our* creation. Our worship of celebrities has gone from a pastime to a devotion, from a form of recreation to a form of veneration, from entertainment to religion.

Detached as we are from God and estranged from loftier pursuits, we have invented new gods here on earth. Where once people were awed by the heavenly stars, today they prostrate themselves before movie stars. Where once man pondered the secrets of the universe, we today seek to uncover the enigma of Marlon Brando. Is it surprising, then, that the objects of this worship begin to believe that they have a right to make up and live by their own rules, even when it becomes completely ruinous?

And we the public, the idolizers, are just as guilty as the celebrities who invite the adulation. The golden calf of Moses' time has been replaced by the Oscar statue of our time.

The essence of the Bible can really be reduced to a single idea: God alone should be the epicenter of our lives, the heart of our existence, the soul of our actions. Brook no counterfeit substitutes.

Gone are the days when humans would bend their knees or prostrate themselves before the celestial host. No, our modern idols have moved from the stone-carved totems of the ancient world to the perfectly sculpted bodies of the Hollywood world. Rather than pray to the heavenly stars, we obsess on the lives of our movie stars. Rather than talk of the beauty of God's creation, we talk about the magnificence of our screen creations. Rather than talk about how we can connect with God, we talk about who Jennifer Aniston is connecting with.

Many believe that it is drugs and failed relationships that spoil celebrities. But I have discovered that it is sycophantic friends and abettors who are the worst poison of all. They reinforce the idea that the celebrity can do no wrong.

Humility of Hubris

Humans are not gods, and when the public expects them to be gods, they must conceal or dismiss their humanity in an effort to not appear ordinary. It is against this backdrop that much of Michael's bizarre behavior must be understood.

Once, when we were walking into the home of my friend, PR guru Howard Rubenstein, for a quiet meeting with members of the press, Michael emerged from his van and put on a black mask. I said, "Please put that silly thing away. It makes you look like Darth Vader." He never wore it in my presence again. He had put it on before, not because, as people speculated, he was a freak about air quality but simply to appear more mysterious. He wanted to always keep people guessing. Indeed, he loved being a trendsetter, bragging to me that he had made it cool for people to wear white socks with the pant legs ending high—"You used to be a geek if you wore white socks and high pants, but now everyone wears them"—and one, instead of two, gloves. Little did Michael realize that even if you are a great trendsetter, but people think you are deranged, you are still the loser. But then making up his own rules was always more appealing to Michael than living by existing ones, no matter what the circumstances.

At the time of the Oxford lecture, which was made possible from my eleven years serving as rabbi at the university, he and I were championing the call for a Children's Bill of Rights and putting children first, a movement to improve the lives of children. I made it clear to Michael that the success of his lecture would depend entirely on his ability to subordinate himself to his message. "Humble yourself and glorify your words."

He agreed. But as we walked into the debating chamber of the venerable Oxford Union, a place where Albert Einstein, the Queen of England, and several American presidents had lectured before him, Michael told me to go in first with the president of the Oxford Union, who should announce him, after which he would arrive as he always does in his concerts, with fanfare and screams.

I told him this was no concert, that he had been invited to one of the most prestigious lecture chambers in the world, that the two-hundred-year-old tradition was for every guest to be escorted by the president into the chamber, and that he would be no exception. But he was adamant. He could not be anything but the star. He could occupy no place but center stage. So we went along with the preposterous arrangement and it immediately cheapened him. And while his lecture was not just a popular but even a critical success, he emerged the loser that night. In the battle of the warring sides of himself, he was destined to lose to the corrupting forces of fame.

After my two years of friendship with Michael, I became extremely disillusioned with celebrity culture in general and what it had done to Michael and the people in his vicinity in particular. It is what led directly to the publication of my 2003 book, *The Private Adam: Becoming a*

Hero in a Selfish Age, which serves as a strong critique and repudiation of the celebrity culture, arguing for everyday, unsung acts of heroism that would never make it into a newspaper. I dismissed the false heroes who were leading our culture off the precipice. My attraction to Michael was largely based on my feeling that he was a different kind of celebrity. More humble, more sensitive, more human. And truth be told, there was that side of him. But very little of that human Michael remained at the end. All that was left was the decaying superstar, the side of him that got away with reckless and irresponsible behavior.

Fear for the Future

When Michael and I were friends, I never feared that he would one day molest a child. The thought of his being a child molester was foreign to me, and even now I find it painful to accept that Michael could sexually abuse a child. No, my fear was of a completely different nature: that Michael would not live to see his fiftieth birthday. That the dark abyss over which he had led his life would finally consume him and he would be lost.

I shudder to think that perhaps there was something that someone could have done to save him. But, barring being found guilty in 2005 and being sent to a penitentiary where all his privileges, including access to phony doctors with their truckload of painkillers, would have been taken away, there seemed to be no hope. In this sense, ironic as it may sound, being found innocent was yet another tragedy in Michael's life.

When he was arrested I thought it might provide the jolt that would save him from implosion. But it was not to be. Michael could never truly hit bottom. Even when he had run through his money, his friends, and his family, he was able to borrow against his future earnings and even his future chance at a comeback to avoid the cold reality that would push him in a new direction.

Losses

In the close friendship we once shared, where I endeavored to reverse the downward spiral, I would often tell him that without an authentic connection to God he would never survive life as a celebrity. But celebrities rarely listen to mortals. And they do not need God, since they are gods themselves. They allow all their relationships to atrophy as they become more and more isolated.

His relationship with his father was the first major relationship he lost. From an early age Michael began to perceive Joseph Jackson—and Michael always called him Joseph rather than Daddy, which his father insisted on—as a harsh manager rather than a tender parent. Next to go was his close relationship with his brothers. Jealousy between Michael and his brothers, egged on by their wives, according to Michael, ensured that The Jackson 5 could not survive as a unit. This also, according to Michael, made him highly suspicious of marriage, thereby ensuring that a grounded wife would not be present to help him through life.

Then he lost his relationship with the Jehovah's Witnesses Church, a key ingredient in keeping him humble and stable. So devoted a son was Michael to his Church that he even placed their required disclaimer at the beginning of his memorable "Thriller" music video, announcing that the video did not represent an endorsement of the occult. A few years later, however, he had repudiated the Church and they had repudiated him. By this time, aside from a loving but distant relationship with this mother, nothing was left. Like a kite at the mercy of the winds, Michael Jackson was completely untethered. And although he would later have two, and then three, children, they could not (nor was it their role to) connect Michael to the people, pursuits, and beliefs that could provide the safe harbor and positive influence all of us need.

The Damaged Celebrity

We are not the first generation of individuals who wish to be famous and who are infatuated with celebrity and notoriety. Throughout history, men and women have endeavored to escape the horrible facelessness of anonymity by becoming recognizable to their fellow humans through grand gestures. The great men and women of history have always sought to rise from the undistinguished morass of the general populace and be noticed, like a towering wave that swells from the pool of the ocean's waters.

Two-and-a-half thousand years ago, Alexander the Great of Macedonia, the first truly famous man in history, took along on his campaigns chroniclers and historians who would later tell the tale of his wondrous conquests. Later, Augustus of Rome minted dozens of coins with his likeness. He wanted his vast achievements as the towering administrator of the greatest empire to be known throughout the world. In an age where the majority of the population was illiterate, the best way of becoming famous was visually rather than verbally. Even in the last century, Charles Lindbergh became the most famous man on earth when he conquered the seemingly endless vastness of the Atlantic Ocean as a lone flyer, and indulged in an orgy of ticker-tape parades and never-ending interviews. So, no, as a generation, we are not distinguished by our lust for fame.

What does make us different, however, is that so many of us relish the loss of our dignity in the quest for celebrity. In the aforementioned historical scenarios, the protagonist always wishes to be famous for some virtue or accomplishment. Celebrity was a means by which one magnified one's own renown and respectability by having the masses know of one's triumphs. Men pursued celebrity with the express intention of promoting their dignity, establishing their legacy, and thereby defining their uniqueness. They promoted their part in the long timeline of human achievement. To be sure, we can debate today whether Napoleon was a liberator or a tyrant, whether one who finds glory on the battlefield is a bully or a victor. But be that as it may, in his own age, military conquest was glorious and thus Napoleon wished for all the earth to know that the glory was his.

Michael Jackson became the most famous man of his generation. But it was a fame radically different from the ones just described. Here was a man who became famous first for his music, then for his dysfunction. He became celebrated first for his genius and talent but then later for his deficiencies and peculiarities. A man so desperate for recognition, so seemingly deprived of love, that if it took being seen with a chimp or telling the world he slept in a hyperbaric chamber to get people to talk about him, he would pay that price. If he had to let it be known that he was buying the bones of the Elephant Man, or run around the world wearing a villain's mask, or grab his crotch a hundred times during a concert, he would do that too to become even more recognizable. Plastic surgery did the rest. In the public's mind, Michael Jackson was transformed from talented boy wonder to human train wreck. Some people embrace eccentricity. Michael put all his creativity into it.

Perversely, he ended up getting everything he ever wanted. His trial on charges of child molestation, among other allegations, made him even more famous than the Beatles. But while some sell their soul for a place in eternity, Michael, through his inability to put any brakes to his plastic reconstructions, sold the very image of God in man.

Michael Jackson became the father of all those who are prepared to flaunt, rather than conceal, their imperfections in the never-ending quest for fame. In that respect, Michael Jackson became, arguably, the most influential man alive, the man whose antics would later invite the age of reality TV and would culminate in cheap stunts like Britney and Madonna kissing on stage, an intoxicated Lindsay Lohan driving her car into a tree, and Jessica Simpson talking about her stool.

Michael gave birth to an entirely new kind of celebrity, the damaged celebrity, being famous not for one's virtues but for one's blemishes. Usually people try to hide their mistakes and their character defects. They want to be famous for the good things and not the bad. Michael's life became the first reality TV show. Before him, we had never heard of someone wanting to be celebrated for their defects. Who has ever heard of desiring to be famous for one's ugliness? Since when is infamous the equal of famous? Since when was facing humiliation and public ridicule considered a valid means to recognition? But basking in the warm glow of the cameras, we don't even notice that we are naked— until, that is, the lights go off. In the darkness of our dignity, we discover what precious commodities we have lost.

Whereas in previous generations, dignity and celebrity were partners, Michael Jackson may one day be best remembered as the man who set them permanently at odds, who took fame and substance and put them in conflict with one another. A man who could have been happy to have risen to the highest ranks of music stardom but decided to intentionally act weird to sustain public interest. As I watched Ed Bradley of *60 Minutes* ask Michael why his album *Invincible* had not even broken into the top ten of the billboard charts, Michael, oblivious to how he was now famous as a freak show rather than as an entertainer, responded: "It's a conspiracy." Michael long ago confused fame with infamy and lived in the twilight zone between those two poles.

Not that he is entirely to blame. Michael's desperation for attention at any cost was presaged by his extreme deprivation of love and attention in the most tender years of his life. His decision, however, to fill the empty pool of love with the poisonous wellspring of tabloid fodder is that for which he must be held accountable.

Out of His Depth

It is the thesis of this book that Michael Jackson, whom people find so easy to revile, is the ultimate victim of the age of celebrity, a man caught up in something that he could not understand and could not control until it ultimately consumed everything he once was. The Michael Jackson we saw toward the end of his life was but a sinister shadow of a once healthy man. That Michael became stranger than almost any celebrity who preceded him was directly linked to him having become more famous than almost anyone who preceded him. The damage was more extensive and more intense.

It is also the contention of this book that this tragedy could have been prevented, not by Michael choosing to be a steel worker like his father before him, but by retaining the wholesome ingredients of a healthy life that could have counterbalanced the emptiness of celebrity. Michael began life with many of those very ingredients—a strong religious faith, deep attachment to family and siblings, a desire to use one's talents for a higher good—and they originally ensured that he did not rot and decay amid his fame.

Unfortunately, as he became a bigger and bigger star, Michael first lost touch with and then consciously repudiated those things and tragically ended up destitute, discredited, and dead. Finally, it is the contention of this book that Michael Jackson serves as a warning to all of us of the damaging effects of the *age* of celebrity, something we are all caught up in.

"Family" of Fans

And herein lies the crux of the problem. Every human being wants to be special, everyone wants to be the center of attention—at least part of the time. It is what the German philosopher Hegel called the thymotic urge, or "the will to recognition." But in days gone by, it was family and human relationships that made one feel like the center of attention. It was the authentic love of relatives and friends that rescued humans from the pain of anonymity. Children had their parents' attention, just as if they were celebrities. Their parents commented on everything they did, as if they were Julia Roberts or Russell Crowe. But a whole generation has now grown up like Michael Jackson, pushed to achieve too early, made to feel by parents that they were machines of productivity at too young an age. Deprived of the wholesome attention that is their birthright, they have grown up lusting for the spotlight and will do almost anything to get it.

Having missed a childhood where he was both his parents' center of affection, Michael had to devote his life to attention-getting measures in order to compensate. Having grown into adulthood without anything wholesome, such as a wife or life partner, to make him feel noticed, he had to do whatever he could to make sure that *we* noticed. Cut off from the family that should have adored him, Michael invented the artificial family of fans that could give him the fix he needed, even if it was a mere shadow of the real thing.

We are all at risk of becoming, or desiring to become, Michael Jacksons—albeit in much lesser keys. *American Idol* works on the premise that *you* can be the next Michael Jackson. Children are sorely neglected in favor of their parents' commercial pursuits. Married couples struggle to hear one another over the din of each other's harried lives. Parents come home from a long day of work and their kids don't run over to greet them, consumed as they are with watching their favorite TV show. The result is that everyone is feeling neglected.

Relationships lack passion and intimacy, and to compensate we seek to make love to the crowds. We want acceptance and even adoration from our friends, families, people we work with, and whatever audience we can find. In the absence of healthy, caring, consistent attention, too many of us have become shameless attention-seekers, even when it is an affront to our dignity. In an impersonal world dominated by the Internet and films, feeling bereft of an inner dignity, people are driven to broadcast their woes or triumphs however they can. (One man in Wisconsin who killed eight people wrote to the police to say that he continued killing because after the first two murders his name had not appeared in the newspapers.)

If we are "lucky" enough to have our fifteen minutes, when it is all over we have to endure the indignity of walking around draped in our dirty laundry, which has become a kind of squalid second skin.

Michael's Redemption Lies in Us Taking Heed

It is my belief that it is our resistance to taking heed, more than anything else, which explains why we are so infatuated with Michael Joseph Jackson. Watching the train wreck of his life and now death, we are watching ourselves in the form of a man who took his pursuit for recognition to an extreme. If James Brown is the godfather of soul, we can see Michael Jackson as the godfather of celebrity without substance, fame without foundation, representing in his sad and damaged life where society was led into the abyss. Watching Michael Jackson's tragedy we are witnessing our own transfiguration. Watching Michael slowly decay we bear witness to our own corruption.

In this respect, let Michael—tragic as his life has become—be a warning to the rest of us.

The only cure for a society hell-bent on fame at any price is to increase the amount of genuine love shown in that society. Parents have got to start listening to their kids when they speak. When your kids come running to you to tell you a seemingly insignificant detail about their teacher, turn off the television for a few minutes and give them your undivided attention. The alternative is to turn on the television a few years later and see your own kid on some reality TV show making a fool of himself because the pain of humiliation is not as great as the pain of neglect.

Husbands and wives have to start giving each other the affection they need. The tragic alternative is that they might find that attention in the arms of a stranger, as more than fifty percent of husbands and wives are doing today. Rather than getting into a cab and immediately getting on your cell phone, speak to the driver. He is not just a means to an end. He was not created by God merely to get you from point A to point B. He is a person with his own dreams, his own ambitions, and his own story.

The essence of a relationship, the essence of marriage, is to be a celebrity. But unlike public celebrity, here you are a celebrity only to one. There is a person to whom you are famous. He or she puts your picture up on the wall and saves your silly mementos and handwritten letters, just like celebrity watchers collect those of Elvis. This person can remember the first time you kissed, and stares at you when you are out in public. When you walk into the room, you immediately become the center of this person's attention, just as if a movie star had walked into the room. And this person is absorbed by your presence.

This is a *real* fan, a devoted fan who will never drop you in favor of the next new thing. If you go bankrupt or develop three chins, this person will stick around. If you suffer public humiliation—even if you are accused of something heinous—this person will stand by you through your trials. Your fame is not ephemeral in this person's eyes. It is eternal. Your share price does not fluctuate in accordance with public demand. The market does not determine your value. This person loves you for your humanity.

Michael Jackson had tens of millions of fans. But what he always lacked was one grand, lifelong admirer—a happy marriage, a stable relationship, a warm embrace to come home to. The same is true with so many of our celebrities in Hollywood. A million fans but not one permanent follower.

Yes, we all want to be a celebrity. But as with an unhealthy celebrity, people only admire you when you are on top of your game. If you lose the Super Bowl, or your looks, or your money, you are abandoned as quickly as you were embraced. Michael Jackson learned this the hard way. Aside from a few thousand die-hard fans, he was, by the end, abandoned by virtually all who once admired him. And the few who stuck with him did so out of pity or for the elusive hunger for a payoff that is the antithesis of meaningful relationship.

Even as I watched Michael eviscerated on the news channels in the years that followed our friendship, I found it painful and lamentable that America had no compassion for him. The utter disfiguration, the teetering near bankruptcy, the squandering of his precious gifts, and most of all the questions about children generated only contempt.

Even Martha Stewart was shown compassion after her arrest and conviction. But to elicit pity, one must first be perceived to be human. And in the eyes of the public, Michael had become pure caricature.

Martha Stewart could never be completely hated because she was never completely loved. Strong emotions can be flipped, and this is precisely what happened in the case of Michael Jackson. The public once loved him. They grew up with him and in their eyes he was always a boy, an innocent and fun-loving man-child.

In his shyness they believed in his innocence. In his naiveté they still remembered their own youth. In seeing him surrounded by children, they were convinced that he was an adolescent at heart. But hell hath no fury like a public duped. A large percentage of the public believed that Michael was not innocent but corrupt, not clean but calculating. Neverland was built not as a shrine to youthful precociousness, but as a lair to lure the unsuspecting. They thought they were getting a choir boy, but then concluded that they had someone as adept at manipulating the public as he was at moving his feet.

As for me, I strongly believed that Michael did not molest his 2003 accuser who figures so prominently in our conversations and that his acquittal, therefore, was righteous and just. But it almost didn't matter because the inspiration he once provided to so many had all but disappeared. He had become the very thing he always most feared, rejected and reviled. And that led Michael to shut himself off from the world more and more, his shadowy existence now feeding his demons.

Unhealthy fame always leads to reclusiveness. But healthy fame leads to the opposite. It inspires people to become trustful and uninhibited and to come out of their shell. When you enter into a relationship with that one big fan—the person who is committed to cherishing you—rather than hiding, you learn to open up. You are no longer afraid to be vulnerable. Your significant other is not just taking; they are giving. To select you, he or she had to deselect every other member of the opposite sex—publicly and permanently. With such phenomenal sacrifice being undertaken on your behalf, you learn to have faith, both in human beings and in the world. Your happiness becomes your partner's happiness. And all your partner wants is to bask, not in your star but in your light.

In the final analysis, healthy fame may never get you your own television show. Nor will it get the maitre d' to save you the table by the fireplace. No strangers will come up to you on the street and ask for your autograph. But it will give you the feeling that no matter what you do and where you go, you will always have a fan club in the privacy and comfort of your own home.

Farewell to Celebrity

Our very civilization is threatened by the cult of celebrity. The court jester has become the king. Those who *play* the heroes have become the culture's actual heroes.

In America today there exists not a single mainstream televised awards ceremony for anything other than movies, television, acting, modeling, and music. Even when brave soldiers are awarded the Congressional Medal of Honor for gallantry, it is not broadcast on TV. When the President awards the Presidential Medal of Freedom to our leading thinkers, writers, and civil servants, it is watched by a handful of people on C-Span. That's a major change for a country whose only actor to become an historical figure, before the age of Hollywood, was John Wilkes Booth.

By making fashion models our role models, Hollywood heroines our heroes, and singers into saints, we have created a shallow and vain society, distinguished not by sacrifice but by indulgence. We have created a culture known not for virtue, but for vanity. And our country is becoming therefore not more dedicated but decadent. The consequences are perilous for the individuals who suffer and for all of us caught up in the distorted national obsession.

For the most part, young people would rather be directors than doctors, rock stars than rabbis. And then we wonder why the youth appear narcissistic and directionless.

To gauge the effect of entertainers being at the epicenter of a national consciousness, just imagine if it were to happen in the life of a single individual. What if entertainment, rather than scholarship, were the foremost preoccupation of a medical student. Instead of working at a library and attending lectures for eight hours each day, our student watched eight hours of TV and DVDs each day. Would you trust him with your kidney?

And now you begin to understand why so many people around the world think Americans are so shallow. Our celebrity-driven culture doesn't focus on education, hard work, sacrifice, or family. It focuses on entertainment, which by its very nature is something you do in your spare time. Entertainment is designed to be on the periphery, never at the center, of national endeavor.

The larger threat to the United States does not come from foreign powers or terrorist plots. Terrorists can harm us but they can never defeat us. The only thing that can threaten the continuity of this great country is if its actual foundations corrode to such an extent that the national edifice falls victim to the forces of historical inevitability. If our nation is built of the marvelous marble of the Greek Parthenon or the Roman Pantheon or the solid stone of Jerusalem's Western Wall, it will last for many centuries, and perhaps millennia, to come. But if it is built of the flimflam material of mere media hype, a sound stage that is all glitz with no substance, it will, God forbid, crumble before our very eyes.

As I've said, no culture is ever healthy if it deifies human beings. It was not for naught that God made as the very First Commandment the injunctions to accept only one God and never to embrace counterfeits: *I am the Lord Your God. You shall have no other gods before me.* God alone should be the epicenter of our lives, the heart of our existence, the soul of our actions. We dare accept no fraudulent substitutes.

Nearly all of us have become closet idolaters, to our own detriment. I used to tell Michael constantly that the act of making himself a god had to end in tragedy. But we who worship at the altar of celebrities must be aware of our own transgression.

Mea Culpa

I, too, as a man of religion who is firmly immersed in the culture, must confront my own veneration of celebrity. Since first deciding to become a rabbi at the age of sixteen, I harbored a dream that one day I would help make spirituality go mainstream, that I would be an instrument in helping Jewish values rise out of the backwater and earn a popular voice in our culture.

Once I became rabbi at Oxford and hosted renowned figures as speakers to our students, I convinced myself that celebrities and the microphone they had to the world offered a shortcut by which to advance a godly message. Why not float noble ideas through the mouthpiece of superstars? All it took was getting the celebrities on board and the rest of humanity would follow.

But I have come to see the error of my own judgment and now believe that celebrity culture is as destructive as it is promising. I realize that I, too, was engaging in the promotion of idolatry. By using a celebrity to talk about values, the message is made less important than the personality. The light of the idea is absorbed and lost in the aura of the star. If the purpose of knowing God is to be weaned off false idols, then God cannot be taught by those who have allowed, and perhaps even encouraged, their own deification.

There are exceptions, wholesome celebrities such as Bono who have leveraged their fame to highlight causes more worthy than themselves. Yet these notable celebrities are so few that they constitute the exceptions that prove the rule.

The Culture Will Change You
Before You Change the Culture

If there is one thing I have learned from my friendship with Michael Jackson, it is this: I, who always prided myself on being above celebrity gossip—finding it rancid and shallow—discovered that I was no more immune to celebrity idolatry than anyone else.

When my relationship with Michael unraveled, one of the people before whom I was most ashamed was Elie Wiesel. I had worked extremely hard bringing the two of them together. Professor Wiesel was kind enough to publicly embrace Michael, a distinct honor from someone who is one of the most respected figures alive. I remember calling him on the phone to discuss the ending of my friendship with Michael.

Professor Wiesel was gracious. He did not rub salt in the wound. He said that he predicted that something like this might happen, and that this was the reason that, in general, he had always stayed away from celebrities and their causes, amid numerous invitations. "Shmuley, you don't want to believe in an 'us' and 'them' mentality," he told me. "You want to believe that God's message can be channeled through any medium. You want to believe that because people are famous—no matter how they became famous—they have the ability to broadcast a wholesome message. But here is something you never reckoned with. I fear that you will discover that the culture will change you before you change the culture."

I had to take a long hard look at myself after that conversation and make important changes in my life, beginning with distancing myself from nearly all celebrity acquaintances for a time until I could regain a substantive footing. I am often described as a man with many celebrity friends, an interesting sobriquet since I have few to none, as I have recommitted myself to a circle of "ordinary" people, among which I number myself.

I spend my time broadcasting my daily radio show on politics, religion, and culture, writing books and articles, lecturing to audiences on contemporary issues, counseling failing marriages, trying to reconnect parents and angry children, and most of all, trying to be a decent husband to my wife and father to our nine children. When the opportunities arise, I accept invitations to appear as a guest on TV and radio, and indeed I am proud to host my own TV show on TLC that focuses on helping families in crisis. But I no longer hunger for those appearances the way I once did and feel embarrassed and ashamed when I do. After all, I spent two years with the most famous person of all and saw where it all led. And if I did not take that message to heart, there is no hope for my ever learning.

The Jews were brought into the world as witnesses to God's presence, and our highest mission is to return God to the center of human life. We are the original Jehovah's Witnesses, our long existence amid pogroms and persecutions bearing witness to our devotion to that most noble of causes and God's continued presence amid our challenged existence. Our national calling is dedicated to a single proposition: that man is created by a loving God to spread law and love. The Jews were meant to inspire all inhabitants of the earth to love not the sparkling, shallow things, such as celebrity, but the simple yet grand things, such as living decent and honest lives, being responsible members of a spiritual community, caring for our spouses and parents, and acting as devoted servants of the public good. The more attention we humans draw to ourselves, the more we subvert the reason for our existence. Similarly, we dare not allow ourselves to live vicariously through our favorite celebrities in place of leading a purposeful and authentic existence.

This does not mean that all hero worship leads to idolatry. Indeed, all my life I have looked up to, and been inspired by, great men and women. I love history and devour human biographies. I love being inspired by lives of courage and commitment, men who fought tyranny, women who spoke truth to power. We all need people to motivate and inspire us. But I now understand that a true hero is the man or woman who knows God as the hero, someone who has subordinated his or her ego to a higher ideal by placing God and humanity at their core. It is fine to try to follow in the footsteps of my great teacher, the Lubavitcher Rebbe, or the Pope, Nelson Mandela, Mother Theresa, the Dalai Lama or Martin Luther King, Jr. Indeed, Hasidic Jews have pictures of the Rebbe in their homes because his saintly life inspires them. But the lives of these people are less arrows pointing to themselves than vectors pointing to the heavens and to their fellow man.

According to Jewish tradition, God hid Moses's burial place, whose location remains a secret until this very day, to ward off the possible deification of Moses and the establishment of his sepulcher as a shrine. Moses wrought great wonders in Egypt, but he was merely a conduit of God's awesome might.

Still, I do not seek to judge any celebrities who have allowed their lives to become public monuments. I am not here to condemn those who have allowed the public to get carried away with a fascination for the minutiae of their lives. Insofar as I have judged Michael in this book it is because the magnitude of the tragedy, which I personally witnessed, cries out and I can no longer be silent about it. But neither will I ever again seek to propagate a love of the Creator solely through men and women who have not yet learned the lesson that God is the source of their glory and that their spotlight comes from He who created all light. Neither can I condone modern men and women allowing their human potential to remain so tragically underdeveloped as they indulge in discussions of whether their favorite actress will win the Oscar, rather than focusing on their need to achieve triumphs in the real game of life.

Saying Goodbye

When Michael invited me and my family to attend his thirtieth anniversary concert in New York the day before September 11, I remember wondering if I still had the power to resist the magnetic attraction of a superstar, if the fireworks display of Madison Square Garden posed a greater thrill for me than the thunder and lightning of Mount Sinai. In the end, one of my proudest moments was when I declined the invitation. I wanted to go back to what I had been before my first meeting with Michael Jackson, a rabbi who tried to spread the light of God rather than bask in the aura of a celebrity.

Our favorite stars might light up the crowd, but their glow is a mere reflection of a more infinite radiance, their rhythm but a hollow echo of a more eternal beat. While enjoying the entertainment value that celebrities can bring into our lives, it behooves us all not to settle for, and certainly not to obsess over, their glow but to seek out the true source of the light. Isaiah put it best: "Lift your eyes heavenward, and see Who created all these."

In seeking proof of the necessity of finding God in our lives, we need look no further than the tragedy of Michael Jackson. For Michael is living proof that spirituality and values in the modern age are no longer a luxury but a necessity. God is not something we can pull out as a Christmas gift only once a year. Faith is no longer something that can be reserved only for the bunker. Prayer is not something that we can resort to only while ensconced in the valley. God must accompany us now and always—even as we ascend the mountain's summit.

When we speak of the need for God for human salvation, we don't mean salvation from only poverty, pain, and affliction. We especially mean salvation from materialism, shallowness, decadence, and the suf-focating selfishness of narcissism and egocentrism.

Michael Jackson was actually an outstanding candidate to come back to God because he was once a pious and devoted religious son, who spent his weekdays in church and his Sundays proselytizing. If he had had any chance of arresting the downward freefall that was his life, it would have first and foremost come about through a humble return to God. Sadly, it appeared that Michael had to hit rock bottom before he was humble enough to take that step and attempt to return to a family of faith that he so desperately needed. And even then it did not happen. Even if he never again became the King of Pop or conquered the world with his music, he might have claimed a title to a different crown that had eluded him throughout his eventful life—namely, the master of his own destiny.

Some will say that I am being too judgmental. Why should Michael have to go back to an organized church when he claimed to be a spir-itual man, even though he was not a regular churchgoer? Indeed, in our conversations, Michael claimed to be highly religious, albeit in his own way. I am dubious of the claim. Proximity to God breeds a distinct humility. Charlatans garbed in religious robes but as distant from God as Pluto is from the sun exhibit an arrogance and a nonrefinement of character that is the hallmark of a counterfeit faith. In our time we have seen enough abuse of those who claim to be religious and spiri-tual but who are nothing but hate-peddlers. Real spirituality means submitting to God as Master of the Universe and living by His rules rather than by those of our own taste. Michael was in desperate need of latching on to the time-honored values and framework of a religious lifestyle to rescue his moribund existence. The Jehovah's Witnesses Church, with its many rules, had grounded him and kept him humble growing up. And a moral straitjacket to curb his destructive excess was exactly what Michael required.

Today, whenever I see myself described in the media as "Michael Jackson's former rabbi," I feel a certain embarrassment from having to face my original insecurity in having believed that I needed a celebrity pairing to be an effective exponent of religious values, and that religion in general, and Judaism in particular, needed a celebrity spokesman to garner mainstream credibility.

Like many others who make the similar mistake of thinking that "if you can't beat 'em, join 'em," and thus try and wed vulgar popular culture with the spiritual enormity of religion, I did not realize the serious dilution of Judeo-Christianity's monotheistic message that would result from being twinned with a culture that promotes human beings as gods.

I have since learned from my mistake and have tried to educate my children to know always that no man but God is the real Thriller.

I was taught as a child that there is no greater privilege than for one's actions to add to God's grandeur and there is no greater failure than to diminish His glory. In the Jewish religion we call it Kiddush Hashem, sanctifying God's presence, and Chillul Hashem, desecrating his sacred name. When I have made mistakes in my life, I have been pained not only by the personal consequences of my actions but especially by the fact that as a rabbi and a Jew I diminished a great world religion. The title I carry is supremely meaningful to me. I did not just take a test to acquire it but rather invested all of myself into being worthy of it. While Judaism will always flourish with spiritual-seekers, it will founder with publicity-seekers. And I know to which camp I must forever belong.

God promised Abraham that his children would be "like the stars of the heaven," not the stars of the silver screen. The former radiate light amid an all-encompassing darkness, and, indeed, the Jewish nation has retained its righteousness in a dark and cruel world. But the latter, our movie stars, are often counterfeit constellations, artificially illuminated facsimiles set in a world of make-believe.

One cannot be religious without being righteous. To the extent that I added to the counterfeit message being promoted in our celebrity-obsessed society by becoming dependent on Michael for a period of two years to be effective as a rabbi, I greatly regret the action and have endeavored to correct it by becoming an outspoken critic of the destructive effect of celebrity culture, as well as becoming a more wholesome and grounded human being.

This is not to say that I condemn Michael and foreswear entirely our once intimate friendship. Rather, it was the dependency that I regret, the belief that I needed him more than he needed me. I believed that religious values would benefit from having a renowned celebrity spokesman and was flattered that a man as famous as Michael Jackson found my spiritual ideas compelling.

A Final Thank You, Michael

Still, after all is said and done, I conclude this book with something that may surprise you. I want to acknowledge a debt of gratitude toward Michael that should not go unpaid.

In the Jewish religion one of the greatest sins is to live as an ingrate. The Bible provides instances where human beings were expected to show gratitude even to inanimate objects. Moses was not allowed to smite the Nile and turn it into blood because it had earlier saved his life when he was a baby in a pitched basket. Similarly, Moses could not wield his staff against the dust of Egypt and turn it into lice because it had saved his life by allowing him to bury the body of an evil Egyptian taskmaster whom he had smitten. How much more so, to use the Talmudic phraseology, must one show gratitude and appreciation to a human being with whom one once enjoyed the solid bond of friendship and a deep bond of affection.

For all his destructive flaws and serious shortcomings, I became a better father as a result of my friendship with Michael Jackson. It was impossible not to, so passionate was Michael about the infinite value of children and so infectious was his enthusiasm for childlike creativity and wonder. For the rest of my life I will never forget Michael making me promise that I would look into my childrens' eyes whenever I told them I loved them. More than anything else, this could have been Michael's lasting legacy and unparalleled gift to the world. How tragic it truly is, therefore, that he corrupted that ideal.

A friend of mine told me that *The New York Post* had ridiculed me, the day after Michael's arrest in November 2003, for a speech I gave a number of years ago where I stated that Michael inspired me to better value my children. But I still stand by those words. I do not believe in blind allegiance either to an active or a former friend. God and morality precede even kinship and friendship, and if someone we love or care about has contravened morality then their actions dare not be defended.

But I still believe in heartfelt gratitude. And I will always be grateful to Michael for inspiring me not just to appreciate the infinite value of my children but to act on that appreciation by prioritizing them always. Amid his undeniable gifts, Michael had led a profligate and largely selfish existence and admitted to things, such as sharing a bed with children, that are unforgivable. That does not make him guilty of pedophilia, and if he was culpable it doesn't annihilate the good he inspired. Any good things I picked up from him along the way remain with me, even as I lament his stunning destructive streak that culminated in his tragic and untimely death. As the great Jewish philosopher Maimonides wrote nearly a millennia ago, "Embrace the truth regardless of its source." The truth that Michael strengthened in me about how my children are my greatest blessing is something for which I will forever be grateful.

My friendship with Michael was based, more than anything else, on how much he cherished children and served as a counterbalance to all the people whom I meet who feel sorry for me for having so many. As a father of a large family I find myself forever apologizing, as if I single-handedly overpopulated the earth or committed a crime. The frequent and loaded stares from scornful onlookers imply that the famine in Africa was caused by *my* selfish fertility.

When I broach this issue with other American families who dare to exceed the two-kids-a-cat-and-a-goldfish national average, they too relate their experiences of suspicious gazes and raised eyebrows. At best one encounters puzzlement. At worst a look of condescension and pity as passersby try to fathom why we would ruin our lives by loading ourselves with the burden of *too many* children, all of whom have to be paid for.

Greater financial prosperity has bought us larger homes but smaller families, fancier cars but fewer baby carriages. But in Michael Jackson I met a man who was the most famous and accomplished entertainer arguably of all time and all he wanted, as he repeatedly told me, were nine kids of his own. I can still remember him reading to Prince and Paris, having every lunch and dinner with them, and refusing to travel without them in tow. He taught me that one's children are one's greatest blessing, the bright light to which we all aspire, the deep glow to which we all are drawn.

ACKNOWLEDGMENTS

Many people deserve thanks for their input into this book. Foremost among them is Michael Jackson for his courage and honesty in sharing so much of his intimate self in the belief that it could help people better understand him and provide valuable lessons in the lives of others. I miss you, Michael, and I mourn your loss. Since you've died I have been reliving so many of our special moments together. May you rest in peace and may your memory be an eternal blessing to your children, family, and the people who truly cared for you.

Frank Cascio, who was Michael's most trusted friend and confidante, was extremely helpful in ensuring that Michael and I got together on a regular basis to make these conversations possible. I was always inspired by Frank's devotion to Michael and today Frank is one of my family's dearest friends.

The people who helped me with the *Heal the Kids* initiative—especially my very dear friend Toba Friedman, who was a Marshall Scholar at Oxford when I was Rabbi there, and Marilyn Piels—deserve special thanks. Both Toba and Marilyn have since married and had children. So I guess all those conversations about how important children are really had the desired effect.

David Steinberger at the Perseus Books Group and Roger Cooper at Vanguard Press could not have been more enthusiastic, helpful, and encouraging in this book's publication. They brought to this project unparalleled sensitivity, devotion, and professionalism. It was truly awe-inspiring to see Roger motivate his expert team to produce a complex book with such alacrity and attention to detail.

Ari Emanuel, my agent and friend at William Morris Endeavor Entertainment, gave outstanding advice and guidance, all mixed with his usual vigor and humor. I especially thank Ari for his personal devotion toward the welfare of me and my family. Mel Berger devoted himself to finding the right home for the book, for which I am truly grateful.

Ron Feiner, my dear friend and attorney of 10 years, assisted both me and Michael in our efforts to heal American families. Throughout the years, Ron has been instrumental in providing me with wisdom, insight, and ongoing guidance.

My dear friend Ric Bachrach has been a constant confidante and trusted advisor in everything I do, both professionally and personally. A man of profound integrity, Ric brought a unique sensitivity in having this material brought to the public with the dignity it deserved.

Janet Goldstein did the impossible of editing my hefty original manuscript for publication in a condensed period of time. I drove Janet crazy with constant edits. But she was a real trooper and kept up both her pace and her sanity.

My friend Glenn Levy provided wise legal counsel as he has at many other crucial junctures in my life.

There is nothing that I could achieve professionally without my very dedicated office staff who work tirelessly to help me realize my vision of bringing spirituality and values to a world that sorely needs them. Chief among them is my personal assistant, Kennia Ramirez, who is there for me and my family at all hours of the day and night. My trusted assistant and colleague of many years, Jason Kitchen, is always at my side for me to lovingly harangue, and our Web and IT director, Dean Bigbee, was extremely helpful in helping to organize the book's material for publication, as was Lara Kasten, who assisted in the transcription of the conversations. My assistant, Erica Carpinello, also transcribed many of the conversations and gave me years of devoted service.

When this book was originally conceived, Jonathan Margolis, my dear friend from the United Kingdom, helped a great deal with the organization of the material.

Michael was close to my children and they cried when he died. I have never published a book without thanking them in the acknowledgements for the inspiration they provide me every single day. Mushki,

Chana, Shterni, Mendy, Shaina, Baba, Yosef, Dovid Chaim, and Cheftz-iba, you give me consistent joy while driving me constantly insane. You are the light of my life and the reason I have dark circles under my eyes (OK, that one is probably my own fault). You are my greatest treasure, and the reason that I had to sell a kidney to keep up. But in all serious-ness, you guys are the best. And I thank Michael for always reminding me that when I tell you I love you I make sure to say it while peering deeply into your eyes, even as you guys wrestle mightily to simply run out with your friends.

More than anyone else my wife Debbie is my wise counselor and de-voted partner in all things. She keeps me anchored, is my moral com-pass, and inspires me every day to be a better man. A woman of sublime dignity and quiet purpose, she was always strangely immune to Michael's celebrity and judged my relationship with him purely on its merits. Did Michael and I truly care for each other, and was our friend-ship leading to something redemptive both for us as well as others? Without Debbie's tethering I would feel adrift.

My teacher, mentor, and guiding light, the Lubavitcher Rebbe, Rabbi Menachem Mendel Schneerson, of blessed memory, who passed away 15 years ago, continues to be my highest spiritual inspiration and the source of desire to spread the light of Jewish values to the mainstream world. No one taught me more about my relationship with God then the Rebbe. The world is darker for his absence and brighter for his teachings.

Finally, I thank God Almighty, Creator of heaven and earth and all contained therein, for the health of my children and family, a wife who loves me, the support of parents, brothers and sisters, and the loving friendships I have made. Not long ago Michael was one of the most precious of those friendships and I ask the Creator, with whom Michael now rests, to comfort him from his pain, shield him from his loneliness, and help him find his way back home.

Rabbi Shmuley Boteach
Englewood, NJ
September, 2009